OTHER BOOKS BY L. J. RATHER

Mind and Body in Eighteenth-Century Medicine: A Study Based on Jerome
   Gaub's *De Regimine Mentis* 1965
Addison and the White Corpuscles: An Aspect of Nineteenth-Century Biol-
   ogy 1972
The Genesis of Cancer: A Study in the History of Ideas 1978

TRANSLATIONS:

Disease, Life and Man: Selected Essays by Rudolph Virchow 1958
The Therapy of the Word in Classical Antiquity, by Pedro Laín Entralgo (with
   John M. Sharp) 1970

THE DREAM OF SELF-DESTRUCTION

All diese philosophischen Sterne zweiter und dritter Grösse verblassen, wenn wir den Namen [Wag-
ner] des erlauchten Mannes nennen, der wie eine
Naturgewalt, ein Sturmherd ohnegleichen die
moderne Welt umgestaltet.

Theodor Lessing

Trompettes tout haut d'or pâmé sur les vélins,
Le dieu Richard Wagner irradiant un sacre
Mal tu par l'encre même en sanglots sibyllins.

Stéphane Mallarmé

Zitate in meiner Arbeit sind wie Räuber am Weg,
die bewaffnet hervorbrechen und dem Müssig-
gänger die Überzeugung abnehmen.

Walter Benjamin

THE DREAM

OF SELF-DESTRUCTION

Wagner's *Ring* and the Modern World

L. J. Rather

Louisiana State University Press
Baton Rouge and London

Designer: Patricia Douglas Crowder
Typeface: VIP Trump
Typesetter: LSU Press
Printer: Thomson-Shore, Inc.
Binder: John Dekker & Sons, Inc.

LIBRARY OF CONGRESS CATALOGING IN PUBLICATION DATA

Rather, L   Joseph, 1913-
    The dream of self-destruction.

    Bibliography: p.
    Includes index.
    1. Wagner, Richard, 1813–1883. Der Ring des
Nibelungen. I. Title.
    ML410.W15R4   782.1'3   79–10118
    ISBN 0–8071–0495–7

To My Wife

Ingeborg Gabrielle Arnold, *Dr. med.* (Munich)
Dresden, 1916: Frankfurt a/M, 1965
Munich, *Nordfriedhof* 178/89

CONTENTS

Preliminary Remarks and Acknowledgments   xv

Prelude   xvii

Chapter I **OVERTURE**   I

    1. THE OLD GODS AWAKEN   I

Growth of interest in Norse mythology in late eighteenth-century Europe. Recovery of *The Song of the Nibelungs,* a medieval German epic poem. Mythology and the myth of race. English and German translations of the Norse Eddas and *The Song of the Nibelungs.* The "curse of gold" seen by Carlyle in 1831 as the central theme of the poem. Carlyle's industrial savior-hero: Plugson of Undershot and the gospel of Mammon. William Morris' poem *Sigurd the Volsung,* a political-social metaphor. Morris calls for the destruction of the capitalist world.

    2. HEINRICH HEINE'S DREAM OF DESTRUCTION   12

Heine warns the French in 1834 that German philosophy has brought about the death of God. The "philosophical wars" to come. Thor now ready to smash the cathedrals of Europe with his giant hammer. Heine claims that the moneyed Jew is the secret ruler of Christendom. His second thoughts in 1852 on Marx, Feuerbach, and the Young Hegelians.

    3. THE MYTH OF RACE   17

Racial mystique in Disraeli's novels of the 1840s: *Tancred* and *Coningsby.* The Sephardic Jew as prototype of "pure" race. "Race is all." The Jews already the secret rulers of Europe. The "Northern" and Jewish races together will dominate the world. Thematic resemblances between Wagner's unfinished drama *The Saracen Woman* (1843) and Disraeli's *Tancred* (1847). Marx on the Jewish question (1843): money is now the real God of Israel; Christendom has become Judaized; European civilization must be emancipated from Judaism before the Jews can themselves be emancipated. Gobineau's myth of race: a "great race" reflects a favorable combination of *purusha*, the male principle, and *prakriti*, the female principle. Downfall of past civilizations in the Old and New Worlds a consequence of racial intermixture and subsequent "degeneration." Gobineau's admiration for the "race of Sephardic Jews." Houston Stewart Chamberlain and *The Foundations of the Nineteenth Century*: Chamberlain rejects the idea of the "pure race"; holds that great races are always the result of interbreeding, but agrees with Disraeli and Gobineau on the fundamental significance of race. Chamberlain's "resurrection of Lazarus": his dream of a coming great race to which the assimilated Jews of Europe will contribute. Lord Redesdale on Chamberlain. Philo-Semitism and anti-Semitism in late nineteenth-century Europe. Virchow versus Chamberlain on race. Trinitarian mystiques: Chamberlain, Hartmann, and Bachofen. The coming "third age," "third kingdom," and "third consciousness" of the human race. Annihilation and the unconscious.

Chapter II **WAGNER AND THE NIBELUNG'S RING**   40

1. THE REDEMPTION OF THE NIBELUNGS   40

Wagner's early life. His beginnings as a "revolutionist." Possibility that Wagner borrowed from the Siegfried romance of Alexandre Dumas *père* while in Paris in the 1840s. Wagner's two essays (1848) on the story of the Nibelungs: Siegfried as Grail-seeker, sun-god, and savior. The hoard of the Nibelungs as Grail treasure. The incest motif. The redemption of Alberich and the Nibelungs. Redemption in Wagner's poem *Siegfried's Death* (1848): Brünnhilde exorcises the curse of gold, power, and possessions symbolized by the Nibelung's ring; Alberich, Hagen, and the Nibelungs not redeemed. Further elaboration of the incest motif.

2. THE NEEDED DESTRUCTION OF THE STATE: WAGNER'S INTERPRETATION OF THE OEDIPUS MYTH   47

Wagner and the Dresden uprising of 1849: the voice of destruction. Wagner's study of the Oedipus myth (1851). Myth and creativity. The politicization of art. Incest and revolution. Antigone as "perfected human being" and goddess of revolution. Antigone's "self-destruction through sympathy." Meaning of the incest bond between Siegmund and Sieglinde in Wagner's *Ring*: the reconciliation of "male" with "female" spirit and the coming of a perfected male-female savior. The union of tone and word, of music and drama, of mind and heart, in the perfected art form of the future. Wagner calls for the "unconscious" to be made "conscious" (1851). Wagner's new understanding of Lohengrin and Elsa. Siegfried-Brünnhilde, the perfected human being. The perfected human being made possible by Wotan's deliberate self-destruction. Wagner's *Ring* as a variation on the Oedipus theme. Siegfried and Jesus as saviors.

3. WAGNER, FEUERBACH, AND SCHOPENHAUER   63

Wagner's dedication of *The Art-Work of the Future* (1849) to Feuerbach. Wagner and Nietzsche. Wagner's "Feuerbachian" explanation of the *Ring*: death must be accepted if a full life is to become possible; sexual love is the highest form of union and the paradigm of knowledge; true knowledge is given by the "I-thou" rather than the "I-it" relationship. Wagner echoes Feuerbach's call for "feeling" to be raised to "consciousness." The close of the first version of the *Ring* poem in relation to Schopenhauer's philosophical denial of the will. The essential ambiguity of works of art.

4. THE PHILOSOPHY OF SCHOPENHAUER AND
ITS RECEPTION BY WAGNER   70
Current misunderstanding of Schopenhauer's philosophy. Initial neglect of his writings in Germany. John Oxenford introduces Schopenhauer to the English in 1853, pointing out that the final goal of "the will to live" is "annihilation." Schopenhauer's circular elucidation of his "single thought." Wagner finds the source of artistic creativity in Schopenhauer's "unconscious will." Relative novelty of Schopenhauer's emphasis on the role of the brain and nervous system in shaping our knowledge of the external world. The four "roots" of the principle of sufficient reason, according to Schopenhauer. The parallel genesis and structure of real worlds and dream worlds. Why Heine called Kant's philosophy a proclamation of the death of God. Schopenhauer's response to Kant on the death of metaphysics. Schopenhauer's journey to the interior Africa of the human heart. What Schopenhauer, William James, Martin Heidegger, Maurice Merleau-Ponty, and Ludwig Wittgenstein have in common. Schopenhauer's Copernican revolution: the cosmos as *macranthropos* replaces the human being as *microcosmos*. Julius Frauenstädt and Ernst Lindner, Schopenhauer's first German-Jewish disciples. The role of the *Vossische Zeitung*. When did Wagner first become acquainted with Schopenhauer's writings? Wagner explains Schopenhauer's philosophy to August Röckel: "Jewish optimism" versus Schopenhauerian pessimism. Wagner revises his concept of self-annihilation.

5. WAGNER, ANTI-SEMITISM, AND RACISM   89
Wagner and the Jews: his friendly relations with Joseph Rubinstein, Carl Tausig, and Hermann Levi. Levi's defense of Wagner. Kinds of anti-Semitism. The anti-Semitism of Karl Marx. The "Platonic" anti-Semitism of Otto Weininger. Wagner's music said to be loved by Jewish anti-Semites because of its "Jewish" features. Theodor Lessing and the concept of Jewish self-hatred (*jüdischer Selbsthass*). Post–World War II views of Wagner's anti-Semitism. Wagner and the rights of animals. Race-hygiene: Nordic and Jewish racism in the United States before World War I.

6. THE CLOSING OF THE "RING"   100
The meaning of the failure of the Nibelungs to achieve redemption. Stein's misinterpretation of Wagner's essay, *Judaism in Music*. "Light-elves" and "dark-elves." Wagner introduces the Schopenhauerian concept of "world-annihilation" into the *Ring*. Wagner rejects Feuerbachian *erōs* in favor of Schopenhauerian *agapē* and explains his changed interpretation of the *Ring* to Röckel. Wagner's presentation of his views on politics, society, and revolution to an American audience in 1879. His lack of faith in the future of Germany. Wagner's doctrine of salvation by art.

Chapter III **MUSIC, DREAMS, AND THE UNCONSCIOUS**   110

1. ORIGINS OF THE IDEA OF THE UNCONSCIOUS   110
Wagner's call (1851) for the unconscious to be made conscious repeated in 1868 by Hartmann and again in 1896 by Freud. Leibniz, Kant, and Schelling on the unconscious. Jean Paul's unconscious as "inner Africa" of the soul. Mid-nineteenth-century English explorers of the unconscious: Hamilton, Mill, Carpenter, and Maudsley. Carl Gustav Carus and the concept of the unconscious. Carus' musical circle in Dresden. His comments on Wagner. Hartmann's philosophy of the unconscious: social reality will be negated when the ends of the unconscious become conscious. Freud claims that only psychoanalysis can make the unconscious conscious (1898). The unconscious and the id. Otto Rank on Freud's intellectual debt to Schopenhauer. Kant, Schopenhauer, and Freud on mental topography. Thomas Mann on Freud and Schopenhauer.

2. SCHOPENHAUER ON DREAMS, THE OCCULT, WIT   118
The unconscious "will" as hidden director of the dream play. *Tat tvam asi* ("thou art that") literally true in dreams: all persons and objects represent the dreamer. In the dream the unconscious "will" *is* fate, in waking life it *shapes* fate. Schopenhauer's "will" and Erigena's "divine ignorance." No random events occur in dreams. How the meaning of the underlying "theorematic" dream undergoes distortion in the remembered "allegorical" dream. Schopenhauer relates wit to the unconscious, in dreams and waking life. Schopenhauer on the occult.

3. SCHOPENHAUER ON SEX AND DEATH   126
The human body as "concrete sexual impulse" and objective counterpart of the drives of the unconscious will. The game of life and death. Eternity: the everlasting present.

4. KABBALISTIC AND SCHOPENHAUERIAN ANTHROPOLOGY   128
The self-destruction of Adam Kadmon. Why Schopenhauer ranks Judaism and Islam below Buddhism, Brahmanism, and primitive Christianity.

5. THE VOICE OF THE UNCONSCIOUS: SCHOPENHAUER
ON MUSIC   131
The meanings of music. Leibniz on music. Schopenhauer on music as unconscious metaphysics. Music as the song of the unconscious self. The opening bars of Wagner's *Ring* and Schopenhauer's cosmological interpretation of musical overtones in *The World as Will and Representation*. Schopenhauer on the metaphysics of Beethoven's music.

6. WAGNER'S THEORY OF MUSIC   136
Wagner's elaboration of Schopenhauer's metaphysics of music. Tone-world versus light-world.

7. THE MEANING OF BEETHOVEN   139
Beethoven as tonal seer. Wagner on Beethoven's C-sharp Minor String Quartet. Wagner's "Feuerbachian" (1849) and "Schopenhauerian" (1870) interpretations of the revolutionary breakthrough in Beethoven's Ninth Symphony. Wagner's affirmation of the world as art.

Chapter IV **WHAT WENT WRONG**   149

1. HOW SHAW FISHED THE GOLD FROM THE RHINE   149
The Wagnerian motif in *Widowers' Houses*. Augier's play *Ceinture Dorée*:
Archer's adaptation and Shaw's modification.

2. SHAW AND WAGNER   152
Shaw's changing interpretations of the *Ring* in the successive editions of
The Perfect Wagnerite, 1898–1923.

3. SHAW ON THE "RING"   155
The Nibelungs under Alberich as the English working class under industrial capitalism. Alberich's *Tarnhelm* as the shareholder's tall hat. What
went wrong? Shaw's explanation of the breakdown of Wagner's allegory:
due to the discovery that neither love nor anarchism is a panacea for the
world's ills.

4. SHAW ADDRESSES THE GERMANS   159
The new chapter, "Why He Changed His Mind," introduced by Shaw into
the German edition (1907) of *The Perfect Wagnerite*: Shaw now suggests
that the breakdown of the allegory of the *Ring* followed on Wagner's discovery that in the real world Alberich-Wotan-Loge had merged to produce
the enlightened modern capitalist.

5. SARTORIUS RECLOTHED   161
Major Barbara (1905), a dramatization of Shaw's views in "Why He
Changed His Mind." Sartorius reclothed: the gospel of St. Andrew Under-
shaft. Salvation through armaments. Undershaft's death and destruction
factory. Shaw explains where Alberich went wrong (1923); explains where
Undershaft and Lazarus went wrong (1929). Where Shaw went wrong.

6. WAGNERISM, WAGNER, AND THE THIRD REICH   167
The party lines on Wagner in Germany and the United States. William
Shirer on Wagnerism in Nazi Germany. His mistaken account of Wagner's operas and music-dramas. On so-called Wagnerian pageantry: Hitler,
Goebbels, and Fritz Lang's film *Die Nibelungen*. German chauvinistic
perversion of Wagnerism already apparent in 1906 to Theodor Lessing.
Shirer's misunderstanding of Wagner's anti-Semitism. *The Ring of the
Nibelung* and *Parsifal* banned by the Nazis in 1942. Marxian and Wagnerian anti-Semitism. Late nineteenth-century attacks on Wagner by the
anti-Semitic press of Vienna: Wagner called the "Rabbi of Bayreuth" and
the "God of the Jews." Lessing on the so-called "Jewish traits" of Wagner's
music.

7. GÖTTERDÄMMERUNG   172
Wagner's dislike of power-hungry political adventurers, or "Robespierres."
Napoleon III and Bismarck both are "Robespierres." Wagner criticizes Bismarck's choice of "war security" rather than peace security. The armaments race begins. Wagner on the function of the police and army in modern states, on property, on gold, paper money, and credit. The "ring of the
Nibelung as stock portfolio." Christians, not Jews, have invented the art
of "coining money out of nothing." The God of the Jews as the real God of

the Christians: Wagner's one-sided view of the God of the Jews (*Juden-gott*). The peoples of Europe "armed to the teeth for mutual destruction." Science exploited by the state chiefly for destructive purposes. The war machinery perhaps out of control. How the approaching self-destruction of European civilization may come about.

Epilogue **WAKING FROM THE NIGHTMARE**   181

German-English Concordance of Cited Works by Wagner and
  Schopenhauer   183
Bibliography   185
Thematic Bibliography   197
Index   207

PRELIMINARY REMARKS
AND ACKNOWLEDGMENTS

The manuscript was begun in 1973 and completed early in 1975. Alterations and additions were made during 1976 and 1977, and a full revision was carried out in the spring of 1978. The poet's precept, "Let the book be suppressed for nine years," has thus been in part obeyed and, I hope, to some benefit. I am grateful to the friends and colleagues who have, at various times, given me their assessments of parts or all of the manuscript. Sidney P. Albert, professor of philosophy at California State University, Los Angeles, has been most helpful on several occasions, with reference especially to my treatment of Shaw. To William Byron Webster, formerly of the Department of German Studies at Stanford University and now music editor of *InterMuse*, and Gerald Gillespie, professor of German Studies and Comparative Literature at Stanford, I am very much in debt for their perennial efforts on my behalf. Dr. Webster has carefully reviewed the entire manuscript and made a number of helpful suggestions. I wish to thank the personnel of the Green Library, the Music Library, the Lane Medical Library, and the Cummings Art Library at Stanford, and the Music Library of the University of California, Berkeley, for the ready assistance and courtesies extended to me. For typing the manuscript, reviewing the translations, and furnishing me with some useful hints in her unpublished M.A. thesis on Jakob Wassermann, I have Patricia Rather to thank; and for aiding me with the proofs, my friend Dr. John B. Frerichs. I am grateful to the staff of the Louisiana State University Press, to my editors Beverly Jarrett and Linda Schexnaydre in particular, for their contributions to the final product of my labors.

Unless otherwise stated, all translations are my own. William Ashton Ellis' valuable translation of Wagner's prose works is somewhat out of date and, like all translations—my own not excepted—has its inaccuracies. I have used the second edition (Leipzig, 1887–1888) of Wagner's *Gesammelte Schriften und Dichtungen* for the most part. I have translated from various German editions, indicated in the notes and bibliography, of Wagner's correspondence with August Röckel, Mathilde Wesendonck, Franz Liszt, Angelo Neumann, and Theodor Uhlig. The larger part of Schopenhauer's work has recently been given excellent new English dress by E. F. J. Payne. Here too I have preferred to make my own translations, using Wolfgang Freiherr von Löhneysen's recently edited German version; but I have included after the bibliography a concordance of my translations with those of Ellis and Payne for the convenience of the reader. I regret that Curt von Westernhagen's *Wagner: A Biography*, translated by Mary Whittall (Cambridge, 1978), reached my hands too late for me to make use of it.

PRELUDE

Shaped from a golden treasure ravished by Alberich the Nibelung from the depths of the Rhine at the cost of forswearing love, the ring in Richard Wagner's music-drama *The Ring of the Nibelung* symbolizes power. And in our world this means, above all, the power of money. In 1881, tangible money having by that time yielded to its spectral manifestation, credit, Wagner could remark that the modern counterpart of the Nibelung's ring was an investor's stock portfolio. Money is a means by which an invisible dominion is exerted over our fellows. In Wagner's version of the myth, the ring is first used by Alberich to enslave his fellow Nibelungs; his ultimate goal is to subjugate the gods and giants as well. Death and corruption of motive attend the passage of the ring from the hands of Alberich to those of the gods and giants and finally to the hands of the hero Siegfried. In the closing scene of Wagner's music-drama, Brünnhilde, with a last outburst of wisdom, renounces the ring and returns it to the depths of the Rhine. Meanwhile Valhalla goes up in flames, and the world of the theater comes to a thunderous end. The Nibelung's ring has by now become a symbol of the great wheel of life, of the endlessly repetitive closed circle of human existence in its present repressive stage, a magic circle in which we find ourselves trapped. Brünnhilde's renunciation of the ring suggests that by renouncing the worship of power and the quest for dominion humanity will break out of the circle and find a new mode of existence. But the close of Wagner's music-drama suggests also that the wisdom of renunciation will reach us too late to stave off universal destruction.

Wagner's story line in *The Ring of the Nibelung* was freely taken, together with many additions and changes of his own invention, from the Norse Eddas and a medieval German epic poem, the *Nibelungen-lied* or *The Song of the Nibelungs*. In the first chapter I have touched briefly on the historical origins of nineteenth-century European interest in Northern myth, legend, and poetry. I have indicated something of the way in which this body of material was used later to construct a secondary "myth," that of the role of Germanic (in the broader sense), Nordic or simply white, racial purity and supremacy. The myth of Jewish racial purity and supremacy—of which Benjamin Disraeli was perhaps the nineteenth century's most fervid partisan—proves, interestingly enough, to have served as a model for such writers on Nordic supremacy as Joseph-Arthur de Gobineau and Houston Stewart Chamberlain, both of whom were great admirers of the Jewish "race."

The heart of my book lies in the second chapter. There I have attempted to show how Wagner, in the light of his own understanding of the Oedipus myth, shaped the story of the Nibelung's ring into an allegory depicting the political, social, and psychological resolution of the Oedipal conflict. Wagner called Sophocles' Oedipus trilogy a "depiction of the whole history of humanity, from the origins of society to the necessary downfall of the state." An understanding of Wagner's little-known study of the Oedipus trilogy is essential to an understanding of *The Ring of the Nibelung*. Part of the story is Wagner's belief that in the perfected world of the future "male" and "female" principles would be in better balance than they were in the aggressive, egoistic, superficially conscious world of his day—or are in ours. Part also is Wagner's call—anticipating that of Sigmund Freud by half a century—for the contents of the unconscious to be raised to the conscious level. The large amount of attention given to Arthur Schopenhauer in the book has a double origin. In the first place, Wagner's early shift of allegiance from the optimistically dialectical philosophy of Ludwig Feuerbach to the so-called pessimistic philosophy of Arthur Schopenhauer led him to rethink and revise the *Ring*: primarily at issue was the precise nature of the "self" to be destroyed. Secondly, Wagner's ideas on the nature of music, on the all-important relationship between music and dreams, and on the significance of the marriage between music and the word in the art form of the future were articulated within the framework of Schopenhauer's philosophy.

In the closing chapter of my book I attempt to show something of the relevance of Wagner's allegory in the *Ring* to the course of European history in the past one hundred years or so, and at the same time to point out how Wagner himself viewed these developments. We are, as Wagner once said, all Nibelungs—"moral dwarfs," George Bernard Shaw added in 1898. In the one hundred years since *The Ring of the Nibelung* was first produced in Bayreuth, the power of the Nibelung's ring has increased enormously. But even in those days, as the reader will learn, Wagner could decry the dull and purblind insistence of Europe's rulers that peace could be maintained only at the price of continual rearmament, note with distress the misuse of science by the modern warfare state, point to the depersonalization inherent in the inhuman scale of modern warfare, and wonder if some blind destructive force in the human heart was bent on encompassing a final *Götterdämmerung* for all humanity.

Some years after the catastrophe of 1914–1918 Sigmund Freud, who had previously expressed no doubts as to the underlying soundness of the nineteenth-century Valhalla, traced the source of the fatal illness of European culture to an inevitably increasing imbalance between the forces of love and death. The death force, the force of destruction and aggression, seemed to feed on the very repression demanded by the development and maintenance of that culture. Would, Freud asked, the drive of aggression and self-destruction be checked in time by its eternal antagonist, love? Freud's assessment of the human condition, set forth in 1930 in *Civilization and Its Discontents*, recalls the devil's claim (made twenty-five years earlier in Shaw's *Man and Superman*) that man's boasted force of life is really a force of death. Among the more notable descendants of Freud's book are Norman O. Brown's *Life Against Death: The Psychoanalytical Meaning of History*, Brigid Brophy's *A Black Ship to Hell*, and Erich Fromm's *The Anatomy of Human Destructiveness*, to name only three.

My book is not of this genre. It is not a psychoanalytical interpretation of human history. Neither is it a psychoanalytical interpretation of Richard Wagner or of his music-dramas, such as may be found in Otto Rank's monumental and as yet untranslated book *Das Inzest-Motiv in Dichtung und Sage* (The Incest-Motif in Literature and Legend). From the standpoint I have taken in this book, psychoanalytical interpretations are part of the story they purport to explain. Nor has it been my intent to assess or evaluate in their entirety the utterances,

actions, or works of Wagner, Schopenhauer, or any other historical figure in the book. Although Wagner has been, in my opinion, as badly
misunderstood by some as Arthur Schopenhauer—and for similar reasons—I am not concerned here with arguing his case. I have presented
some evidence that may change the reader's mind. But my primary
intent in writing this book has been to depict a peculiar nineteenth-
century pattern of mythic correspondences, which I have called the
"dream of self-destruction." The technique I have used might be termed
montage, constructivist, or documentary; that is, the book consists
largely of hidden, paraphrased, or open quotations from the writers
with whom it is concerned. I had in mind Walter Benjamin's ideal of a
completely objective book. On a larger scale, this technique was employed by Karl Kraus in *Die letzten Tage der Menschheit* (The Last
Days of Humanity) and by Thomas Mann in *Doktor Faustus* to depict
the breakdown of European culture in, respectively, the Great War and
World War II. Wagner's *The Ring of the Nibelung* owes its central position in the book no less to the complexity of its theme, made still more
complex by Wagner's shifting values over the twenty-eight years of its
composition, than to the multiple interconnections between Wagner's
ideas and the course of nineteenth-century intellectual and artistic
history.

Such unity as may be claimed for the present work is more dream-
like in character, more musical (in the Wagnerian sense) than logical,
and secured less by a linear thread of logic binding the parts together
than by multiple interlinkages between the many repetitions and trans-
formations of a few fundamental themes audible throughout the nineteenth century, and still to be heard in our own.

But why in general do human beings anticipate an end of the world? And, granting this, just why a terrible end?
Immanuel Kant, *Das Ende aller Dinge* (1784)

If there exists within us a dark power that so very inimically and treacherously lays a guiding thread with which it seizes us fast and draws us along a path fraught with danger and destruction that we would not otherwise have trod—if there exists such a power, then it must take shape within us in the likeness of our own self, indeed it must become this self; for only then do we believe in it, and grant it the room it needs to fulfill that hidden end.
E. T. A. Hoffmann, *Der Sandmann* (1816)

Nevertheless it must arouse our misgivings that the advancing art of war continues to turn away from the mainsprings of moral forces toward the development of mechanical force. Here the rawest forces of the underlying powers of nature are brought into artificial play, into which, despite all mathematics and arithmetic, the blind will, breaking loose after its fashion with elemental power, could someday mix itself.
Richard Wagner, *Religion und Kunst* (1880)

The engineer's brain carried the calculations to the utmost point. Behind surged forces beyond control. The failure is dictated from the other side. Undiscoverable from here. The formula is correct—and the gas explodes! Don't you understand? . . . In the gray misty distance bursts of fireballs rush together—plainly in self-destruction.
Georg Kaiser, *Gas* (1918–1920)

The most cursory study of dream-life and of the phantasies of the insane shows that ideas of world destruction (more accurately destruction of what the world symbolizes) are latent in the unconscious mind. . . . The first promise of the atomic age is that it can make some of our nightmares come true. Civilized man may still rejoice to find on waking that his nightly struggle with primitive instincts is "only a dream" but he wakes to find that his unconscious mind has stolen a march on him.
Edward Glover, *War, Sadism and Pacifism* (1946)

Above them the monstrous deceptions twitched on and off, and around them the black soulless buildings stood wrapped in a cold dream of their own destruction. . . . "Destroy the world!" he cried in his heart.
Malcolm Lowry, *Under the Volcano* (1947)

Why, other than for want of love, is our whole civilization headed for destruction?
Richard Wagner, *Was nützt diese Erkenntniss?* (1880)

Just as torches and fireworks grow pale and lose their brightness in the sun, so intelligence, even genius, and beauty likewise, are eclipsed and thrown into the shade by goodness of heart.
Arthur Schopenhauer, *Die Welt als Wille und Vorstellung*, II (1844)

The Dream of Self-Destruction

Chapter I
OVERTURE

Near the middle of the eighteenth century a German epic poem, once popular in the Middle Ages, was rescued from near oblivion and in 1757 put into print.[1] In 1827 it was translated from the original Middle High German into modern German by Karl Simrock and entitled the *Nibelungenlied*. Not distant in spirit from the *Morte d'Arthur* or *Chanson de Roland*, it is a tale of love, loyalty, and revenge, ending in disaster and death. Taking into account here the chief characters only, *The Song of the Nibelungs* centers at first on the deeds of the heroic Prince Siegfried, the son of Siegmund and Siegelinde, rulers of the Netherlands. Siegfried journeys to the Burgundian court on the Rhine. Just before his arrival Hagen, the faithful retainer of the Burgundian rulers, tells King Gunther of Siegfried's greatest feat: he has slain the knights Schilbung and Nibelung and taken possession of the Nibelung hoard, after having reduced its guardian, the dwarf-knight Alberich, to submission. The treasure includes the sword Balmung and a cap of invisibility (*Tarnkappe*) that endows its wearer with the strength of twelve men. Siegfried is welcomed at the court; and after overcoming the Saxon enemies of Burgundy, he falls in love with Gunther's sister, Kriemhild. Before he can have her for his bride, he must assist Gunther in his own quest for the hand of Brunhild, queen of Iceland. The heroic queen has so far easily defeated all her suitors in contests of strength. With the aid of the *Tarnkappe*, and in the name of Gunther, Siegfried

1. Henry and Mary Garland, *The Oxford Companion to German Literature* (Oxford, 1976), 635, 802.

overcomes her. After the joint consummation of the marriages—and Gunther has to call for Siegfried's help again, for on the wedding night Brunhild binds him hand and foot and suspends him from a nail on the wall—the two women begin to quarrel over precedence.

Enraged by Brunhild's assertion that Siegfried is a mere vassal, Kriemhild reveals that it was Siegfried, not Gunther, who overcame Brunhild in Iceland and once again at the Burgundian court. Enlisting Hagen and Gunther, Brunhild then seeks revenge. Hagen tricks the secret of Siegfried's invulnerability from Kriemhild and kills him with a stab in the back; further, he takes possession of the Nibelung treasure and hides it in the depths of the Rhine. Years later, meditating revenge against the murderers of her husband, Kriemhild marries Etzel, king of the Huns. She lures Hagen, Gunther, and the Burgundians (now called the "Nibelungs") to Etzel's court, where they are slaughtered to the last man.[2] That whoever holds the treasure becomes a "Nibelung" is implicit in the poem.

Scholars recognized that *The Song of the Nibelungs* was based on tales and poems written in Old Norse, dating back to the pre-Christian era of northern Europe. Of this fund of myth and legend the prose Edda had never dropped entirely out of sight. The so-called elder or poetic Edda, however, was not recovered until the middle of the seventeenth century. Other Old Norse versions of the story of the Nibelungs and Volsungs, which pieced out the fragmentary account given in the prose Edda, were also available. The poetic Edda tells of gods, giants, and dwarfs, as well as of heroic men and women. It begins with a poem of great force and cosmic magnitude, the Völuspa, Ragnarök, or "twilight of the gods"—a sibylline prophecy by the Völva foretelling the imminent downfall of the Northern gods, the spread of chaos among men and women, and the eventual destruction of the world by fire. The medieval *Song of the Nibelungs*, it is worth repeating, is an epic poem dealing with mortal men and women. There are no gods, giants, dwarfs, or

2. Karl Simrock (trans.), *Das Nibelungenlied* (54th ed.; Stuttgart, 1898). I have adopted Simrock's spelling of the proper names. It is worth noting that Hagen's unconditional attachment to the fortunes of Gunther was designated *Nibelungentreue* by the German chancellor Prince von Bülow in 1909 and used to indicate the strength of the bond between Germany and Austria-Hungary. See Wilhelm von Massow (ed.), *Fürst Bülows Reden* (5 vols.; Leipzig, 1910–15), V, 127–28.

supernatural beings in the tale. What little there is of the marvelous lies in the background.

Of interest mainly to scholars in the original, the Eddas had been made available in modern languages even before the nineteenth century began. Paul Henri Mallet, a French scholar working under the patronage of King Frederick V of Denmark, produced a work in which the Eddas were included in a French translation. Bishop Thomas Percy's English translation of Mallet's book was published in 1770 under the title of *Northern Antiquities*; it contains a Latin version of the poetic Edda. Amos Cottle's English translation of the poetic Edda was published in 1797. In the 1820s appeared a Danish translation of the poetic Edda by Finnur Magnússon, professor of Northern literature at Copenhagen. The German translation of 1837 by Ludwig Ettmüller was written in *Stabreim*, the alliterative verse style later used by Wagner when he rewrote the story for his own dramatic purposes.[3]

The northern European people's search for "roots" had thus begun. By the end of the nineteenth century there were few educated adults in Europe and the United States who were not familiar with the whole pantheon of Northern gods, heroes, and heroines—Thor, Balder, Brunhild, Sieglinde, Siegmund, Sigurd, Siegfried, and all the rest—as the changing pattern of given names in the nineteenth century suggests. And before the second half of the century had begun, there were signs that this corpus of myth and legend was being used to weld a kind of tribal unity among the Northern, or "Nordic," peoples of Europe. Out of Nordic myth, a myth of Nordic unity and eventually supremacy was being constructed. The peculiarly German exploitation of the myth of Nordic supremacy during the rule of the Nazis should not allow us to forget that long before Hitler the same myth had been exploited, with equal ruthlessness and considerably more success, by the ruling classes

3. Paul Henri Mallet, *L'Introduction à l'histoire de Dannemarc, où l'on traite de la religion, des loix, des moeurs et des usages des anciens Danois* (2 vols.; Copenhagen, 1755–56). Thomas Percy, *Northern antiquities: or, A description of the manners, customs, religion and laws of the ancient Danes, and other northern nations; including those of our own Saxon ancestors* (2 vols.; London, 1770). Amos Simon Cottle (trans.), *Icelandic Poetry; or, The Edda of Saemund* (Bristol, 1797). Finnur Magnússon, *Den aeldre Edda: En samling af de nordiske folks aeldste sagn og sange, ved Saemund Sigfüsson kaldet hin Frode* (4 vols.; Copenhagen, 1821–23). Ludwig Ettmüller, *Die Lieder der Edda von den Nibelungen* (Zurich, 1837).

in England, Europe, and the United States. Consider such phrases as "the lesser breeds," "the white man's burden," "our little brown brothers," and "manifest destiny," widely current before Western hegemony collapsed (morally at least) in World War I. To be reminded that the treatment accorded to "inferior races" by the leaders of the National Socialist German Workers Party was not without precedent, we need only recall the genocidal exploitation of the Belgian Congo under Leopold II or the laws against racial intermixture, the contempt for the "half-breed," and the fate of Indians and black Africans in the United States. We should not allow the disgrace into which "racism" has fallen in our own day to conceal from us the eminent respectability that it enjoyed in the nineteenth century, when its proponents were men of position, power, and moral authority.

In 1831 a long account of Karl Simrock's newly published translation of *The Song of the Nibelungs* appeared in the *Westminster Review*. It came from the pen of the great Scotch admirer of things German, Thomas Carlyle, who can serve as witness here for the growth of nineteenth-century Europe's nostalgia for its Northern past. Carlyle says that the resurrection of the *Nibelungenlied* in the mid–eighteenth century was the beginning of a "stream of publications and speculations, still rolling on, with increased current, to the present day." Toward the end of that century an antiquarian tendency, a "fonder, more earnest looking back into the Past," had begun to manifest itself in the literature of all European lands. In Germany as in England, he continues, the "distinct symptoms" and "manifold effects" of the new movement in thought were easy to see. Calling the *Nibelungenlied* a "Northern Epos" or "Northern Iliad," Carlyle observes that "the whole story of the *Nibelungen* is fateful, mysterious, guided by unseen influences. . . . Vain were it to inquire where that *Nibelungenland* specifically is: its very name is *Nebel-land* or *Nifl-land*, the land of Darkness, of Invisibility."[4]

The tragic and dramatic character of this medieval epic made a strong impression on Carlyle. The last ten of the thirty-nine *Aventiuren* constituting the *Nibelungenlied* were, he notes, "almost like an image of Doomsday." And indeed they are, for what the poet of the *Ni-*

4. Thomas Carlyle, review of Karl Simrock's translation of "Das Nibelungenlied" (1827), *Westminster Review* (July, 1831), 1, 3, 16–17, 44.

belungenlied had done, consciously or unconsciously, was to transfer from a divine to a human milieu the cosmic downfall described in the Völuspa or Ragnarök. The fiery end of the Nibelung-Burgundians at Etzel's court corresponds to the death of the gods, when Surtur the Black comes up from the south with his flaming sword and sets off the universal holocaust. It corresponds also, on one level of meaning at least, to the downfall of the gods at the close of Wagner's *The Ring of the Nibelung*. But in Wagner's version lovelessness and the lust for gold and power are root causes of the ultimate disaster. The poet of the *Nibelungenlied*, whoever he was—Carlyle mentions Wolfram von Eschenbach, the twelfth-century author of *Parzifal*, and "Klingsohr of Ungerland, a minstrel who once passed for a magician," as two possible candidates—stood in the tradition of the Minnesänger, minstrels and troubadours. In the *Nibelungenlied*, says Carlyle:

The catastrophe is dimly prophesied from the beginning; and, at every fresh step, rises more and more clearly into view. A shadow of coming Fate, as it were, a low inarticulate voice of Doom falls, from the first, out of that charmed Nibelungen-land: the discord of two women is a little spark of evil passion, that ere long enlarges itself into a crime; foul murder is done; and now Sin rolls on like a devouring fire, till the guilty and innocent alike are encircled with it, and a whole land is ashes, and a whole race is swept away.[5]

In the light of Carlyle's comment on the antiquarian tendency that had surfaced throughout northern Europe at the close of the eighteenth century, we can understand something of the interest aroused by the *Nibelungenlied* even outside of the German-speaking lands. But for the Germans themselves, whose homeland had been dismembered for centuries and repeatedly devastated by outside powers during the seventeenth century, the poem had special significance. For the non-Germans of Europe, says Carlyle, the poem did no more than shed some new light on an "almost forgotten age . . . a fair rainbow land"; but for some Germans, in whose medieval tongue it was written, the *Nibelungenlied* was "naturally an object of no common love. . . . After long ages of concealment they have found it in the remote wilderness, still standing like the trunk of some almost antediluvian oak; nay with boughs on it still green after all the wind and weather of twelve hundred years.

5. *Ibid.*, 17, 27.

To many a patriotic feeling, which lingers fondly in the solitary places of the Past, it may be a rallying point and its 'Lover's *Trysting-tree.*'"[6] Almost from the moment of its discovery, then, there is evidence that the myth was being politicized—lending force to Richard Wagner's remark, two decades later, that in our age *everything* becomes politicized.

Although Carlyle was a critic of English capitalism and a spokesman for social reform, he drew no social moral from the story of the Nibelungs, as Richard Wagner would do in the 1850s and William Morris again in the 1870s. Nor did he draw any "racist" moral, any doctrine of Nordic unity, as would Morris and his followers. It is true that Carlyle called special attention to the curse attached to the hoard of the Nibelungs and thereby made explicit what was merely implicit in the *Nibelungenlied* itself. The hoard or treasure of the Nibelungs proves fatal to all its possessors. It brings

death to the two sons of Nibelung; to Siegfried its conqueror: neither does the Burgundian Royal House fare better with it. Already, discords threatening to rise, Hagen sees prudent to sink it into the Rhine; first taking oath of Gunther and his brothers, that none of them shall reveal the hiding place. . . . But the curse that clave to it could not be sunk there. The Nibelungen-land is now theirs: they themselves are henceforward called Nibelungen; and this history of their fate is the *Nibelungen Noth* (Nibelungen's Need, extreme need, or final wreck and abolition).[7]

By the 1840s Carlyle was making frequent use of material from the Eddas and the story of the Nibelungs—now presumably more familiar to his readers—for metaphorical expression of his social, political, and philosophical views. In Carlyle's writings on heroes, hero worship, and the heroic in history, the social aspect of his criticism is most prominent; but he also contrasts the mechanistic materialism of nineteenth-century Europe unfavorably with the organic view found among the ancient Northern peoples. Throughout Carlyle's writings the "life-Tree Igdrasil" (Yggdrasil is Odin's horse) symbolizes his view of nature as a living organism. He writes that

Igdrasil, the Ash-Tree of Existence, has its roots deep down in the kingdom of Hela or Death; its trunk reaches up heaven-high, spreads its boughs over the whole universe: it is the Tree of Existence. At the foot of it, in the Death-

6. *Ibid.*, 45.
7. *Ibid.*, 30.

kingdom, sit the three *Nornas*, Fates—the Past, Present, Future; watering its roots from the Sacred Well. Its "boughs", with their buddings and disleafings, —events, things suffered, things done, catastrophes,—stretch through all lands and times.

And Carlyle asks his readers to consider the grandeur of this vision in comparison with the spiritual poverty of the nineteenth century's "*Machine* of the Universe."[8]

Like many men in the 1840s, including Wagner and Karl Marx, Carlyle believed that the society of his time, money-based, wealth-seeking, and coldly egotistical, was on the brink of destruction. In 1843 he used a newly published compilation of medieval writings as the takeoff point for a book of social criticism entitled *Past and Present*. There he reminds his readers that King Midas, too, had asked for gold and gotten more of it than he wanted, along with a pair of ass's ears. Humanity has confronted the sphinx of nature but failed to answer her questions rightly. We have lost touch with "the eternal inner Facts of the Universe, and followed the transient outer Appearances thereof." In consequence we are now "spell-bound, reeling on the brink of huge peril." The boasted wealth of England is like a mock-servant; it has made no one happier, wiser, better, or more beautiful: "We have more riches than any Nation ever had before; we have less good of them than any Nation had before. Our successful industry is hitherto unsuccessful; a strange success, if we stop here! In the midst of plethoric plenty, the people perish; with gold walls and full barns, no man feels himself safe or satisfied. . . . Have we actually got enchanted then; accursed by some god?" And Carlyle goes on to say that not only in Europe is the "brutish empire of Mammon" crumbling but also in the United States. "In Yankeeland itself," he adds, "my Transcendental friends announce . . . that the Demiurgus Dollar is dethroned."[9]

8. Thomas Carlyle, *Thomas Carlyle on Heroes, Hero-Worship, and the Heroic in History*, ed. H. D. Gray (New York, 1906), 20. This series of lectures was first published in 1841.

9. Thomas Carlyle, *Past and Present* (New York, 1918), 7–10. Carlyle's words are echoed by Marx in a speech published in the *People's Paper*, April 19, 1856: "In our days everything seems pregnant with its contrary. Machinery, gifted with the wonderful power of shortening and fructifying human labour, we behold starving and over-working it. The new-fangled sources of wealth, by some strange weird spell, are turned into sources of want." Cited in English, in *Karl Marx Friedrich Engels über Kunst und Literatur*, ed. Michail Lifschitz (Berlin, 1948), 75. A generally favorable review of Car-

In spite of Carlyle's lurid picture of the abyss yawning in the path of a heedless Europe—a Ragnarök and last judgment that may be "delayed some day or two, some century or two" yet will inevitably come —his attitude toward the burgeoning industrial society of nineteenth-century England is not entirely negative. Indeed he sees the Captain of Industry as the new hero of the age. True, this hero is as yet a naked egoist and an unashamed buccaneer, but he can perhaps be socialized. "Plugson" is Carlyle's name for this hero, master of Plugson and Co. of St. Dolly Undershot and possibly the eventual savior of Europe. Carlyle's attitude toward Plugson is ambiguous but in the end positive. On the one hand, the master of St. Dolly Undershot has fallen victim to the "Gospel of Mammon" with its vain hope of unifying humanity by means of a "cash-payment . . . union-bond." But on the other, he is a beneficent, though rugged individualist who provides thousands of workmen with raw material, machinery, and weekly wages, and in so doing asks no help from the government. Plugson promises that, if given elbow room, he will spin out the "sinews of war" and "conquer like a giant"; Carlyle, on his part, offers to help if Plugson will stop worshipping a primitive Mammon and convert to enlightened, paternalistic capitalism. "Tools and the Man," not "Arms and the Man," is the "proper Epic of this world"; such are Carlyle's parting words to Plugson of St. Dolly Undershot.[10] Carlyle's hero worship forces him to have a hero at all costs. And in the modern world, the world of capitalistic industry, he can find no one more capable than Plugson. Tamed and reformed, that buccaneer can perhaps become the proper leader of a middle class solely devoted to the pursuit of profit. But is this enough? We are left with an uneasy feeling by Carlyle's promise that Plugson will go into the armaments industry and conquer for us "like a giant." Does this mean that one set of slaves will be released from bondage at the expense of another, that exploitation of the worker at home will be ameliorated only by increasing it abroad? Or something even worse?

Another critic of English society who drew inspiration from this corpus of myths was William Morris, writer, artist, and socialist. As

---

lyle's book, by Friedrich Engels, was published in 1844 in the *Deutsch-Französische Jahrbücher*. See "The Condition of England: *Past and Present* by Thomas Carlyle, 1843," in *Karl Marx Friedrich Engels Collected Works* (Moscow, 1975–), III, 444–67.
    10. Carlyle, *Past and Present*, 217–26, 240.

early as 1858, at the age of twenty-four years, he wrote a poem entitled "The Defence of Guenevere." The focus of his interest in the Middle Ages later shifted to Norse mythology; and in 1870, together with his teacher Eiríkr Magnússon, he published an English translation of the story of the Volsungs and Nibelungs. The avowed purpose of the work was to trumpet the glorious past of the Northern races of Europe. We recall that, although Carlyle had termed the Middle High German *Nibelungenlied* a northern Iliad, he had seen it as peculiarly relevant to the modern Germans (*die Deutschen*). But Morris and Magnússon, in the preface to their translation of the old Norse legends, call the Volsung saga a "great Epic of the North" and state that it should be to "all our race what the Tale of Troy was to the Greeks." They hope that their work

may serve to create and powerfully promote interest in the history and literature of our Northern ancestors; that Englishmen, Americans and Germans may come to know and appreciate with honorable pride the deeds, the valor, the glorious record of that liberty-loving, intellectual and virile race from which we are descended. May it no longer be said that Americans, Germans and Englishmen hold in higher esteem the story of Greek, Roman and Persian conquerors, the deeds of alien peoples, than the heroism, the mythology, the poetic grandeur of our ancient Gothic forebears.

And the 1906 edition of their translation has an introduction by H. Halliday Sparling in which we are told that the North should be, for the English-speaking peoples, "if not a holy land, yet at least a place more to be regarded than any part of the world beside." The story of the Volsungs and Nibelungs, adds Sparling, "inspired William Morris in producing the one great English epic of the century; and Richard Wagner in the mightiest among his music-dramas."[11]

Sparling's "English epic" is of course not the translation just mentioned but *The Story of Sigurd the Volsung and the Fall of the Nibelungs*, a long poem that presents William Morris' interpretation of the legend.[12] It was published in 1876, the year that saw the first complete performance of Wagner's trilogy, *The Ring of the Nibelung*. Like Wagner and Carlyle before him, Morris rejected the plutocratic order of

11. Eiríkr Magnússon and William Morris, *The Volsunga Saga* (London and New York, 1906), I, 24–28.
12. William Morris, *The Collected Works* (24 vols.; London, 1910–1915), XII.

nineteenth-century Europe. Like Wagner, Morris preached a gospel of salvation by art. Late in life he became an avowed follower of Karl Marx, whose economic and political doctrines had, Morris wrote, given an evolutionary basis to the desire of earlier socialists for the replacement of unrestricted competition by a spirit of cooperation. Morris' hatred of modern civilization and his hope for its eventual destruction—the leading passion of his life, so he wrote in 1894—rested on both aesthetic and moral grounds. He speaks of our civilization's mastery and misuse of power, of its impoverished commonwealth and bloated private sector, of its stupendous organization "all for the misery of life," of its "eyeless vulgarity which has destroyed art." What has been the culmination of the age-old strivings of humanity in our time? A "sordid, aimless, ugly confusion," a "dull squalor," a "counting-house on top of a cinder-heap," replies Morris, in phrases that recall Charles Dickens' *Our Mutual Friend*. This doomed society can by no stretch of the imagination be rescued by mere meliorative reforms—by abolishing the monarchy, the House of Lords, and the huge standing army of Great Britain, all in the name of democracy. For, says Morris, the United States of America has neither monarchy nor House of Lords, and its tiny standing army is "chiefly used for the murder of red-skins"; and for all that it is "a society corrupt to the core . . . at this moment engaged in suppressing freedom with just the same reckless brutality and blind ignorance as the Czar of all the Russias uses." Unless the special privileges conferred on a small number of people by the capitalist system are abolished, "nothing at all would have been accomplished."[13] The real enemy of humanity is riches—riches that go hand in hand with poverty and slavery and are quite another thing than wealth; in the name of riches, money, and profit the real wealth of England is being destroyed and degraded. If matters are allowed to continue in this way, the earth's surface will be made hideous everywhere; and in the end master will be no better off than slave. Humanity may then be delivered from its plight by some terrible cataclysm. But in all likelihood it will once again wearily trudge the circle, until at last "some accident, some unforeseen consequence of arrangement made an end of it altogether."[14]

13. Morris, *Collected Works*, XXIII, 30–31. In a footnote, Morris calls attention to the "legal murder," in 1888, of the Chicago anarchists.
14. *Ibid.*, 74, 95–96, 158–59, 279.

The resemblance of all this to the thoughts and images turning in Wagner's mind when, twenty or more years earlier, he shaped *The Ring of the Nibelung* is—as we shall see later—striking. Morris, in writing his own Nibelung poem, did not take the same liberties with the mythic material that Wagner allowed himself in the *Ring*. But he did alter, re-arrange, and shift emphasis to lend the tale a moral for his time. As Eshleman says, *The Story of Sigurd the Volsung and the Fall of the Nibelungs* states the evils of nineteenth-century European and English imperialistic capitalism, as Morris saw them.[15] As in Wagner's *Ring*, Morris' theme is the baneful and ultimately fatal effect of lovelessness, envy, greed, and the lust for gold and power. When the god Loki seizes the hoard of the Nibelungs from the Elf-king Andvari (Alberich in Wagner's *Ring*), Andvari tries to make off with the golden ring of power still on his finger. But Loki commands:

Come hither again to thy master, and give the ring to me;
For meseems it is Loki's portion, and the Bale of Men shall it be.

Bale is *bane* or *bain*, the curse, woe, or evil fate of humanity:

Then the Elf-king drew off the gold-ring and stood with empty hand
E'en where the flood fell over 'twixt the water and the land,
And he gazed on the great Guile-master, and huge and grim he grew
And his anguish swelled within him, and the words of the Norns he knew;
How that gold was the seed of gold to the wise and the shapers of things,
The hoarders of hidden treasure, and the unseen glory of rings;
But the seed of woe to the world and the foolish wasters of men,
And grief to the generations that die and spring again.

In Morris' poem Sigurd is told this tale by Regin, the brother of Faf-ner and the son of Reidmar, king of the dwarfs. Sigurd is also told by Regin that Loki was in turn forced to yield the ring to Reidmar. Fafner, after killing his father, took possession of the ring and turned into a dragon, the "Gold-wallower." Regin has forged the sword Wrath and put it into the hands of Sigurd so that he may kill the dragon and win back the treasure, after which the dwarf plans to kill him. Sword in hand, Sigurd rides out to meet his fate:

And for me were the edges smithied, and the Wrath cries out aloud;

15. Lloyd Wendell Eshleman, *A Victorian Rebel: The Life of William Morris* (New York, 1940), 128–34.

And a voice hath called from the darkness, and I ride to the Glittering Heath;
To smite on the door of Destruction, and waken the warder of Death.

On the Glittering Heath—a traditional hiding place of the Grail-treasure
—Sigurd meets and slays the dragon Fafner. He then takes possession
of Andvari's golden hoard. Morris follows the remorseless path of the
old tale to its conclusion:

Ye have heard of Sigurd afore time, how the foes of the Gods he slew;
How forth from the darksome desert the Gold of Waters he drew;
How he wakened Love on the Mountain, and wakened Brynhild the Bright,
And dwelt on Earth for a season, and shone in all men's sight.
Ye have heard of the Cloudy People, and the dimming of the day
And the latter world's confusion, and Sigurd gone away;
Now ye know of the Need of the Nibelung and the end of the broken troth,
All the death of kings and of kindreds and the Sorrow of Odin the Goth.[16]

The "Need of the Nibelung," plainly enough, is Morris' way of expressing the dire need of nineteenth-century European humanity.

2. HEINRICH HEINE'S DREAM OF DESTRUCTION

In 1834—three years after Carlyle's assessment of the *Nibelungenlied*
and at a time when Wagner was a struggling young musician of twenty-
one years—a prophetic essay on the history of religion and philosophy
in Germany appeared in a French periodical, the *Revue des deux mondes*. It came from the pen of Heinrich Heine, a thirty-seven-year-old
German Jew who had been living in self-imposed exile in France since
1831. Heine's intent was to explain to the logical French mind something of the peculiar and obscure character of German thought, and at
the same time to issue the French a warning. Brilliant, witty, and en-
tertaining throughout, the essay takes on a dithyrambic, prophetic, and
strangely foreboding tone toward its close. Heine warns the French that
a spiritual earthquake of extraordinary magnitude is slowly building up
in German lands. He warns them of a catastrophe to come in comparison with which the French Revolution will seem like a harmless idyll.
German philosophy, he tells them, has brought about the death of God.
The metaphysical spirit has been slain by the Kantian critique of human reason, by Immanuel Kant's proof that we can never know things

16. Morris, *Collected Works*, XII, 83, 102, 306.

as they are in themselves but only in the phenomenal forms conferred on their manifestations by the knowing subject. Even time and space are not the ultimate realities they seem to be. They, too, are dependent on the structure of the mind that knows them. Heine foresees that the dethronement of the Christian God will be followed by an awakening of the old Northern pagan gods from the long slumber in which they have been held by the talisman of Christianity. That talisman is already crumbling into dust. Before Heine's inner eye the "old stone gods arise . . . rub the dust of a thousand years from their eyes. . . . At last Thor springs up with his giant hammer and smashes the Gothic cathedrals." The *furor Teutonicus*, the "berserk madness" of the ancient Northmen, will walk abroad.[17]

A threat from "Germany" must have seemed rather remote to the French of the 1830s, for there was as yet no such national entity on the horizon. For centuries the small German states had been the playground of foreign military powers. The peoples of the German-speaking lands had been half-exterminated in the Thirty Years War; Louis XIV had devastated the Palatinate in 1688; a century later Napoleon I brought Germany and the whole of Europe under his control and reached out to seize Russia. In 1834 Napoleon had been dead for only thirteen years. A consequence of his short-lived triumph of the will had been the demise of the moribund Holy Roman Empire of the German Nation. "Germany" was a mere aggregate of duchies, principalities and kingdoms—headed by Catholic Bavaria in the south and Protestant Prussia in the north—often at odds with one another. The German peoples were regarded by their neighbors as a stolid, industrious, orderly, and peaceful folk, with a curious streak of dreaminess in their character. (As a German, Heine himself felt called on to warn his readers not to dismiss him as a mere phantast.) What could France, by far the most populous, wealthy, and militarily powerful nation of Europe, have to fear from dreamers beyond the Rhine?

To understand something of the reason for Heine's disquiet, we must inquire into the death of God, an event that, according to Heine, took place in 1781 with the publication of Kant's *Critique of Pure Reason*. The appearance of Kant's book had signaled a "January 21st of De-

17. Heinrich Heine, "De l'Allemagne depuis Luther," *Revue des deux mondes*, 1. *trimestre* (1834), 473–505; 4. *trimestre* (1834), 373–408, 633–78.

ism," says Heine, recalling the execution of Louis XVI on January 21, 1793. "It is the Jehovah of old who readies himself for death":

We have known him since his cradle in Egypt, where he was raised among calves and divine crocodiles. . . . We have seen him . . . become in Palestine the little god of a poor shepherd folk. . . . We saw him emigrate to Rome, the capital, where he renounced every kind of national prejudice. . . . We saw him purify and spiritualize himself still more, become paternal, merciful, a benefactor of humanity, a philanthropist—But nothing could save him! Do you not hear the ringing of the bell? To your knees! They are bringing the sacraments to a dying God.[18]

The vacant throne of religion is now fought over by philosophers. After Kant had come J. G. Fichte with his "absolute ego," spinning the world out of itself like a spider. Then came the German philosophers of nature, some of whom had revived certain dangerously obscurantist social doctrines, such as Joseph Görres, who claimed that the nation-state was an organic whole, a giant tree whose members subsisted only through their relation to the whole—precisely the idea behind the "corporative hierarchy of the Middle Ages," remarks Heine. After the nature-philosophers had come Georg Friedrich Hegel, and the great circle of philosophy had been closed by the Hegelian dialectic.[19]

Now, says Heine, we must await the beginning of philosophical (we would say ideological) wars. For the Germans are a methodical folk. Their thought precedes action as lightning precedes thunder. True, it is German thunder and it will come slowly. But it will come. And when it does, there will be a crash like one that has not been heard since the beginning of the world:

There will appear Kantians who will no more hear of piety in the world of facts than in the world of ideas, and they will pitilessly overturn with sword and axe the soil of our European life to extirpate the last roots of the past. Armed Fichteans, whose fanaticism of will can be checked neither by fear nor self-interest—for they live in the spirit and despise matter, like the early Christians whom neither earthly joys nor bodily torture could tame—will come on the same stage. . . . But most frightening of all would be the philosophers of nature who would intervene in the action of a German revolution and identify themselves with the work of destruction. For if the hand of the Kantian strikes hard and sure because his heart is unmoved by any respect for

18. *Ibid.*, 408.
19. *Ibid.*, 674–75.

tradition, if the Fichtean boldly scorns all danger because for him it does not exist in reality, the philosopher of nature will be terrible in that he puts himself in touch with the primal powers of the earth, in that he conjures up the hidden forces of tradition and is able to evoke all those of German pantheism.[20]

It is at this point that Thor will begin smashing the Gothic cathedrals of Christian Europe.

We would be wrong in supposing that Heine did not want the Gothic cathedrals to be smashed and the past uprooted. At this time he believed in the necessity and desirability of a revolution against the old order. Medieval Christianity, says Heine, had dishonored the human body along with all else that was material, had made Venus into a whore, and had forced Tannhäuser to think her a devil. The senses have been made to play the hypocrite. But humanity is now reaching out for a new understanding of itself; it is seeking for a way to wed the material and the spiritual: "The most immediate goal of all our modern institutions is thus the rehabilitation of the material, its religious recognition and moral sanctification, its reconciliation with the spirit. Purusha and Prakriti will be united anew. As the ancient myth of India so ingeniously demonstrates, it was from their violent parting that evil, the great rent in the world, arose."[21] It is clear, then, that Heine in a certain sense *wants* the Gothic cathedrals—those visible symbols of the rule of medieval Christianity—to be smashed. His uneasiness seems to rest on a fear that the forces about to be released in Germany will be beyond control.

What Heine has to say next requires some familiarity with the position occupied by a small number of specially privileged, so-called court Jews before the emancipation of the Jews from the ghettos of Western Europe. By the time of Heine's essay the court Jews, who had for generations been handling the financial affairs of various petty European rulers, were far less important than certain powerful families of Jewish international bankers, most notably the Rothschilds of England, France, Germany, Austria, and Italy. According to Hannah Arendt, the last war financed by a Jew was the Prussian-Austrian war of 1866. The Prussian Parliament had refused to extend Bismarck the necessary credits, and he had turned to Gerson Bleichröder for assistance—the same Bleich-

20. *Ibid.*, 676.
21. *Ibid.*, 387–88.

röder who, through his connection with the Rothschilds, was to provide Bismarck with a news conduit to Disraeli in England in the seventies and who, again in conjunction with the Rothschilds, was to arrange for the payment of reparations to Prussia after the French defeat in 1871. The peace treaties of Versailles were the last in which Jews were prominent as advisors; the last Jew who owed his national prominence to his international financial connections was Walther Rathenau, foreign minister of the Weimar Republic.[22] In Heine's time such Jews appeared to some people as an invisible government that manipulated the strings of power behind facades of emperors, kings, and parliaments:

Christianity had yielded all that was material to Caesar and the Talmudist bankers, contenting itself with denying supremacy to the former and stigmatizing the latter in public opinion. . . . But behold! in the end the hated sword and despised money gain supreme power, and the representatives of the spirit are forced to come to terms with them. Yes, and this agreement has even become a firm alliance. It is not only the priests of Rome, but also those of England and Prussia, in the end all privileged priests, who have compacted with Caesar and his consorts to oppress the people.[23]

Heine, partly ironically, goes on to claim that the greatest triumph in Europe had been celebrated by the Jews. This people had not only resisted heathen Rome but in the end had conquered it. The "poor rabbi of Nazareth," the derided king of the Jews, crowned with thorns, had in the end become the God of the Romans. Not the king of this world, of course, Heine continues, although that position too had been occupied by the Jews. And even Christian Rome has been conquered and made tributary to the Jew. Go to 15 rue Lafitte at the beginning of any year's quarter, Heine tells his readers:

You will see stopped before the high portal a heavy vehicle from which a large man descends. He climbs a staircase leading to a smaller room where a blond young man is sitting with grand seigneurial nonchalance in which there is something so solid, so positive, so absolute that it is as if he had all the money of the world in his pocket. And in effect he does have all the money of this world in his pocket, because his name is M. James de Rothschild, and the large man is Monsignor the ambassador of His Holiness, the Pope, who

22. Hannah Arendt, *The Origins of Totalitarianism* (2nd ed.; Cleveland & New York, 1958), 20–21.
23. Heine, "De l'Allemagne," 4. *trimestre* (1834), 386–87.

brings as his representative the tribute of Rome, the interest on the Roman loan.[24]

Heine's essay, with some minor changes of wording, appeared in German in 1834. Almost twenty years later he brought out a second German edition. It was based—the original German version no longer being obtainable—on the essay in the *Revue des deux mondes*. Although, as Heine tells his readers in the preface, his views on religion and the death of God have changed, he has decided to leave the essay unrevised, aside from minor alterations. It is worth noting that Heine has lost his faith in Hegel and turned back to the Bible for inspiration. He recommends his "much more impenitent friend Marx" and such Young Hegelians as Ludwig Feuerbach and Bruno Bauer, "those godless self-deifiers," to study the legend of Nebuchadnezzar. Nothing more is said of the coming catastrophe. The aborted revolutions of 1848–1849 had, after all, come and gone. But it does seem that Heine is now more concerned about Young Hegelians than about armed Kantians, Fichteans, and nature-philosophers.[25]

3. THE MYTH OF RACE

As we have seen, it was the hope of William Morris and his circle that an acquaintance with the Norse gods and heroes would serve to awaken pride of race among the Northern peoples of Europe, including those who had moved on to the United States and Canada. The English, Germans, and Scandinavians were the chief representatives of the group that Morris had in mind. Forty years earlier the Germans, so Carlyle has told us, were already rallying around the racial trysting tree of the *Nibelungenlied*. There is little evidence that notions of racial purity or pride of race played a significant ideological role in Europe before the nineteenth century. The noble families of Europe, including those south of the Alps and west of the Rhine, were the exception. They were largely of Germanic origin; with them pride of blood had been cultivated since the fall of the Roman Empire. Pride of race among the Jews was even

24. *Ibid.*, 402.
25. Heinrich Heine, *Werke*, ed. Hermann Friedemann, Helene Herrmann, Erwin Kalischer, Raimund Pissin, and Veit Valentin (15 vols. in 5; Berlin, 1927), VII-IX, 163–67.

more ancient. Unlike its upstart counterpart among the Northern peoples, it was not confined to a few leading families. For all orthodox Jews purity of blood was the sine qua non of the existence of the Jewish people; hence the relative disinterest of Judaism in proselytizing, as compared with Christianity and Islam.[26] Racial pride was inherent in their position as the chosen race, the people chosen by Jahweh to take possession of the earth and the fullness thereof. Here we single out for comment the views of three important nineteenth-century "racists": Benjamin Disraeli, Count Arthur de Gobineau, and Houston Stewart Chamberlain—an English Jew who obtained high position and was subsequently ennobled, a French nobleman, and a British admiral's son who wrote in German and became a citizen of the German Reich.

Disraeli was the spokesman for the Young England wing of the Tory party in the 1840s when his novels began to make a stir. Later, as Queen Victoria's prime minister in 1867, he authorized a punitive expedition to Ethiopia. From 1874 to 1880 Disraeli, now first Earl of Beaconsfield, implemented the aggressive English foreign policy. The British Empire was at the very peak of its expansionist phase: the war against the Afghans (1878), the Zulu War (1879), the purchase of the Suez Canal (1875), and the crowning of Victoria as empress of India (1876) are some of the high points of Disraeli's second period as prime minister. Disraeli's father, a literary critic, was a Christian convert; and Benjamin had been duly baptized into the Christian faith. But if we accept the views expressed in Disraeli's novels *Coningsby* (1844) and *Tancred* (1847), membership in the Jewish "race" is quite independent of overt religious affiliation. In *Coningsby* the spokesman for Disraeli's racial mystique is the immensely wealthy and cultured Sidonia, scion of an international banking family of Sephardic Jews. Sidonia comes from an old and illustrious Spanish Jewish family that has included among its

26. The Jews proselytized actively in ancient Rome, if we are to believe Horace (*Satires*, I, iv., 143–44) and the New Testament (Matthew, 23:15). According to the Marxist historian Abram Leon, the Jews were banished from Rome in 139 B.C. for being overzealous in recruiting proselytes. The economic importance of the Jews lay in the sphere of commerce and later, usury, says Leon. In medieval times, he writes, feudalism was "mother earth" for the lord and Jew alike: "If the lord needed the Jew, the Jew also had need of the lord." See Abram Leon *The Jewish Question: A Marxist Interpretation* (1950; reprint ed., New York, 1970), 77, 114. Making allowance for such exceptions as the Khazars and the Falashas, Jewish proselytizing fell off sharply after the first few centuries of the common era.

apparently Christian members in the past an archbishop of Toledo and even a Grand Inquisitor. But throughout its long sojourn in Spain this family, "in common with two-thirds of the Aragonese nobility, secretly adhered to the ancient faith and ceremonies of their fathers." We need not inquire into the truth of these claims, for we are dealing here with fiction rather than fact; but a sizable number of Jews in Spain had actually done something of the sort. Had he known of them, Disraeli might have pointed to the Jews of the Dönmeh in Salonika, who followed the example of their seventeenth-century Messiah Sabbatai Ṣevi, converting to Islam yet keeping their Jewish identity intact.[27]

Sidonia's racial views are expounded in large part in *Coningsby* and *Tancred* by an authorial voice. We learn that there are five chief varieties of the human race: "to wit, the Caucasian, the Mongolian, the Malayan, the American, the Ethiopian; the Arabian tribes rank in the first and superior class, together, among others with the Saxon and the Greek. . . . But Sidonia and his brethren could claim a distinction which the Saxon and the Greek and the rest of the Caucasian nations have forfeited. The Hebrew is an unmixed race. . . . An unmixed race of a first rate organization are the aristocracy of nature." We see that a christening has not weakened Disraeli's adherence to the traditional Jewish belief in the importance of racial "purity." Alone of the white peoples, the Hebrew race had refrained from intermixture with other peoples and so preserved the purity of its lineage. Hence its claim to be an "aristocracy of nature." Disraeli's "Arabian tribes" correspond to the Semites in general; we find Sidonia at times referring to the Hebrews as "Arabs." With a hint of condescension, Sidonia informs Coningsby that he, blue-eyed and golden-haired, is the scion of a "sufficiently pure" Northern race, a representative of a "famous breed, with whom we Arabs have contended long." And in the end the "Arabs" have triumphed. Adopting the role of Coningsby's mentor or elder brother, Sidonia tells him that the "Jewish mind" now exerts an enormous and far-reaching influence on the affairs of Europe. The first Jesuits were Jews. The "mysterious Russian diplomacy" is now organized and carried on largely by Jews. There are Jewish ministers in the courts of St. Petersburg, Madrid, Paris,

27. Benjamin Disraeli, *Coningsby; or, The New Generation* (London, 1927), 220–21; Gershom Scholem, *Sabbatai Ṣevi, the Mystical Messiah* (Princeton, N.J., 1973), xiii.

and Berlin. In Germany the Jews "almost monopolise" the professorial chairs. And further, "that mighty revolution which is at this moment preparing in Germany . . . is entirely developing under the auspices of Jews." It is made plain to Coningsby by Sidonia that the world is governed by very different personages from those thought to be in control by people who have no knowledge of what is taking place behind the scenes; Europe is in fact ruled by an invisible government of Jews. And, Sidonia adds, "even musical Europe is ours"; the great musicians of the day, "Rossini, Meyerbeer and Mendelssohn, are of Hebrew race."[28]

Sidonia-Disraeli's stature as a prophet is diminished somewhat when we recall that the "mighty revolution" being readied in German lands under the auspices of the Jews, although it did indeed take place in Berlin, Dresden, and other German cities in 1848 and 1849, fizzled out quite ingloriously—leaving, incidentally, Wagner in political exile and his friends Michael Bakunin and August Röckel in prison under sentence of death. Yet it is plain that Disraeli, like many others, was aware that real trouble was brewing in Europe. Interestingly enough, he seems to have thought the position of England was even more precarious than that of France. In France at least—so Sidonia tells Coningsby—the throne is occupied by a hero-king, a veritable Ulysses. (Not unsurprisingly the reference is to that reactionary expansionist, the conqueror of Algeria, Louis Philippe, who—despite Sidonia's faith in him—was forced in the February Revolution of 1848 to abdicate and flee to England, where he enjoyed the friendship and protection of Queen Victoria.) As the leading British Tory and imperialist of his time, Disraeli appears to have believed that the salvation of Europe lay in the triumph of the allied principles of racial purity and aristocracy. He knew, of course, that there was considerable antagonism between the Jews and the other inhabitants of England. But he held it as an article of faith that the two great races of England, the racially pure Jews and the (not quite so pure) representatives of the Caucasian race, could and should work together in amity (just as Chamberlain in Germany was to suggest some forty years later). Sidonia warns Coningsby that if the "Northern race" fails to understand that Jews are Tories by nature—for "Toryism, indeed, is but copied from that mighty prototype which has fashioned

28. Disraeli, *Coningsby*, 232, 264–67, 281.

Europe"—if, still worse, the Northern race once again begins to perse-
cute the Jews, the latter will, with each succeeding generation, "become more powerful and dangerous to the society which is hostile toward them."[29]

As Philip Guedalla pointed out in 1927, to Disraeli the Jew was a
proto-Christian and the Christian a perfected Jew. Guedalla remarks
that Disraeli's Semitism is sometimes a shade malicious, as when he
proclaims that the life of a British peer is mainly regulated by "Arabian
laws and Syrian customs." In *Tancred*, indeed, Disraeli's racism reaches
its peak. But it is by no means pure Semitism. Tancred—who, despite
his name and origin, has "dark, intelligent eyes"—is the young son of
the Duke and Duchess of Bellamont and Lord Montacute in his own
right. Troubled by the moral deterioration of nineteenth-century England, he undertakes a pilgrimage to the Holy Land. The indefatigable
Sidonia comes to his aid, putting him in touch with the prior of Terra
Santa at Jerusalem—a "Nueva" of the fourteenth century whose "blood
is no longer clear, but has been modified by many Gothic intermar-
riages"—and with "the one banker" of the Near East, a Jew who despite
his wealth and power is, Sidonia assures Tancred, "mine." After incul-
cating the proper spirit of humility in Tancred by informing him that
the bishops of England were, a few centuries back, "tattooed savages"
and understood neither the old nor the new learning, Sidonia sends
him on his way. The novel closes with the doubtful promise of a coming union of Tancred, in Palestine, with the beautiful Jewess Eva. On
his knees before a daughter of his "Redeemer's race," Tancred proposes
that their "united destinies shall advance the sovereign purpose" of
their lives. Perhaps the male and female representatives of the two great
races will unite to generate the coming race—the crude, hardly formed
son of the North uniting with the daughter of the oldest race. Perhaps
not. There is much for Tancred to learn: from Sidonia that "all is race;
there is no other truth," that with the decay of race is coupled the decay
of empire, that the "decay of a race is an inevitable necessity unless . . .
it never mixes its blood," that the times call for a "man"; from Eva that
"Hebrews have never blended with their conquerors"; from the authorial voice that "some flat-nosed Frank," son of a race "spawned perhaps

29. *Ibid.*, 319–20.

in the morasses of some Northern forest hardly yet cleared," has dared
to talk of progress merely because, "by an ingenious application of some
scientific acquirements, he had established a society which has mistaken comfort for civilization." From Tancred himself we hear that
"Arabia alone has remained free and faithful to the divine tradition"
and that some day "the sacred quarter of the globe will recover its pri-
meval and divine supremacy." We must bear in mind that for Disraeli
the Arabs were merely "Jews on horseback." As Guedalla points out,
Disraeli seemed, in his novels at least, incapable of distinguishing a
Jew from an Arab.[30]

Coningsby and Tancred by no means span the measure of Disraeli's
political, social, and racial dreams and ideas. A complete study of the
novels in relation to Disraeli's actual colonial and imperial policies
may be found in a doctoral dissertation published in Germany in 1935.[31]
But before leaving Disraeli to explore some similar ideas in Arthur de
Gobineau and Houston Stewart Chamberlain, a remarkable thematic
resemblance between Disraeli's Tancred and Wagner's The Saracen
Woman deserves comment. The first sketch was made by Wagner in
Paris in 1841. In 1843 he completed the text, which was intended to
serve as an operatic vehicle for Frau Schroeder-Devrient, the singer
whom he so much admired. For one reason or another Wagner abandoned the project. The text itself was lost, and it did not turn up until
five years after Wagner's death. In the following year, 1889, it was published for the first time in the Bayreuther Blätter.[32] The Saracen Woman
has a solid historical base. Manfred, natural son of the Hohenstaufen
Emperor Frederick II and leader of the Ghibelline party in Italy, was
the last of the Hohenstaufen kings of Sicily. After the Sicilian Vespers
(1282), Manfred's son-in-law, Peter III of Aragon, founded a new dy-

30. Benjamin Disraeli, Tancred; or, The New Crusade (London, 1927), viii, 46, 54,
128–29, 197, 233, 441, 500.
31. Hans Rühl, Disraelis Imperialismus und die Kolonialpolitik seiner Zeit (Leipzig, 1935). Bruno Bauer, a former Young Hegelian, wrote in 1882 that the heroes of Disraeli's novels, Sidonia especially, represented Disraeli's fantasies of himself as leader.
Bauer says that this "most talkative of dictators" gave his romances to the Young England party as a catechism and that the sum of their wisdom is that a political leader
must "despise human beings, and march forward over the heads of the people." See
Bruno Bauer, Disraelis romantischer und Bismarcks sozialistischer Imperialismus
(1882; reprint ed., Darmstadt, 1969), 60, 247.
32. Richard Wagner, Richard Wagner's Prose Works, trans. William Ashton Ellis
(8 vols.; London, 1899), VIII, 250–76.

nasty on the island. So much is history. In Wagner's sketch Manfred's inspiration in his battle against the papal forces is a mysterious Saracen woman, Fatima by name. He falls hopelessly in love with her, but she resists his advances. Just before her death (she is stabbed by a rival), Fatima reveals herself to be Manfred's half-sister, the natural daughter of Frederick II (presumably a product of his stay in Jerusalem). The failed union of Wagner's Manfred and Fatima has its counterpart in the possibly successful union of Disraeli's Tancred and Eva. Wagner's introduction of an incest motif into the story of Manfred and Fatima foreshadows the multiple incestuous relationships introduced into *The Ring of the Nibelung*. And oddly enough, Manfred is a "Nibelung"—for Wagner was shortly thereafter to identify the historical Wibelungs (the German Ghibellines) with the legendary Nibelungs.

Disraeli's overheated fancy—as Guedalla observes in his introduction to *Tancred*—roams about in a borderland lying somewhere between past and present, fact and fiction, Christianity and Judaism, Arab and Jew, Europe and Asia—a fancy sometimes alert, sometimes drowsy with poppycock. But this "spiritual No Man's Land," as Guedalla calls it, was familiar country to the spirit of the times. We shall find that Disraeli is not the only dreamer wandering about in this land. Heine and Wagner are there, perhaps also Carlyle and Morris. Karl Marx is there. At times Marx's utterances are distinguishable from those of Heine, Disraeli, and Wagner only by their bitter tone as he pours out the vials of his prophet's wrath on a society in which man is dominated by the thing he worships above all else—*money*—that alienating, alienated, and alien essence which has "robbed the whole world, the human world as well as nature, of its proper worth." Writing in 1843 on Bruno Bauer's *The Jewish Question*, Marx states that "the God of the Jews has been secularized and has become the god of this world." The bill of exchange is the real god of the Jew. His god is an "illusory bill of exchange." Money, continues Marx, "is the jealous god of Israel before whom no other god may exist." On the subject of emancipation of the Jews, Marx says that the Jews have already emancipated themselves, "insofar as Christians have become Jews." In a rapid series of paradoxes he claims that Christianity arose out of Judaism and has now sunk back into Judaism: "The Jew is the practical Christian, and the practical Christian has again become the Jew." The universal domination of Judaism has converted man and nature into "alienable and saleable objects subservient to egoistic need." Hence the social emancipation of the Jew calls for "the emancipation of society from Judaism." In what seems like an anticipation of the thesis set forth by Wagner in his essay *Judaism in Music* (1850), Marx states that "contempt for theory, for art, for history, for man as an end in himself . . . is contained abstractly in the Jewish religion" and has become the *"actual conscious* standpoint" of the monied man.[33] It is of course not true that Marx, Disraeli, and Wagner were in agreement on all points. But they are so obviously denizens of a particular spiritual milieu that we could almost place them from their "style" alone, just as a connoisseur is able to date a painter or musician.

The racial theme sounded by Disraeli in the 1840s was taken up and developed on a grand scale in the 1850s by Arthur de Gobineau, nobleman, diplomat, and man of letters. Gobineau's *chef-d'oeuvre* is his essay on the inequality of human races. Whereas Disraeli attributes everything of value to the Jews, Gobineau attributes everything to the Aryans: "Everything great, noble and fruitful in the works of man on this earth . . . is the development of a single germ and the result of a single thought; it belongs to one family alone, the different branches of which have reigned in all civilized countries." Gobineau's essay is brilliant, fanciful, and shot through with ideas later taken up by such writers as Houston Stewart Chamberlain, Oswald Spengler, and Arnold Toynbee. The human race has three subdivisions, according to Gobi-

33. Karl Marx, *Writings of the Young Marx on Philosophy and Society*, trans. and ed. L. D. Easton and K. H. Guddat (Garden City, N.Y., 1967), 216–48. The Marxian proletariat, like the Marxian "Jew," can achieve emancipation only at the price of self-abolition. The proletariat becomes "victorious only by abolishing itself and its opposite . . . private property," say Marx and Engels. The world-historical role of the proletariat does not imply that socialist writers "regard the proletarians as *gods*." They continue: "Rather the contrary. Since in the fully-formed proletariat the abstraction of all humanity, even of the *semblance* of humanity, is practically complete; since the conditions of the life of the proletariat sum up all the conditions of life of society today in their most inhuman form; since man has lost himself in the proletariat, yet at the same time has not only gained theoretical consciousness of that loss, but through urgent, no longer removable, no longer disguisable, absolutely imperative *need*. . . is driven to revolt against this inhumanity, it follows that the proletariat can and must emancipate itself. But it cannot emancipate itself without abolishing the conditions of its own life." See "The Holy Family," *Karl Marx Friedrich Engels Collected Works*, IV, 7–211; esp. 36–37. The Jews, likewise, can become fully emancipated only by abolishing the socio-economic conditions determining the existence (including the religious life) of the "Jew."

neau: the white, the yellow, and the black. All higher civilizations are the work of the white race. In the history of humanity, only ten "complete societies" or civilizations have arisen. Seven of these lie, or lay, in Europe and Asia: the Indian, the Egyptian, the Assyrian, the Greek, the Chinese, the Roman, and the Germanic. The remaining three lay in the New World: the Peruvian, the Mexican, and the Alleghanian. Gobineau supposes that the Aryans intermixed with the black peoples of India and Africa and the yellow peoples of China to contribute the germ of the future civilizations in those lands. The Assyrian civilization, including the Phoenician, Carthaginian, and Hebrew, was Semitic in origin. The Medes, Persians, and Zoroastrians were of Aryan stock; the Greeks of Aryan stock modified by Semitic elements; and the Romans a mixture of Aryan, Semitic, Celtic, and Iberian elements. Among the New World civilizations Gobineau calls the Aztec the highest, even though he himself preferred the less ferocious religious culture of the Incas of Peru. The Roman Empire in Europe, with its racial hodgepodge, eventually came under the dominion of an Aryan stock of peoples, namely the "Germanic races, which in the fifth century transformed the Western mind."[34] It is worth noting that Gobineau, borrowing as he frequently does from Wilhelm von Humboldt, distinguishes a culture from a civilization. A culture is characterized by the development of arts and sciences; it represents a higher level of advancement than does a civilization.

The speculative strain in Gobineau's thought becomes most evident when he speaks of civilizations as magnified images of human beings—androgynous beings, in which either male or female principle may predominate. These superorganisms, each in its time, have "all believed in their own immortality." The Incas and their families, as they traveled swiftly along the fifteen-hundred-mile road that still links Cuzco to Quito, were no doubt convinced that their conquests would last forever, says Gobineau. And yet—"Time, with one blow of his wing, has hurled their empire, like so many others, into the uttermost abyss." How do these great entities come into being? Gobineau replies that a mere aggregate of tribes becomes a civilization only when "one of the two currents of instinct, the material and the intellectual, flow-

34. Arthur de Gobineau, *The Inequality of the Human Races*, trans. Adrian Collins (New York, 1915), xiv, xv, 211–12.

ing with greater force than before," fuses with the other. Two separate
groups of human beings, originally borne along by one or the other of the
two currents, intermingle and interbreed. Different qualities come to the
surface, "according as the power of thought or action is dominant. . . .
We may use here the Hindu symbolism, and represent what I call the
'intellectual current' by Prakriti, the female principle, and the 'material current' by Purusha, the male principle. There is, of course, no praise
or blame attaching to either of these phrases; they merely imply that
one principle is fertilized by the other."[35] Gobineau's use of the *puru-
sha-prakriti* metaphor recalls Heine. Wagner too, at the time of Gobineau's writing, was involved in working out his own interpretation,
musical and otherwise, of the male-female conjunction.

Why do these superorganisms die? What is the reason for their apparently inevitable decline and fall, leaving the earth littered with "wrecks
of civilizations that have preceded our own"? Some thinkers, says Gobineau, have proposed that civilizations die of intrinsic "degeneration."
Just as individual organisms die—when they do not die by violence or
disease—in consequence of an internally determined breakdown of
their structural-functional elements, so also do social organisms perish. No external agency is needed to bring them down. Gobineau calls
this account correct but circular. It really says no more than that a civilization dies "because it is degenerate and is degenerate because it dies"
—leaving unanswered the question of why it became degenerate in the
first place. Nevertheless, he was in agreement with the idea that there
is but one fatal disease of civilizations, namely degeneration. Every
civilization "acquires, on the very day of its birth, hidden among the
elements of its life, the seed of an inevitable death." What, then, are the
inevitable causes of societal degeneration? Until an answer to this question is obtained, says Gobineau, we must admit that the "science of
social anatomy is in its infancy." Gobineau's own answer to the question is hardly compatible with the claim that a "seed of an inevitable
death" permeates any network of relations, however ingeniously contrived, among human beings. For his answer is one that we have already heard from the mouth of Sidonia-Disraeli: it is racial intermix-

35. *Ibid.*, 86, 167.

ture that inevitably leads to the degeneration of society and the decay of civilization. Races are unequal in their endowments. The intermixture of "blood" causes a civilization erected by a superior breed to fall into the hands of a lesser breed. The inferior breed is unable to sustain the life of the social organism; the civilization stumbles on its path, falls, and dies.[36]

The history of the Jews supplied Gobineau with a paradigm of the benefits of racial purity. It is a pity, he remarks, that the Christians have not been able to develop among themselves the sentiment that they too are a chosen people, whose obligation is to remain racially pure. Consider what the belief had done for the ancient Israelites:

> Modern travellers know what an amount of organized effort was required from the Israelite farmers. . . . Since the chosen race ceased to dwell in the mountains and plains of Palestine, the well where Jacob's flocks came down to drink has been filled up with sand, Naboth's vineyard has been invaded by the desert, and the bramble flourishes in the place where stood the palace of Ahab. And what did the Jews become, in this miserable corner of the earth? They became a people that succeeded in everything it undertook, a free, strong, and intelligent people, and one which, before it lost, sword in hand, the name of an independent nation, had given as many learned men to the world as it had merchants.

Oscar Levy's introduction to Gobineau's essay is instructive. Writing at the time of the outbreak of the Great War, Levy sees Gobineau as a true prophet—a man who had discerned behind the impressive material and technical facade of the nineteenth century a "muddle of moral values." But, unlike Wagner, he was a stern, uncompromising, and gloomy prophet. "Old Wagner, who introduced him to the German public," notes Levy, "thought of brightening his gloom by a little Christian faith, hope and charity, in order to make the pill more palatable to that great public, which he, the great Stagemanager, knew so well." Other Germans too, including Chamberlain, had poured water into Gobineau's wine or "sweetened it with patriotic syrups." Even Disraeli, who reminded Levy so much of Gobineau in other respects, had failed to develop the necessary "scepticism against the Church and its Semitic values." And now that catastrophe has overtaken us, concludes

36. *Ibid.,* 23–25.

Levy, we must turn back "to those prophets who accused our forefathers of being on the road to destruction, all the more so as these prophets were likewise true poets, who tried as such to point out the right road, endeavouring to remedy, as far as their insight went, the evil of their time."[37]

As will be shown later, Wagner was less optimistic about the future of Europe in general and of Germany in particular than Levy's words indicate. Levy is correct in suggesting that Wagner looked for solace in the virtues of faith, hope, and love. Levy's estimate of Chamberlain is perhaps less disputable. In comparison with Gobineau before him and Spengler after, Chamberlain believed that the imminent collapse of European civilization—feared and predicted by so many others in the decades preceding the First World War—could be averted.

Biographers of Houston Stewart Chamberlain (who married Richard Wagner's daughter Eva in 1908), at least those who contribute biographical notes to encyclopedias, usually refer to him as a violent anti-Semite; but the reader of Chamberlain's *The Foundations of the Nineteenth Century* who expects to find Nazi-style diatribes against the Jews will be disappointed. As with Gobineau, the Jews are for Chamberlain the paradigm of a successful race; with Disraeli, Chamberlain foresees the fruitful union of Jew and Aryan. The introduction to the *Foundations* by Lord Redesdale, the future father-in-law of the British fascist leader Sir Oswald Mosley, makes interesting reading. Redesdale tells how he once called upon a "distinguished Jewish gentleman" who had just come from a meeting with "Mr. D'Israeli, as he was then." What had they talked about? "'Oh,' said my host, 'the usual thing—the Race.'" At a remote stage of its existence, continues Redesdale, the Jewish race took form from several diverse elements; since then it had remained stable and unchanged for thousands of years—"one of the wonders of the world." And one rigidly observed law sufficed for this purpose: "The Israelite maiden may wed a Gentile: such an alliance tends not to the degeneracy of the race: but the Jewish man must not marry outside of his own nation, the seed of the chosen people must not be contaminated by a foreign alliance." No one was more convinced of the noble purity of "the Race" than Lord Beaconsfield, adds Redesdale, and with

37. *Ibid.*, vii, viii, 59.

what conviction did he insist in *Coningsby* on the "influence of the Jew working alongside of the European!"[38]

Redesdale agreed with most of what Chamberlain had to say in the *Foundations*, although he considered that the Ashkenazim had been dealt with unfairly and "those intensely aristocratic Jews of Spain and Portugal, the descendants of the men whom the Romans, dreading their influence, deported westward," favored. The Ashkenazim, or German Jews, had in fact played a greater role in Europe than the Sephardim; and although their characteristic talent had been the acquisition of money, the charities of Europe would be in a sad plight without them. "Of the treasure which they have laid up they have given freely," he says. Politically, too, they had been important. Redesdale reminds his readers that the two Jewish bankers who had represented the Germans on the one side and the French on the other in 1870 were not Sephardi but Ashkenazi Jews. He asks: "Who and what then is the Jew, this wonderful man who during the last hundred years has attained such a position in the whole civilized world?"[39]

That question is only one of the many investigated by Chamberlain in *The Foundations of the Nineteenth Century*. His book is an essay in universal history embracing politics, art, science, and religion. The overall structure of Chamberlain's book and many of its individual features anticipate Oswald Spengler's *Decline of the West*, which was published two decades later. Chamberlain, however, lacks both Spengler's black historical pessimism and his gifts as a writer of prose. For Chamberlain each great culture is the product of a race (*Rasse*)—a term that in his writings and elsewhere is equivalent to the English "breed." Chamberlain holds that the biological laws governing plants and animals apply equally to human beings. Great "races" or "breeds" of animals come about by chance or are due to the interaction of factors controlled by breeders. He points out that the race (*Rasse*) of English thoroughbred horses (*Vollblutpferde*, or full-blooded horses) was developed by crossing English mares with Arabian stallions (the reverse of Disraeli's proposal, one is tempted to remark). And one of the "noblest

38. Houston Stewart Chamberlain, *Die Grundlagen des neunzehnten Jahrhunderts* (2 vols.; Munich, 1899); Houston Stewart Chamberlain, *The Foundations of the Nineteenth Century*, trans. John Lees (2 vols.; London, 1911), I, xxxiv.

39. Chamberlain, *Foundations*, I, xxxv, xxxvi.

creatures that nature possesses," the Newfoundland dog, originated from the crossing of Eskimo dogs and French hounds. After it had become fixed and purebred by constant inbreeding, it was brought to Europe by fanciers and perfected by artificial selection.[40]

Advocates of racial purity in the human sphere who fail to take proper account of history and experimental biology become, says Chamberlain, victims of a "mystical conception of a race pure in itself, which is an airy abstraction that retards instead of furthering" our understanding. It is on this point that Chamberlain differs most sharply with Gobineau, or with a view that he ascribes to Gobineau, namely the

fantastic idea, that the originally "pure" noble races crossed with each other in the course of history, and with every crossing became irrevocably less pure and less noble. From this we must of necessity derive a hopelessly pessimistic view of the future of the human race. But this supposition rests on total ignorance of the physiological importance of what we have to understand by "race." A noble race does not fall from Heaven, it becomes a noble race gradually, just like fruit-trees, and this gradual process can begin anew at any moment, as soon as accident of geography and history or a fixed plan (as in the case of the Jews) creates the conditions.[41]

Chamberlain holds that a great race, once established by chance or destiny, can preserve itself only by carefully controlled inbreeding. What he objects to in Gobineau is the claim that the major races had been established once and for all at the beginning of historical time and that thereafter the inevitable result of racial intermixture would be cultural degeneration, decay, and death.

Chamberlain could hardly have held otherwise and still retained his strong faith in the special virtues of "the Germans" in general (*die Germanen*)—the "Teutons," as Lees translates the term—and the inhabitants of Germany (*die Deutschen*) in particular. As a result of the studies in anthropology, archeology, and ethnology that had been so avidly pursued in the second half of the nineteenth century throughout Europe, he was well aware of the mixed racial background of the European "nations." Saxony—"quickened throughout by a mixture of Slavonic blood"—had given Germany some of its greatest figures, Chamberlain notes. Swabia, the home of Mozart and Schiller, is inhabited by a half-Celtic race; Burgundy owes its greatness to a mixture of Teutonic

40. *Ibid.*, 281; *Grundlagen*, I, 282.
41. Chamberlain, *Foundations*, I, 263, 281.

and Romance elements; the Franks have mixed with Gallo-Romans in the past; and so on. The widened and deepened historical perspective of post-Darwinian Europe made it impossible for Chamberlain to believe in a primal race of Aryans that had taken form once and for all at some time in the early history of the world. Gobineau's concept of race, on the other hand, belongs almost in the historical framework of the Old Testament. Nor did Chamberlain make the extravagant claim that one race alone had been the seed of all higher civilizations. Chamberlain's notion of how a great race comes into being carries with it the corollary that such a race may spring up at any time. Moreover, he was of the opinion—in the *Foundations* at least—that in the European "new world" and "new civilization" which he saw on the horizon a further intermixture of races would occur. That world, says Chamberlain, would not be purely Germanic. In the nineteenth century other races had appeared on the European scene, in particular the Jews and the formerly Teutonic Slavs—now "un-Teutonized by mixture of blood." The new world of which he spoke had its roots as far back as the thirteenth century and would yet "perhaps assimilate great racial complexes and so lay itself open to new influences from all the different types."[42]

Like Disraeli, Chamberlain was an assimilationist. And, again like Disraeli, he believed that Europe must come to terms with the Jews. "To this day," indicates Chamberlain, "these two powers—Jews and Teutonic races—stand . . . now as friendly, now as hostile, but always as alien forces face to face." Again echoing Disraeli, he points out that Judaism is one of the "most conservative ideas in the world," and the Jews have made sacred that "idea of physical race-unity and race-purity, which is the very essence of Judaism." Unlike Disraeli and Gobineau, who half-identified Jews and Semites, Chamberlain holds that the "national character" of the Arabs is quite different from that of the Jews. Although he disagrees with the belief he ascribes to Gobineau, namely that Judaism has always had a disintegrating effect on other peoples, Chamberlain does see the Jews as a powerful and potentially dangerous minority, always and everywhere to be reckoned with and feared. His numerous citations on this subject, ranging from Cicero to the Hohen-

42. *Ibid.,* lxvi, 272–73.

staufen and Hohenzollern emperors, from Herder to Goethe and Bismarck, are fascinating and revealing, such as his account of Goethe's indignation in 1823 at the new law permitting marriages between Germans and Jews.[43]

Chamberlain points out that resistance to assimilation has been even stronger on the Jewish side. At the beginning of the nineteenth century, when Napoleon sent an ultimatum to the Jewish council of elders in France demanding the total fusion of the Jews with the rest of the French nation, the French Jews rejected the article prescribing absolute freedom of marriage of Jews with Christians. Their daughters, they said, might marry outside of the Israelite people—but not their sons. And the dictator of all Europe had to yield, notes Chamberlain. Deuteronomy 7:3 forbids all marriages between Jews and non-Jews, but Exodus 34:16 forbids only that of sons. Likewise, in Nehemiah 13 it is only the marriage of a son to a non-Jew that is stigmatized as a sin against God. The question really is one of physical descent, says Chamberlain, for the Talmud itself tells us that proselytes are as injurious to Judaism as ulcers are to a sound body. Nevertheless, the old problem continues to raise its head, especially since the nineteenth-century renaissance of the Jewish peoples of Europe:

The Jewish Renaissance is the resurrection of a Lazarus long considered dead, who introduces into the Teutonic world the customs and modes of thought of the Oriental, and who at the same time seems to receive a new lease of life thereby, like the vine-pest which, after leading in America the humble life of an innocent little beetle, was introduced into Europe and suddenly attained to a world-wide fame of serious import. We have, however, reason to hope and believe that the Jews, like the Americans, have brought us not only a new pest but also a new vine. Certain it is that they have left a peculiar impress upon our time, and that the "new world" which is arising will require a very great exercise of its strength for the work of assimilating this fragment of the "old world."

The above citation, less its two final sentences, was apparently the most anti-Semitic—in the Nazi sense of the term—utterance that the Nazi "philosopher" Alfred Rosenberg could find for inclusion in his book on Chamberlain.[44]

43. *Ibid.*, 254–57, 343–46; Johann Wolfgang Goethe, *Goethes Gespräche*, ed. Wolfgang Herwig (4 vols.; Zurich, 1965–), Vol. III, Pt. 1, 581.

44. Chamberlain, *Foundations*, I, lxxxiii–lxxxiv, 332–33; Alfred Rosenberg, *Hous-*

Because the Jewish race established purity of the blood as its guiding principle at the start of its career, it alone of all races possesses real "physiognomy and character." In our day, Chamberlain continues, when so much nonsense is uttered about the question of race, we should "let Disraeli teach us that the whole significance of Judaism lies in its purity of race." Disraeli has expounded his ideas in *Tancred*; he has told us in *Coningsby* that race is all, that there is no other truth, that every race that carelessly suffers its blood to be mixed will go under.[45] Chamberlain is as dithyrambic as Disraeli in his praise of the paradigm of racial purity, the Sephardic Jew:

In contrast to the new, growing Anglo-Saxon race, look for instance, at the Sephardim, the so-called "Spanish Jews"; here we find how a genuine race can keep itself noble for centuries and tens of centuries, but at the same time how very necessary it is to distinguish between the nobly reared portions of a nation and the rest. In England, Holland and Italy there are still genuine Sephardim but very few, since they can scarcely any longer avoid crossing with the Ashkenazim (the so-called "German Jews"). Thus, for example, the Montefiores of the present generation have all without exception married German Jewesses. But everyone who has traveled in the East of Europe, where the genuine Sephardim still as far as possible avoid all intercourse with German Jews, for whom they have an almost comical repugnance, will agree with me when I say that it is only when one sees these men and has intercourse with them that one begins to comprehend the significance of Judaism in the history of the world. This is nobility in the fullest sense of the word, genuine nobility of race![46]

Before Chamberlain's eyes seems to float the ideal figure of Disraeli's Sidonia, and perhaps also that of George Eliot's Daniel Deronda (1876).

Although Lord Redesdale calls Chamberlain a "strong anti-Semite," this was by no means Chamberlain's own belief:

I have become convinced that the usual treatment of the "Jewish question" is altogether and always superficial; the Jew is no enemy of Teutonic civilization and culture. . . . I think we are inclined to underestimate our own powers in this respect and, on the other hand, to exaggerate the importance of the Jewish influence. Hand in hand with this goes the perfectly ridiculous and revolting tendency to make the Jew the general scapegoat of our time. In reality

---

ton *Stewart Chamberlain als Verkünder und Begründer einer deutschen Zukunft* (Munich, 1927), 110.

45. The statement "race is all" occurs in *Tancred*, not in *Coningsby*.
46. Chamberlain, *Foundations*, I, 271, 272–73.

the "Jewish peril" lies much deeper; the Jew is not responsible for it; we have given rise to it ourselves and must overcome it ourselves.

Chamberlain considered that he had avoided the twin extremes of philo-Semitism and anti-Semitism: he had brought forward neither the "good" Jew nor the "bad" Jew. "Nothing," he states, "is falser than judging a people by individuals." In spite of his emphasis on race, Chamberlain, like Marx and Wagner before him—and for that matter Oscar Levy after him, who as late as 1915 could speak disparagingly of the "Semitic values" of the Christian Church—believes that a man could "become a Jew without being an Israelite." The term *Jew*, he says, denotes a way of thinking and feeling. And it is "senseless to call an Israelite a 'Jew,' though his descent is beyond question . . . if the law of Moses has no place in his heart." Citing Romans 2:28, 29, Chamberlain says that he is not a Jew who is one only outwardly; he is a Jew who is one inwardly.[47]

In Chamberlain's mind the notion of race occupied a region lying somewhere between anthropology and psychology. There were those in Germany who were made uneasy by this vagueness of categories. One was Rudolf Virchow, a pathologist who also achieved eminence in politics (as a leader of the German Progressive Party), anthropology, ethnology, and archeology. From his anthropological studies, largely based on the measurement of skulls, Virchow concluded in 1893 that racial thinking of the kind later exemplified by Chamberlain showed a certain lack of "sound common sense"; it represented, in fact, a reversion to the outworn nature-philosophy (*Naturphilosophie*) prevalent in early nineteenth-century Germany. Virchow's words now seem prophetic:

Our time, so sure of itself and of victory by reason of its scientific consciousness, is as apt as former ages to underestimate the strength of the mystic impulses with which the soul of the nation is infected by isolated adventurers. Even now it is standing baffled before the enigma of anti-Semitism, whose appearance in this time of equality of rights is inexplicable to everybody, yet which, in spite of its mysteriousness, or perhaps on account of it, fascinates our cultured youth. Up to the present moment the demand for a professorship of anti-Semitism has not made itself heard; but rumor has it that there

47. *Ibid.*, xxxv, lxxviii, 489, 491–92.

are anti-Semitic professors. He who knows the "Naturphilosophie" in all its minute branchings is not astonished by such phenomena.[48]

Virchow was skeptical also of the prevailing belief that in the remote past an Indo-Germanic, Indo-European, or Aryan race had emigrated from the mountains of Asia to the European mainland, where it had formed the trunk from which the many-branched peoples of Europe had sprung. That theory, says Virchow, although widely held, has "lately received some damaging blows and none more destructive than from the quarters of pre-historic archeology."[49]

Although respecting Virchow as a scientist and scholar, Chamberlain believed that Virchow had misunderstood the point at issue. Our very ability to show that racial intermixture has occurred proves, he holds, that we have at our disposal reliable indices of past races (skull configuration, mainly) and that we do not have to rely wholly on such relatively transient indices as skin and hair color, noses, the fleshy configuration of the face. "Scientific anatomy," says Chamberlain, "has furnished such conclusive proofs of the existence of physical characteristics distinguishing the races from each other that they can no longer be denied." Further, evidence unearthed by philologists and mythologists convinced Chamberlain, as it had so many others, that specific patterns of culture are linked to specific physical patterns of race. Heretofore only the Jewish people have possessed a recorded history, and the sad fact is that the Holy Book of the Christians takes one race, and one race alone, seriously. The New Testament is hardly more than an appendage to the history of the Jews and their long struggle with Jahweh. But now, says Chamberlain, echoing the words of Morris and Magnússon two decades earlier, "the brilliant series of Teutonic and Indian scholars has, half unconsciously, accomplished a great work at the right moment; now we too possess our 'holy books,' and what they teach us is more beautiful and nobler than what the Old Testament sets forth."[50] Nothing could be more revealing than Chamberlain's "too."

48. Rudolf Virchow, "The Founding of the Berlin University and the Transition from the Philosophic to the Scientific Age," *Smithsonian Report*, 1894, pp. 681–85.

49. Rudolf Virchow, "Anthropology in the Last Twenty Years," *Smithsonian Report*, 1889, pp. 555–70.

50. Chamberlain, *Foundations*, I, xcii, xciii. The derivatory character of German racism was pointed out in 1932 by a German Jew, Jakob Wassermann, who stated:

Jahweh, says Chamberlain, is an arbitrary and capricious autocrat who demands Job-like submission from his worshippers; and the Jew, like his God, is the very embodiment of the "will." The strong-willed Jew makes Jahweh pitch his tent once and for all among the Hebrews. The Jewish God, the very incarnation of arbitrariness, issues commands that are not only arbitrary but inconsistent. On the one hand, the chosen people are ordered not to kill; on the other, they are ordered to engage in the wholesale slaughter of neighboring peoples: "Beside moral commands which breathe to some extent high morality and humanity, there stand commands which are directly immoral and inhuman, others again determine the most trivial points: what one may eat and not eat, how one shall wash, etc., in short, everywhere absolute arbitrariness."[51] In contrast the Indo-Germanic and Aryan gods are themselves subject to law and necessity. Above them stands the goddess Themis; she who signifies the rule of law is more eternal than the eternal gods themselves; she alone lastingly holds sway over all things. Unlike Jahweh, the God of the Jews, the Indo-Germanic gods are always conscious of a higher law than their own arbitrary caprice. Here "the will obeys, it does not command," says Chamberlain, raising an old theological issue—the question of whether God wills the good because it *is* good, or whether good is good *because* God wills it. Chamberlain does not say that the will obeys the intellect; rather, it obeys a law *recognized* by the intellect. Since a people's god is simply that people projected on a divine or cosmic scale, the Jew represents the embodiment of the will, just as the Aryan represents the embodiment of the intellect. The will—the will to live, the will to power—is, says Chamberlain, deeply seated in the Jew; and it is for this reason that a "moderately gifted Indo-European is

---

"German anti-Semitism supposes itself to be based on the Germanic ideal of race, but it is in reality, as a folkish procedure, through and through Jewish; only the Jews, the priest-folk *kat exochen*, knew and lived under the principle of god-given exclusiveness and national election, which has now indeed so bitterly been brought home to them in the end." See Jakob Wassermann, *Rede an die Jugend über das Leben im Geiste* (Berlin, 1932), 30–31.

51. Chamberlain, *Foundations*, I, 240. This passage anticipates Proust's account of Françoise's code of ethics, which is said by the narrator to recall "those ancient laws that, along with such ferocious prescriptions as to massacre infants at the breast, forbid with exaggerated delicacy the seething of a kid in its mother's milk, or the eating of the nerve of the thigh in an animal." See Marcel Proust, *À la recherche du temps perdu* (3 vols.; Paris, 1968), I, 28–29.

so peculiarly characterless in comparison with the most poorly gifted Jew."[52]

Another curious feature of Chamberlain's book is worth noting here. Homer, he reminds us, said that everything is divided into three. The number *three* is not a chance number like *seven* (the seven planets, the septentriones) or ten (derived from the fingers); it expresses, rather, a fundamental phenomenon that could not have failed to "impress itself at an early time on races that were inclined to poetry and metaphysics." Prior to the advent of Christianity came the Indian doctrine of the Trimurti, the triple godhead of Brahma, Vishnu, and Shiva. The Christian Church had "steered successfully past the most dangerous cliff, Semitic monotheism," to the Trinity. The Christian Trinity "might rather be called an experience than a symbol"—an experience of nature, that is, for the myth-creating Indo-European spirit had remained true to nature symbolism even after its exposure to the angry Semitic Jahweh, God of the Jews. The number *three* expresses a myth of physical and metaphysical experience; this was recognized by Hegel, although with him "the proceeding very soon degenerates . . . into trifling," that is, the "so-called necessary progression of the thesis, antithesis and synthesis, or again the deity of the Absolute as father, the different existence as son, the return to itself as spirit."[53]

Chamberlain has here identified a concept of great mythic power. Behind the Christian Trinity of Father, Son, and Holy Ghost lies an earlier trinity of mother, father, and child; and behind that perhaps the still earlier duality of mother and child—when the role of the father in parenthood was unknown. A generation before Chamberlain, in 1861, the Swiss cultural historian Johann Bachofen had attempted to interpret the whole corpus of Egyptian and Greek myth (including the myth of Oedipus) as the unfolding of a tripartite relationship expressing "telluric, lunar and solar" stages of cultural development:

The lowest state is the purely telluric, the highest the solar. To the first corresponds generation in a state of nature, as it displays itself in a swamp; thus the wild, illegitimate union of the sexes with exclusive emphasis on material motherhood. The highest stage is, on the contrary, the pure sun-principle, to which corresponds father-right, and thus legitimate union of the sexes with

52. Chamberlain, *Foundations*, I, 239–42.
53. *Ibid.*, 24–27.

clear-cut subordination of the mother, who moves entirely into the background, a step that came to full expression in the Apollonian cult—pure, pertaining to the changeless heights of light—and in the spiritualized, motherless Athena. . . . Between the two lies an intermediary stage in which both are united. This is the moon-region, between earth and sun, that of *psychē* between *sōma* and *nous*.[54]

Another aspect of the myth of "threes"—apparent somewhat after the time of Chamberlain's writings in the dreams of Stefan George and other Germans who hoped to realize a mystical "Third Kingdom"— goes back to a twelfth-century Italian monk, Joachim of Floris, who obscurely prophesied the coming of a Third Age, the Age of the Holy Ghost, in which the hierarchy of the Church would wither away, opposites would be reconciled, and infidel and Christian would be united. The first age is represented by the Old Testament; it extends from Abraham to Christ and is under the dominion of God the Father. The second age is represented by the New Testament; it extends from Christ to an unknown figure in the future and is under the dominion of God the Son. The third age will be the reign of the Holy Ghost; its close will be followed by the end of all things.[55]

A sociopsychological scheme bearing a Florian imprint had been set forth in 1868 by Eduard von Hartmann, a German philosopher who owes much to Schopenhauer. Hartmann's scheme has three stages, and to move from one to another requires an elevation of the level of consciousness. The illusion that happiness is obtainable takes three forms; each form is equivalent to a stage in human psychological development. The first form of the illusion is that happiness is available here and now, under the aegis of the state; the second, that it is available in the next world, under the aegis of the church; the third, that it will be available here below after church and state have been discarded in favor of "society." Like others who had been influenced by the Young Hegelians, Hartmann conceives of "society" as a new development in the history of the world, a kind of Third Reich; its appearance on the world scene is so novel, says Hartmann, that it has gone almost unrecognized.

---

54. Johann Jacob Bachofen, *Das Mutterrecht: Eine Untersuchung über die Gynaikokratie der alten Welt nach ihrer religiösen und rechtlichen Natur* (2nd ed.; Basel, 1897), 119.

55. Herbert Grundmann, *Studien über Joachim von Floris* (Leipzig, 1927), 58–59.

Hartmann defines society as "the *organization of labour* in the widest sense"—from the simplest kinds of manual labor to the labor of teachers, artists, and investigators. The third form of the world's illusion is that happiness will be available for everyone in a socialist future, after the spirit of egoism has succumbed to the spirit of communalism, after "freedom of competition" has been replaced by the systematic division of the world's work. In the third stage, says Hartmann, "instinct" will paradoxically be restored to its rights and the "affirmation of the will to live proclaimed provisionally true"; optimism and pessimism will be united. Nevertheless, Hartmann's *ultimate* goal is the same as Schopenhauer's Nirvana, for a still higher stage of consciousness will enable us to transcend the third illusion. The wheel of existence will stop turning; the world-process will come to an end.[56] We shall see that Wagner was still subject to the third illusion when, in 1848, he first conceived of *The Ring of the Nibelung*. But by 1856, with Schopenhauer's help, he had cast it off.

56. Eduard von Hartmann, *Philosophy of the Unconscious*, trans. William C. Coupland (3 vols.; London, 1931), III, 12, 81, 94, 102–103.

Chapter II

WAGNER AND
THE NIBELUNG'S RING

1. THE REDEMPTION OF THE NIBELUNGS

In an autobiographical sketch written by Richard Wagner in his twenty-ninth year (just after his opera *Rienzi* had been accepted at Dresden in 1842), we read that he received little formal instruction in music during his childhood. He entered a classical secondary school, the *Kreuzschule* in Dresden, at the age of nine and was thereafter busied chiefly with the study of Latin, Greek, ancient history, and classical mythology. By his own account he showed some evidence of musical ability at an early age: when he was seven years old, his stepfather, Ludwig Geyer, who was then on his deathbed, heard him playing a simple tune on the piano and asked the boy's mother whether Richard might perhaps have musical talent. Geyer had earlier tried to teach Wagner to draw. He showed very little talent in this direction, but Geyer continued to believe (so Wagner's mother told him) that the boy was specially gifted. Wagner's first creative efforts were in the field of drama. Before he was sixteen, he had learned English in order to read Shakespeare in the original and had sketched out a great tragedy derived chiefly from *Hamlet* and *King Lear*. Of this tragedy Wagner remarks: "The plan was exceedingly grandiose; two hundred and forty people died in the course of the piece, and I found myself required in working it out to have most of them return as spirits, because otherwise I should have run out of characters in the last acts."[1]

Later on he became actively engaged in the study of music, and Lud-

1. Richard Wagner, *Gesammelte Schriften und Dichtungen* (10 vols.; 2nd ed.; Leipzig, 1887–88), I, 4–19.

wig van Beethoven's compositions made an overpowering impression on him. He resolved also that his tragedy would not be released until it had been provided with suitable music. At about this time the July Revolution of 1830 took place in France, and unrest spread to Germany. Says Wagner: "With one stroke I became a revolutionist and reached the conviction that every halfway aspiring human being ought to be concerned exclusively with politics. I was only happy in the company of political littérateurs; I also began an overture that dealt with a political theme." On top of all this Wagner was aroused by the reading of E. T. A. Hoffmann's tales to a pitch of the "wildest mysticism." He had daytime visions of tonics, thirds, and dominants taking on visible form and revealing to him their secret meaning.[2]

Wagner's interest in the Siegfried myth as a vehicle for his ideas, musical and otherwise, apparently dates from his first stay (1839–1842) in Paris. In 1841 a romance by Alexandre Dumas, loosely based on the story of Siegfried and entitled *Les merveilleuses aventures du comte Lyderic*, was published in a Paris family magazine. It has been conjectured that Wagner's interest in Siegfried was aroused by this story and that he borrowed from it in writing the *Ring*. But Newman has pointed out that many poets and composers worked with the Nibelung story in the first half of the nineteenth century—Felix Mendelssohn was on the point of writing an opera on the subject in 1840, and Heinrich Dorn's opera *Die Nibelungen* was actually produced in 1854—and that in 1844 the aesthetician Friedrich Vischer issued a call for a truly German opera based on the *Nibelungenlied*.[3] The urge would have come to Wagner in one way or another. Dumas placed his romance in Merovingian France. Lyderic is the son of Salwart, prince of Dijon. Salwart is slain by brigands while journeying through a forest with his wife and child. Lyderic's mother, Ermengarde, hides the infant under a bush for safekeeping. Nourished by a doe and guarded by a nightingale, the child is eventually found by a pious hermit who names him Lyderic—"joyous singer"

2. *Ibid.*, 5, 6, 7.
3. Ernest Newman, *The Life of Richard Wagner* (4 vols.; New York, 1933–47), II, 27. Newman incorrectly gives the title as the adventures of "Prince" Lyderic. Friedrich Engels, too, was attracted by the figure of Siegfried. In 1840 he wrote approvingly of Siegfried's "defiance of convention" and called him "representative of German youth" ("Siegfried's Native Town," *Karl Marx Friedrich Engels Collected Works*, II, 132–36). Fragments of a drama by Engels entitled "The Invulnerable Siegfried" are said to be extant. See *Karl Marx Friedrich Engels über Kunst und Literatur* (Berlin, 1948), 473, 524.

in old German, according to Dumas—in memory of the guardian night-ingale. Lyderic grows up in ignorance of his true parentage. He is enor-mously strong and fond of all animals, other than beasts of prey. While traveling through the forest toward the forge of "Maître Mimer, armu-rier," Lyderic is advised by the nightingale of his obligations to his par-ents (we may have here the original of the forest-bird in Wagner's *Sieg-fried*). Lyderic is eventually restored to his rights and becomes the first count of Flanders.[4] The *Nibelungenlied*, it may be recalled, locates Prince Siegfried's home in the Low Countries.

In the summer of 1848 while assistant *Kapellmeister* at the court theater in Dresden, Wagner wrote a mixed study of myth and history entitled *Die Wibelungen*. Here he identifies the historical "Wibelungs" with the mythical "Nibelungs." He rejects the claim, made by Bishop Otto of Freising, that the medieval party of the Wibelungs (Ghibellines), which was opposed by the Welfs (Guelphs), took its name from the German town of Waiblingen. As for the original meaning of the Nibe-lung myth, Wagner finds Siegfried to be a sun-god or god of light. The mythical hoard of the Nibelungs is the glory of the earth itself, which we recognize at the break of day when Siegfried slays the dragon of dark-ness that has spread its wings over the visible treasures of the world. At the end of each day the light-god is once again treacherously killed and drawn down into the dark realm of death to become himself a "Nibe-lung." And on the following day he arises again. Later, after myths of gods have yielded place to myths of earthly heroes, the familiar Sieg-fried of the Norse sagas takes form:

Here we recognize Siegfried as he wins the hoard of the Nibelungs, and through it power without limit. This hoard and the power residing in it remain the heart to which all further shapings of the saga are related as to an immovable center-point: all striving and struggling is directed toward the hoard of the Nibelungs as the epitome of all earthly power; whoever possesses it, whoever commands through it, is or becomes a Nibelung.[5]

Now, says Wagner, when Christian myth was superimposed on the myths of the pagan North, a new development occurred: the mythical

4. Alexandre Dumas *père*, "Les merveilleuses aventures du comte Lyderic," *Musée des familles*, September, 1841, pp. 373–77; October, 1841, pp. 1–14; November, 1841, pp. 33–44.

5. Wagner, *Gesammelte Schriften*, II, 119, 124.

treasure of the Holy Grail underwent fusion with the mythical hoard of the Nibelungs, and the uneasy Western world passed from Rome to Jerusalem in search of salvation. Still dissatisfied, it turns farther east in its search; the legendary Grail has been withdrawn from the degenerate West to the chaste original homeland of the Northern peoples; that is, to the Aryans in the East. At the close of the essay Wagner accomplishes still another mythic identification: he sees the Emperor Friedrich Barbarossa, sword at his side, guarding the hoard of the Nibelungs—the Grail treasure—in the caverns of the Kyffhäuser.[6]

Later in the same year Wagner drew up an outline for a drama based on the story of the Nibelungs.[7] This was the nucleus around which *The Ring of the Nibelung* crystallized. The outline contains several new elements introduced by Wagner. Of these the most important is the incest motif: Siegfried, "he who shall bring peace through victory," the savior-hero, is the offspring of a brother and sister, the Volsungs Siegmund and Sieglinde. In the complete *Ring* itself, the incest motif was given still further elaboration, although several of the other elements introduced in the outline were dropped or altered. In the outline Siegfried is clearly a Grail-seeker, for the hoard of the Nibelungs, the object of his quest, is said to lie on the Glittering Heath (*Gnitahaide*) guarded by a dragon, and the Glittering Heath is a Grail locale. (Wagner equates *Gnitahaide* with *Neidhaide*, "heath of envy.") The Grail reference is concealed in the *Ring*: there the treasure, guarded by a dragon as before, lies in a *Neidhöhle* or "cave of envy." Another difference between the two versions is that in the outline Siegfried's death not only expiates the sin of the gods but also releases the Nibelungs from their servitude to the power of the ring. (The half-Nibelung Hagen, it is true, does not share in this release.) In the final version of Wagner's *Ring*, the stage action portrays the universal destruction prophesied in the Eddas: Ragnarök, *Götterdämmerung*, the twilight of the gods.

In more detail, Wagner's outline of 1848 is as follows. Deep beneath the earth, "like worms in a dead body," dwell the Nibelungs ("children of the mist"), a restless, busy race of dwarf-smiths. One of their num-

6. *Ibid.*, 151, 155. Siegfried's role as Grail-seeker is touched on in Jessie Laidlay Weston's *The Legends of the Wagner Drama: Studies in Mythology and Romance* (1903; reprint ed., New York, 1977), but not in her better-known work *From Ritual to Romance* (Cambridge, Eng., 1920).
7. Wagner, *Gesammelte Schriften*, II, 156–66.

ber, Alberich, seizes the gold of the Rhine and forges from it a ring that makes him absolute master of the race of Nibelungs. Now working for him alone, they are forced to heap up the hoard of the Nibelung (*Nibelungenhort*). Alberich also forces his brother, Reigin-Mime, to fashion an important item from the hoard, namely the cap of concealment (*Tarnkappe, Tarnhelm*), which allows its wearer to take on any shape at will.

Thus equipped, Alberich sets out to conquer the world. The race of giants becomes fearful, not so much of Alberich as of a prophecy that his weapons will one day come into the hands of a race of human heroes and bring about the downfall of the giants. The gods, who also aspire to supreme power, take advantage of this fear. Wotan contracts with the giants for the building of an impregnable fortress, from which the gods are to rule the world. In return, the giants demand the hoard of the Nibelung. The gods then seize Alberich and, at the price of his life, extort the treasure. Alberich attempts to withhold the ring; but knowing that the ring is the secret of his power, the gods insist on taking possession of it. In yielding up the ring at last, Alberich places a curse on it: all its possessors shall be doomed. Wotan tries to withhold the ring from the giants, but he is kept from doing so by the admonitions of the three fates (*Schicksalsfrauen*) or Norns. The giants, knowing nothing of the use of power, leave the hoard on the *Gnitahaide* under the guardianship of a dragon. Alberich and the Nibelungs remain slaves of the ring. Alberich broods ceaselessly over ways to regain it; the other Nibelungs are helpless, miserable, fruitlessly active. Meanwhile, the gods in their mighty fortress have put the world in order and achieved a peace of sorts. But "the peace through which they achieved power is not based on reconciliation. It was brought about by force and guile. The intent of their higher world-order is moral consciousness, but they themselves are tainted by the very injustice that they punish. From the depths of Nibelheim ominously sounds the awareness of their guilt: for the servitude of the Nibelungs is unbroken."[8]

Power has been taken from Alberich, but "the soul, the freedom, of the Nibelungs lies unused beneath the belly of the sluggish dragon." The gods cannot set matters right without committing still further in-

8. *Ibid.*, 157.

justices. They resolve, therefore, to create a race of human heroes who shall freely will to expiate the guilt of the gods. The hero must come from the race of the Volsungs. With one of Holda's apples, Wotan causes a childless Volsung couple to bear the twins Siegmund and Sieglinde. Sieglinde becomes the wife of Hunding, who is not of the Volsung race. The marriage remains childless. Then, "in order to produce a true Volsung," Siegmund and Sieglinde mate. Wotan (Fricka does not appear in the outline) condemns Siegmund to die at the hands of Hunding in expiation of his crime. The Valkyrie, or wish-maiden (*Wunschmädchen*), Brünnhilde, who has vainly intervened to protect Siegmund (thus requiring Wotan himself to shatter Siegmund's sword), is also punished. She is expelled from the band of Valkyries, thrown into a deep sleep, placed on a cliff, and surrounded by a ring of fire. Siegfried, the offspring of the incestuous union, is committed by the dying Sieglinde to the care of Reigin-Mime. Mime raises Siegfried in the forest, teaches him the smith's art, and eventually gives him the shattered fragments of his father's sword. Siegfried then forges the sword Balmung (the Nothung of the *Ring*) from the fragments. At Mime's behest, he kills the dragon and wins possession of the hoard. A taste of the dragon's blood enables him to understand the song of the forest-birds; they tell him that Mime plans to kill him and take the hoard. Thus forewarned, Siegfried kills Mime. With only the ring and the *Tarnkappe*, he sets out through the forest. The birds then tell him of Brünnhilde. Siegfried passes unharmed through the fire and arouses the sleeping Valkyrie. She imparts her secret wisdom and warns him to be faithful and to avoid deception; in return Siegfried gives her the Nibelung's ring. The two pledge their faith to each other, and the hero departs in search of further adventures.

Siegfried journeys to the land of another race of heroes, the kingdom of the Gibichungs on the Rhine. Gunther, the king of the Gibichungs, and his sister, Gudrun, are children of the former king and his queen, Grimhild. But Hagen, their gloomy, sinister half-brother and close advisor, is an elf-son (*Albensohn*), for Grimhild was once overpowered by Alberich (the text of the *Ring* adds that he forced his way into her favors with gold). And it is on his elf-son that Alberich now pins his hope of regaining the ring.

Hagen tells Gunther that Brünnhilde is his destined queen and persuades Gudrun that Siegfried is to be her spouse. When Siegfried arrives at the hall of the Gibichungs, he is given a drink that causes him to forget Brünnhilde and fall in love with Gudrun. Siegfried and Gunther then become blood brothers, and Siegfried pledges himself to win Brünnhilde for Gunther in return for the hand of Gudrun. Using "for the first and only time his power as lord of the Nibelungs," Siegfried assumes Gunther's appearance with the help of the *Tarnhelm* and makes his way through the magic fire a second time. Brünnhilde resists, but her superhuman powers and her wisdom have departed with her virginity. After a short struggle Siegfried takes the ring from her finger. To Brünnhilde's surprise, they spend the night together separated by the sword Balmung. On the following day they journey to the hall of the Gibichungs, Gunther surreptitiously taking Siegfried's place on the way. Brünnhilde next sees Siegfried with Gudrun, the ring on his finger. She tells Gunther that he has been betrayed by Siegfried. Urged on by Hagen, the three plot to kill Siegfried. Hagen slays Siegfried with a stab in the back—Siegfried's only vulnerable point, as he has learned from Brünnhilde. Siegfried regains his memory before dying, and Gunther learns for the first time of Siegfried's earlier relation to Brünnhilde. Hagen and Gunther quarrel over possession of the ring, and Gunther is slain.

Brünnhilde is now aware of the reason for Siegfried's betrayal. Some of her lost wisdom returns, and she cries out: "Hear then, you glorious gods, your injustice is wiped out thanks to him, the hero who took your guilt on himself! He gave it into my hands to finish the work: let the servitude of the Nibelungs be loosed; the ring shall no longer bind them. Alberich shall not receive it; he shall no longer oppress you; in return he also shall be as free as you." Brünnhilde returns the ring to the "wise sister of the depths" and calls on the All-father to rule now and forever in peace. She steps into the funeral pyre, carrying only the *Tarnhelm*. In the stage background, we see Brünnhilde, on her horse and once again clad as a Valkyrie, carrying Siegfried to Valhalla. Hagen makes one last attempt to seize the ring, but he is drawn under the waves by the "three water-women." [9]

In the outline Alberich does not forswear love, as he does in the music-drama, in order to win the gold of the Rhine. The ring of power

9. *Ibid.*, 166.

forged from the gold keeps both Alberich and the Nibelungs in servitude. Their release from servitude, after Brünnhilde has returned the ring to the Rhine, is one of the central features of the outline. In the *Ring* trilogy the Nibelungs appear only in the prelude, *The Gold of the Rhine*—if we discount Hagen's dreamlike visitation by Alberich in *The Twilight of the Gods*—and nothing is said of their release from servitude. Again in the outline, the sin of the gods is expiated by Siegfried's death, and the eternal rule of Wotan seems to have been secured; in the music-drama Wotan, Valhalla, and the gods go up in flames. Between the outline and the music-drama lies Wagner's poem *Siegfried's Death*, which was finished in November, 1848. In both outline and poem, Siegfried is the central character. In the final version of the *Ring*, however, Wotan has become the pivot around which the music-drama turns. In all Wagner's versions, Siegfried is the product of an incestuous union. And in the outline we are told that *only* from such a union can the savior-hero issue. In the *Ring*, moreover, Wagner compounds the incest motif by making Wotan both the father (through a mortal woman) of Siegmund and Sieglinde and the father (through Erda) of Brünnhilde. And when Siegfried first awakens Brünnhilde, he takes her to be his *mother*. Why this emphasis by Wagner on the incest motif? In the original Norse saga, Sigmund and Signy, the children of the Volsung, do indeed have a son (Sinfjotli) who dies early in the course of the tale; but Sigurd the hero is the son of Sigmund by Hjordis, daughter of King Eylimi. In the variant *Thidrek* saga, Siegfried is the son of Siegmund and of Sisibe, the daughter of King Nodung of Spain. And in the medieval *Nibelungenlied*, Siegfried is the son of the otherwise unrelated King Sigmund and Queen Sieglinde.

2. THE NEEDED DESTRUCTION OF THE STATE: WAGNER'S INTERPRETATION OF THE OEDIPUS MYTH

Ernest Newman has shown that Wagner's role in the Dresden uprising of 1849 was not the trifling thing that Wagner himself, and certain of his biographers, attempted to make it seem at a later date. There is little doubt that Wagner was involved, if only peripherally, in supplying weapons to the rebels. Newman asserts that Wagner was the author of an unsigned article entitled "The Revolution," which appeared in the *Volksblätter* on April 8, 1849, shortly before the outbreak of the uprising in Dresden. Here the "sublime goddess Revolution" is called on to complete the destruction of a world already half in ruins. Speaking through Wagner's mouth, the goddess—repeating the phrase "I will destroy" more than ten times—promises to destroy the whole present order, "for it has sprung from sin, its flower is misery and its fruit is crime." The present order "makes millions the slaves of a few, and makes these few the slaves of their own power, their own riches"; it "makes labour a burden and enjoyment a vice"; it compels half of mankind to perform the useless and harmful work of "soldiers, officials, speculators and money-makers . . . while the other half must support the whole edifice of shame at the cost of the exhaustion of their powers and the sacrifice of all the joys of life." Down to its last trace "this insane order of things, compact of force, lies, care, hypocrisy, want, sorrow, suffering, tears, trickery and crime" must be destroyed. Says the goddess: "I annihilate what exists, and whither I turn there wells forth fresh life from the dead rock. . . . Whatever is must pass away . . . and I, the eternal destroyer, fulfill the law and create eternally youthful life." [10]

An answer to the question of the relation between incest and revolution can be found in Wagner's theoretical treatise on opera and drama, which he completed in 1851. [11] Wagner was at the time living in Zurich as a political exile. Although he had much to say later in regard to the meaning—meanings, really, since his interpretation underwent a change after he adopted Schopenhauer's philosophy—of *The Ring of the Nibelung*, Wagner avoided discussion of the incest motif. But an indirect answer appears in his analysis of the Oedipus legend in Sophocles' trilogy: *Oedipus the King, Oedipus at Colonus*, and *Antigone*. The third chapter of Wagner's treatise deals with the political significance of the Oedipus legend. As always with Wagner (in both his creative and theoretical writings), we find something less than clarity. His theoretical writings are works of art and are always highly polyvalent in significance. But this means also, from a purely analytic and intellectual point of view, that they are at times confused and confusing.

Wagner held that the natural and unspoiled human being was by nature a creative artist. He believed that the human beings of past "mythic" times had been truly creative; he hoped that the human be-

10. Newman, *Life*, II, 54–203.
11. Wagner, *Gesammelte Schriften*, IV, 1–103.

ings of the future would regain that power. The external senses and the brain, says Wagner, empower the human being to form a creative view (*Anschauung*) of the external world and so to reduce its infinite complexity to manageable proportions. Superimposed on this "natural" form of creativity is a secondary form of "artistic" creativity, through which human beings communicate their views. A people (*Volk*) is characterized by a set of views shared in common. In the earliest stages of the development of humankind, perceived reality was shaped by the popular imagination into plastic, visible forms—hence the various legendary depictions of gods, heroes, and human beings. Greek tragedy was based on Greek legend, just as medieval miracle plays were based on Christian legend. Wagner finds that medieval knightly romances, such as the story of Tristan, and the *Nibelungenlied* resulted from the grafting of Christian myth to the tree of Northern legend.[12]

Every people thus creates a mythic world and a real, socially organized world. One of the most striking features of the European world has been the development of two disparate forms of organization, one religious and the other secular, church and state. Wagner sees them as dialectical opposites, each contributing to the growth of the other as they try to define the limits of their authority. Each would like to swallow the other entirely. But their very existence testifies to a fundamental split in vision. Wagner finds that the struggle between church and state is a struggle of life against death:

The Christian Church, too, had striven for unity: all proclamation of life was supposed to funnel into her, as life's central point. But she was not a central but an end point of life; for the secret nature of true Christianity was death. At the opposite end point, however, stood the natural source of life itself, which death could only master by destroying. But the force that eternally directed life toward Christian death was none other than the *state* itself.

Wagner is saying here that the political state is death-oriented, although at first sight it seems to be the life-oriented foe of death-oriented Christianity. Here we have an additional reason why he believed that the destruction of the state was the historical task of our time. The end result

---

12. Wagner's greatness as a theoretician in the realm of the sociology of knowledge has not gone entirely unrecognized. See W. Stark, *The Sociology of Knowledge* (London, 1958), 10; Stark observes that for Wagner "the problems of creative art are in the last analysis identical with the problems of public life."

of the Western historical development has been the bourgeois society (bürgerliche Gesellschaft) of our own day. When the artist withdraws the cloak of custom from that society, an ugly formless chaos is disclosed: a "corrupted, crippled human being" in a society that is no longer a "living organism."[13]

Before probing the significance of the myth of Oedipus in Sophocles' trilogy of plays, Wagner discusses Greek legend and tragedy, Christian legend and tragedy, Germanic legend and knightly romance, the new view of human nature expressed in Shakespeare's plays, the subsequent development of descriptive and realistic novels, and finally, what he sees as a necessary outcome, namely the complete fusion of politics and literature in our own time. He concludes: "In this way the art of the creative writer (Dichter) has become politics. No one can 'poeticize' without 'politicizing.' . . . In a purely political world, not to be a politician comes to hardly more than not existing at all; whoever still slinks away from politics today only belies his own existence. The creative writer cannot again be present among us until we no longer have politics."[14]

Politics, continues Wagner, is the secret of our history and the central issue of our time; Napoleon rightly told Goethe that the place held by fate in the ancient world is held by politics in the modern world. Wagner does not explain precisely what the reader is to understand by his equation of "politics" with "fate" or "destiny." Taken in its broadest sense, the equation seems to mean that the human being of today, insofar as he or she is truly such, can no longer unquestioningly accept the rule of human law, custom, or morality—as if it were imposed from without by divine necessity or built into the very structure of the human world. For the "human" world is now seen as a human creation. Everything in it is open to question and negotiation; it has become "politicized." Even where the laws of physics and biology are concerned, the human being is no longer willing to accept without question the "natural" constraints of space, time, race, sex, or whatever. Here too there is room for negotiation. The "natural" superiority or inferiority of races, once unquestioningly accepted, reduces to a political question of the same order as the question of the superiority and inferiority of the

13. Wagner, Gesammelte Schriften, IV, 43, 51–52.
14. Ibid., 53.

various social classes. Even the attempt to substitute "anatomy" for "destiny" in the case of the relations between the sexes fails, and this realm too becomes "politicized" in the second half of the nineteenth century. How far Wagner went along any of these lines is another question; but in 1851 his aim, indisputably, was to liberate the free individual from bondage to the state, that corrupt guardian of custom and law.

The myth of Oedipus, Wagner tells us in 1851—five years before the birth of Sigmund Freud—is a myth without compare, a myth that is "always true" and "inexhaustible for all times": "Even today we need only interpret the Oedipus myth, and in keeping with its innermost nature, to win a comprehensible picture of the entire history of humanity, from the beginning of society to the necessary downfall (*Untergang*) of the state. In the myth the necessity of this downfall is sensed in advance; to carry it out is up to actual history."[15]

The myth is as follows. Laius, king of Thebes, warned by the Delphic oracle that his son will one day kill him and marry his wife, Jocasta, orders the newly born child of Jocasta to be cast away on a mountain. But the infant is found and rescued by a shepherd of Corinth and given the name Oedipus. Learning of the prophecy on reaching manhood and supposing that it refers to his foster-father King Polybus, Oedipus flees Corinth. On the way to Thebes he meets, quarrels with, and kills Laius. Oedipus then delivers Thebes by answering the riddle of the Sphinx. He marries Jocasta and becomes king of Thebes. From this incestuous union spring two daughters, Antigone and Ismene, and two sons, Polynices and Eteocles. When the blind seer Tiresias reveals the truth to Oedipus and Jocasta, Oedipus tears out his eyes and Jocasta commits suicide. The kingship reverts to the two sons, who agree to rule by turns. When Eteocles refuses to vacate the throne at the appointed time, Polynices and his supporters march on Thebes. The brothers fight and are slain. Creon, the uncle of Oedipus and brother of Jocasta, then becomes king. He decrees that the body of Eteocles shall be buried with honors; that of Polynices shall be abandoned to birds of prey. Whoever disobeys the decree shall be buried alive. Antigone defies him and buries the body of her brother. Despite the pleas of Creon's son, who

15. *Ibid.*, 64–65.

loves her, she is condemned to be buried alive. After the death of Antigone, Creon's son attempts, unsuccessfully, to kill his father. He then turns his sword on himself. Next, Creon's wife commits suicide. The trilogy ends with Creon's acknowledgment that the rule of his house is over.

For Wagner, the self-destruction of Creon's son is the symbolic self-destruction of the state. That destruction is the result of the surfacing of a long-buried and increasingly severe conflict between arbitrary (*willkürlich*), purely conventional morality, represented by the state, and nonarbitrary or spontaneous (*unwillkürlich*) morality, represented by the fully aware human being. But even the conventional morality of the state has its ultimate source in the spontaneous moral sense of the individual human being, and the state is bound to destroy itself when it becomes so corrupt that it cuts itself off entirely from its source. The moment of destruction comes with the appearance of a free and fully developed individual human being who resists the corrupt moral edicts of the state in the name of true morality and thus raises the moral consciousness of society to a new level. The state, now become a monster, is destroyed and replaced by a comradely society (*Gesellschaft*) of human beings. So it is that Wagner hails Antigone as a goddess of revolution: "Holy Antigone! I summon you! Let your banner wave, that we may, beneath it, both destroy and redeem!"[16]

Fundamental to Wagner's analysis of the Oedipus myth is the distinction drawn between two kinds of morality. One, championed by the state, is a corrupt, frozen, dead version of the other, which Wagner sees as the spontaneous, living morality of a fully aware human being. The various crimes committed by the protagonists of the Oedipus drama thus fall into two categories. When the Pythia informs Laius that he will be killed by his own son, the concealed premise of her prophecy is that he will follow the dictates of state morality. An absolute ruler, says Wagner, identifies the well-being of the state with his own well-being, and this is the germ of all crimes committed in the name of the state. In the name of the state, then, Laius has decided that "*peace* and *order*, even at the price of the basest crime against human nature and even customary morality—at the price of the deliberate murder of a

16. *Ibid.*, 55–64.

child by its father—were more worthy of consideration than that most natural of human sentiments which tells us that the father should sacrifice himself for his children, not the children for him."[17] Laius disposes of his son in secret, so as not to offend the Thebans. But, says Wagner, even had the Thebans known of the deed, they too would have accepted it in the name of peace and order. At the very beginning of the drama, then, Wagner finds that corrupted custom has blocked the source of true morality: state (conventional) morality has replaced natural (human) morality.

In contrast to the crime of Laius—which he, Jocasta, and the Thebans could justify in the name of the security of the state and leave unpunished—are the crimes of Oedipus and Jocasta. The incestuous union between Oedipus and Jocasta is, says Wagner, not a crime at all. Certainly it is not a crime against nature, for the children issuing from the union are in no way abnormal or deformed. Nor is it a crime against the spontaneously arising sentiment that normally prevents sexual union between brothers and sisters and between parents and children, for the original crime of Laius had made the development of that sentiment impossible. And the same crime has transformed parricide into homicide by presenting Laius to his son as a hostile stranger—which is precisely what he had shown himself to be in the beginning. (It is obvious that the same considerations apply to the incestuous union of Siegmund and Sieglinde, who are brought up apart.) But Oedipus and Jocasta cannot see their union in this light; hence, their drastic self-punishment. When Eteocles later refuses to abide by his sworn oath to yield the throne to Polynices at the appointed time, Wagner sees another triumph of state morality: Eteocles has identified his rule with himself. Again the Thebans acquiesce in the name of peace and order. Creon understands what the Thebans want, says Wagner; and his command that Eteocles is to be buried with all honors, while the body of Polynices is to be abandoned to dogs and birds of prey, is politically a very shrewd act. For in this way Creon

affirmed his power as he justified Eteocles, who had guaranteed peace to the citizens by breaking his oath, and gave it to be clearly understood that he, likewise, was willing to guarantee the maintenance of peace and order in the

17. *Ibid.*, 61.

state by taking on himself alone any crime against human morality. With his command he gave at the same time the strongest and most decisive proof of his affirmative attitude toward the state: he struck humanity in the face and cried: Long live the state![18]

But precisely at this point a woman, Antigone, rises up who knows nothing of reasons of state, a woman whose love for Polynices is neither sexual, parental, filial, nor merely that of sister for brother. Her love is the "richest flowering of purely human love." She has attained a new level of consciousness. She is fully aware of the "spontaneous necessity" of her act. She knows "that she had to obey this unconscious compelling necessity of self-destruction through sympathy (*Selbstvernichtung aus Sympathie*). In this state of consciousness of the unconscious (*Bewusstsein des Unbewussten*) she was the perfected human being—love in its highest fullness and supreme power."[19] And it is her act that leads to the symbolic destruction of the state. A destruction that is necessary, according to Wagner, because the political state was surviving solely through the vices of society. It had become an autonomous organism, the oppressor of an as yet unborn society that would subsist on the virtues of fully human, individual men and women. The Greeks attempt to arm themselves against destiny by means of the political state, says Wagner, and the myth tells of their failure.

The same timelessly true myth has a message for us today. The political state has now become our destiny. And its interests conflict sharply with those of the free individual. The essence of the political state is the arbitrary exercise of power (*Willkür*); the essence of free individuality is inner necessity (*Notwendigkeit*). The task of the future is plain. We must recognize that individuality has been right in its age-old battle with the state. Just as did Antigone, we must rise to a new level of consciousness and organize a new society:

But to organize society in this sense means to base it on its eternally inexhaustible source, the free self-determination of the individual. To bring the *unconscious part* of human nature in *society* to *consciousness*, and to recognize in this consciousness nothing other than the *necessity, common to all members of society, of free self-determination of the individual* amounts to the destruction of the state, since the state stepped through society to the

18. *Ibid.*, 62.
19. *Ibid.*, 63.

fore by denying free self-determination to the individual. The state lives on
the death of the individual.[20]

We can now see why the apparently criminal union between Siegmund and Sieglinde, like that between Oedipus and Jocasta, is unnatural only by convention and not by nature. The violation of conventional
morality involved in the birth of Siegfried and of Antigone is reflected
in the subsequent violation of conventional morality involved in the
overthrow of the state by Antigone and of the corrupt order of the gods
by Siegfried. The child of each of the two incestuous unions is in both
instances a savior: Antigone the savior-heroine and Siegfried the savior-
hero. Such is one of the rationales of the incest motif in *The Ring of the
Nibelung*.

An additional rationale may be found in Wagner's essay on opera
and drama. The human being of our time, says Wagner, has discovered
that nature is a "living organism" rather than a "mechanism constructed
for an end." Accordingly, the relation between the human being and
nature must become one of communion, love, and mutual enjoyment.
The cold, egoistical, pure understanding (*Verstand*) cannot bridge the
gap with its instrument of communication, the word. Communication
is possible in this case only through "feeling" (*Gefühl*), using the inarticulate language of tones. But, adds Wagner, it was from "feeling" that
"understanding" first arose; that is, somewhere far back in the history
of the human race the tone was the mother of the word. Now, at a higher
level of development, the masculine element of understanding turns
back to fructify the feminine element of feeling in order to bring forth
the "purely human" (*Reinmenschliche*)—the male-female representative of the human species. There is an analogy (perhaps a merely trivial
one, Wagner admits) between this process and the generation of the
perfected human being Antigone by the return of Oedipus to the womb
of Jocasta, his mother. In any case, Wagner sees this apparently circular
return as in reality a spiraling upward to a new level of human development. "Tonal language," he writes, "is the beginning and the end of
verbal language, just as feeling is the beginning and the end of understanding." And in the same way, "myth is the beginning and the end of
history." The highest goal of the creative artist—the vision that Wag-

20. *Ibid.*, 66–67.

ner now has in mind for his future work—is "the most understandable representation in drama, justified by the clearest human consciousness and corresponding to the intuition of eternally present life, of newly discovered myth." [21]

Wagner now saw his task clearly. He would represent the timeless validity of the Siegfried myth in a trilogy of music-dramas, just as Sophocles had done before him with the Oedipus myth. The savior-hero Siegfried would replace the savior-heroine Antigone, both representative of the liberated and perfected human beings of the future, both the issue of incestuous unions. Both symbolize a return to the original source with the object of beginning the cycle again at a higher level. History would fructify myth; verbal language (Wortsprache) would fructify tonal language (Tonsprache); understanding would fructify feeling. The closed circle would yield a new tonal-verbal language, representing a new level of "understanding-feeling," of "myth-history," and the attainment of a perfected "male-female" human being. The mythic history of this perfected human being would be given in a dramatic trilogy of his own, The Ring of the Nibelung, differing from the trilogy of Sophocles in that music would be married to the word and resembling it in that Siegfried would accomplish the eternally necessary task accomplished by Antigone—the task of making the old order yield place to the new.

In a subsequent communication to his friends written at the close of 1851, Wagner described in detail the course of his intellectual development up to that time and told them what was to come. [22] On returning from Paris to Dresden in 1842, he had plunged into the study of German history and Northern myth. He had made plans for a drama based on the life of the first Hohenstaufen emperor, but had given it up when he saw that his real task was to deal with mythic significance rather than historical fact. Next he had turned to the old legends—the Norse Eddas and sagas and the medieval German Nibelungenlied—which were now available in modern German. From the first, the figure of Siegfried had interested him; but as long as he had known Siegfried from the medieval Nibelungenlied alone, the possibility of making the hero the protagonist of a drama had not occurred to him. Only after he

21. Ibid., 85, 88, 91, 101–103.
22. Ibid., "Eine Mittheilung an meine Freunde," 230–344.

had cast off the medieval trappings and penetrated to the heart of the
Siegfried myth did this happen. But his dramatic representation of the
eternal truth of myth could not rest on the use of words alone. A marriage of music to drama was called for—a real marriage, not simply an
artificial conjuncture as in ordinary operas:

> This marriage can only be successful if the musical language is immediately
> connected to whatever is companionable and related in verbal language; the
> bond has to be made precisely where in verbal language itself an imperative
> desire for actual, sensuous expression of feeling is already manifest. . . . A
> content graspable by the understanding alone also remains communicable
> by verbal language alone. But the more it expands to become a force of feeling,
> so much the more decisively does it require expression that in the end only
> tonal language can make possible with the required fullness.[23]

The ultimate marriage that Wagner was trying to consummate can
be seen as a marriage between the divided halves of the self, one that
would reconstitute the whole human being in its primal form: a marriage between the head (intellect, consciousness, the "male" principle,
the arbitrary or *das Willkürliche*) and the heart (feeling, the unconscious, the "female" principle, the spontaneous, or *das Unwillkürliche*).
We have seen a somewhat similar union envisioned by Heine in 1834:
man, *purusha* (Sanskrit, "man") is to be reunited with nature, *prakriti*
(equivalent to the Sanskrit *pradhana*, or "fundamental substance"). At
this stage in Wagner's development the union was symbolized by the
union of two lovers, one female and the other male. But the incest motif hints that the real union must take place within each and every individual human being—half being, in reality—and in such a way that
the "male" and "female" principles can at last be reconciled: the (Jungian) animus and anima will have at last come to terms with each other.
The results of such a union will be revolutionary in all respects—from
the minutest detail of interpersonal relationships between women and
men, men and men, and women and women, to the whole structure
of our arts, sciences, and civilization. Wagner's paradigm for this all-
embracing union is the union of tone and words to produce the revolutionary art of the future—the music-drama—to which his life's work
as an artist was now dedicated.

23. *Ibid.*, 312–13, 318.

Wagner's *Communication to My Friends* (he was then thirty-eight years old, with all of his greatest works before him) is surely the most extraordinary example of artistic self-awareness ever committed to paper. Looking back on his early work, Wagner now sees the protagonist of *The Flying Dutchman* (1841) as a combination of Ulysses, Wandering Jew, and the chapbook Faust (he should have added Wotan, the Wild Huntsman, to this list), all of whom have missed salvation. The Dutchman's success may be questioned. Although his call is answered by Senta, he and his ship plunge, Pequod-like, into the depths as the opera ends. In *Lohengrin* (1841–1847) salvation is once again not achieved: Lohengrin reaches down from the Grail heights to Elsa; but their temporary union is disrupted—partly by their doubles, Telramund and Ortrud, partly by Elsa's own lack of faith. Elsa is "the other half of his (Lohengrin's) own being . . . the unconscious (*das Unbewusste*), the spontaneous (*das Unwillkürliche*), into which Lohengrin's conscious, deliberate (*willkürliche*) being yearns to be redeemed. But this yearning, again, is itself the unconscious necessity, the spontaneous (*das Unwillkürliche*) in Lohengrin, through which he feels himself akin to Elsa."[24]

Elsa's union with Lohengrin ends in disaster. But Wagner now sees, he tells his friends, that Elsa's jealous outbreak has revealed to him the essence of a love that Lohengrin himself had failed to grasp—Lohengrin, but not Wagner:

I had discovered her; the lost arrow that I had shot toward a suspected, as yet unknown, noble treasure was precisely my Lohengrin, whom I had to abandon in order to arrive with certainty on the track of the *truly womanly* that would bring salvation to me and all the world, after male egoism (even in the noblest form) had shattered before this principle in self-destruction. Elsa— the woman—the woman hitherto not understood by me, but now understood —this most necessary essential expression of the purest sensual spontaneity (*Unwillkür*)—had made me a complete revolutionary. She was the spirit of the people, from whom I too yearned, as an artistic human being, for my salvation.[25]

Wagner remarks at this point that only through the power of "unconscious consciousness" (*unbewussten Bewusstseins*) did he achieve understanding of Elsa's true significance for Lohengrin. As would happen

24. *Ibid.*, 301.
25. *Ibid.*, 301–302.

again in the creation of the *Ring*, Wagner had conceived and brought forth in *Lohengrin* a work under the sole guidance of reasons of the heart; only later had they surfaced as reasons of the head. In spite of all appearances to the contrary, Elsa represents an Antigone-like figure—a heroine who insists on giving Lohengrin his right name. Looking ahead a few years to *Siegfried*, it is easy for us to recognize a still plainer dramatization of Wagner's newly won understanding of the balance between male and female principles called for by the spirit of the age. When Siegfried, armed with the sword Nothung, shatters Wotan's upraised lance, "male egoism . . . in its noblest form" is once again shattered. The dramatic action also symbolizes the self-destuction of Wotan; he himself, through the operation of his unconscious will (that is, Brünnhilde) had put the sword in Siegfried's hand. The shattering of Wotan's lance destroys the last barrier to Siegfried's union with Brünnhilde. The perfected human being of the future, Siegfried-Brünnhilde, is male-female or female-male. *Purusha* and *prakriti* are in balance at last. A new race of human beings inherits the earth.

It was clear to Wagner that the Oedipus myth had been too thoroughly exploited before him to serve as raw material for the great music-drama that he now felt himself gestating within. Still another reason for looking elsewhere was his desire to work with mythic material more immediately relevant to the European past. He was left with a choice between the Christian myth of Jesus and the pagan myth of Siegfried. Since (as he told his friends in the communication) the figure of Jesus was already imprinted on the popular mind in fixed and unalterable form, he had chosen Siegfried to be the protagonist of his projected drama of salvation. (But the figure of Jesus remained immensely appealing to Wagner as a prime symbol of the denial of the kingdom of this world; and in the year that he wrote *Siegfried's Death*, he also sketched out a *Jesus of Nazareth*.) Wagner's dislike of European capitalism, militarism, and autocracy was by now so intense that his salvation, as he saw it, lay solely in a "flight from this life . . . through self-destruction" —not, as he explained to his friends, self-destruction as mere suicide but rather as a protest against the loveless modern world, as a "denial of lovelessness in general." Wagner chose symbolic instead of actual self-destruction and wrote *The Ring of the Nibelung*. "I intend," Wagner told his friends in 1851, "to produce my myth in *three complete dramas*, before which a great prelude will be placed . . . [and] to perform those three dramas, together with the prelude, in the course of three days and one fore-evening."[26]

Hardly more than a year after this announcement, Wagner had finished writing the words of the prelude and the three parts of *The Ring of the Nibelung*. He would, as we shall see, alter the closing lines of *The Twilight of the Gods* on several occasions to come. The music was as yet to be composed. And one piece of the stage action—Wotan seizing and brandishing the sword Nothung (forgotten by Fafner when he departs with the Nibelung's hoard) just before crossing the bridge to Valhalla—was not introduced until the first full performance of the prelude and trilogy in 1876. Early in 1853, Wagner distributed privately printed copies of the *Ring* to a handful of friends, Franz Liszt among them. To Liszt, who was by this time his most influential partisan in Europe, Wagner wrote in February of 1853: "Mark well my new poem —it contains the beginning and the end of the world!" And a little later, in a letter to August Röckel, Wagner wrote that he, like Wotan in *The Twilight of the Gods*, had withdrawn himself from political action. Wagner adds: "Look closely at him [Wotan]! He resembles us to a hair; he is the sum of the present-day intelligentsia; Siegfried, on the contrary, is the human being of the future—desired and wished for but not to be made by us—who must create himself through our destruction."[27]

From the above lines it is plain that, although Wagner has not yet given up hope in Siegfried (the human being of the future, who, as Wagner later explained to Röckel, is really only half of a human being and must be complemented by Brünnhilde), he has come to identify himself with the dying Wotan rather than with the triumphant Siegfried. Wagner has decided that he is too much a part of the old order to be comfortable in the new, and he includes Röckel and the whole of the "intelligentsia" along with himself. The chief theme of *The Ring of the Nibelung* has become Wotan's realization that not only is it beyond his power to right the wrong (his extortion of the hoard from Alberich) on which the empire of the gods was founded, but also that he himself

26. *Ibid.*, 331–32, 343–44.
27. Richard Wagner, *Richard Wagners Briefe*, ed. Erich Kloss (17 vols. in 9; Leipzig, 1910–13), X, 209; Richard Wagner, *Richard Wagner an August Röckel*, ed. La Mara [Ida Maria Lipsius] (Leipzig, 1903), 38.

must go under before the new order can come into being. Wotan's original plan was to create a free human being who would slay the dragon and return the hoard, symbolized by the Nibelung's ring, to the depths of the Rhine. But Fricka, Wotan's wife and goddess of convention, outraged by Sieglinde's desertion of her lawful husband and the incestuous union between Siegmund and Sieglinde, forces Wotan to abandon his plan. Urged on by Fricka, Wotan raises his lance—the lance engraved with the runes of sacred compact—and breaks the sword in his son's hands. By doing so Wotan renders himself impotent. From this point on in the action he is a mere spectator, a "Wanderer." When, stirred momentarily by jealousy or pride, he again raises his lance in order to prevent Siegfried from reaching Brünnhilde, the reforged sword in the hands of his grandson shatters the lance into fragments; and Wotan is seen no more. At the time of the letters to Röckel and Liszt, Wotan was Wagner's symbol of male egoism and individualism, which, albeit in its "noblest form," had to be "shattered in self-destruction" in order to create the fully human, male-female principle symbolized by Brünnhilde-Siegfried. Wotan is Lohengrin reinterpreted in the light of Wagner's new understanding.

Let us briefly rehearse the features common to the Siegfried legend (in the form given it by Wagner) and the Oedipus legend. Laius, king of Thebes, is told by the oracle that he will die at the hands of his son. He exposes his infant son (later to be named Oedipus) to seemingly certain death on a mountaintop. But Oedipus is rescued by a shepherd and taken to Corinth. There he reaches manhood, free of the obligations that would have been laid on him at Thebes. In all innocence he can kill his father and marry his mother, neither of whom he has ever seen. From the incestuous union between Oedipus and his mother springs the savior-heroine Antigone, who (in Wagner's eyes) is the first human being of the future, the overthrower of the state, the goddess of destruction and rebirth. Siegfried, grandson of Wotan and nephew of Brünnhilde, as well as issue of an incestuous union between Siegmund and Sieglinde, "creates" himself as he grows up in the forest, free of all bonds of the past. Still playing on the incest motif, Wagner has Siegfried take Brünnhilde at first sight to be his mother. Making his way toward Brünnhilde, Siegfried does not recognize as his grandfather the tedious old man who attempts to bar his way. Nor does Oedipus, unwittingly on his way toward union with his mother, recognize the stranger who bars his way as his father. Further, to Wagner the original crime of Laius (the exposure of Oedipus) results from the identification by Laius of the well-being of the state with his own well-being. In the name of this identification, Laius renounces the love he owes his son and becomes, as Wagner says, an "unnatural father." Instead of preserving the state, this action has in its train a series of crimes that culminates in the downfall of the state. Wotan, likewise, is willing to commit almost any crime in order to establish and preserve his supreme power. He deceitfully promises Freia to the giants as a reward for building Valhalla; he robs Alberich of the gold of the Rhine—piously informing Alberich that the gold belongs to the Rhine daughters in any case—to pay the giants in place of Freia; and, like Laius, he denies the love due his own son, Siegmund, when Fricka reminds him of the source of his power. But, as Pearl Wilson remarked in 1919, "The thought of giving up his fortress never occurs to him."[28] Wotan's doom, like that of Laius, is made certain by the very measures he takes to avert it.

A final word remains to be said concerning Wagner's elaboration of the incest motif in the *Ring*. In Wagner's first sketch, written in 1848, Siegfried is the son of a brother-sister pair, Siegmund and Sieglinde. It has already been stated here that neither in the medieval *Nibelungenlied* nor in the several versions of the Volsung saga is Siegfried the product of an incestuous union. But it is true that a Volsung king had a son and a daughter, the twins Sigmund and Signy, and that after the death of the king at the hands of Siggeir, who then took Signy for his bride, she—plotting revenge through her sons but unable to give birth to one from Siggeir strong enough for the task—went to her brother Sigmund, magically disguised, and afterward gave birth to a son, Sinfiotli. Together Sigmund and Sinfiotli overthrew the forces of Siggeir; Sinfiotli was later poisoned by Sigmund's wife, whose brother he had slain. Wagner's decision to make Siegfried the outcome of an incestuous union was deeply motivated, for he must have known that it would be offensive to many in his audience. And so it was, as Newman has pointed out in his biography. Arthur Drews, in a study of the conceptual content of

28. Wagner, *Gesammelte Schriften*, IV, 65; Pearl Cleveland Wilson, *Wagner's Dramas and Greek Tragedy* (New York, 1919). Wilson points out numerous correspondences between Wagner's *Ring* and the *Oresteia* but shies away from the incest motif.

Wagner's *Ring*, mentions a straightforward (if somewhat simpleminded) attempt to come to terms with the Siegmund-Sieglinde union. Wagner, says the author of this explanation, had meant to exemplify the immoral relationships bred by a capitalistic economic order that crammed working men and women together like cattle in the slums of London and Liverpool. Drews's own interpretation is that even a union between brother and sister cannot detract from the all-embracing significance ascribed by the composer to the union of the sexes.[29]

3. WAGNER, FEUERBACH, AND SCHOPENHAUER

Just when it was that Wagner's attention was drawn to the writings of Ludwig Feuerbach (1804–1872) is uncertain. In 1849 Wagner dedicated his essay *The Art-Work of the Future* to Feuerbach and in 1851 tried to persuade him to visit Zurich, where Wagner was living in exile.[30] Like many other Germans, Wagner took no serious account of the work of Arthur Schopenhauer (1788–1860) until the mid-1850s. Up to that time his philosophical interests centered almost exclusively on Feuerbach. Wagner did indeed, as we shall see, experience something like a conversion when he finally made contact with the philosophy of Schopenhauer. But to anyone familiar with the ideas expressed in *Opera and Drama* and *A Communication to My Friends*, both written in the early 1850s, a Schopenhauerian note is already audible. An important part of the ethical message of Schopenhauer's philosophy is, in fact, contained in Wagner's phrase "self-destruction through sympathy" (*Selbstvernichtung aus Sympathie*), used in 1851 to designate Antigone's moral imperative. The same imperative was obeyed by Wotan in the *Ring*.

29. Ernst Koch, *Richard Wagners Bühnenfestspiel "Der Ring des Nibelungen" in seinem Verhältnis zur alten Sage wie zur modernen Nibelungendichtungen betrachtet* (Leipzig, 1875); Newman, *Life*, II, 432; III, 207. And so also was Thomas Mann's parody of the story ("*Wälsungenblut*") in 1906, where the twins Siegmund and Sieglinde are scions of a wealthy German-Jewish family. Arthur Drews, *Der Ideengehalt von Richard Wagners "Ring des Nibelungen" in seiner Beziehung zur modernen Philosophie* (Leipzig, 1898), 22–23. Karl Marx had his own reasons for objecting to Wagner's treatment of the incestuous relationship between Siegmund and Sieglinde. He stated that Wagner had falsified primitive thought with the words: "Was it ever heard that a brother embraced a sister as a bride?" (These are not precisely Fricka's words to Wotan in *Die Walküre*, but they are close enough.) The truth is, Marx continued: "In primitive times the sister *was* the bride, *and that was moral.*" Friedrich Engels, *The Origin of the Family, Private Property and the State, in the Light of the Researches of Lewis H. Morgan* (London, 1940), 36; also *Karl Marx Friedrich Engels über Kunst und Literatur*, 168.

30. Newman, *Life*, II, 431, note.

The kind of love that motivated Antigone to defy Creon's edict and bury the abandoned body of her brother is very close to Christian *agapē*. But it is quite clear that in 1851 Wagner had not yet separated *erōs*— sexual love, or love involving desire—from *agapē*. Nor did he do so until several years later, as his correspondence with August Röckel from 1853 to 1856 will show.

A brief comment on the relationship between Wagner and a third philosopher, Friedrich Nietzsche (1844–1900), will first be made for the benefit of the reader who may wonder why Nietzsche is passed over in the present work. Nietzsche and Wagner first met in 1869, when Wagner was fifty-six years old. Nietzsche was a brilliant youth of twenty-four, newly appointed to the chair of classical philology at Basel. For an understanding of the writings of Wagner, an understanding of Feuerbach and Schopenhauer is essential. For an understanding of Nietzsche, the writings of Schopenhauer and Wagner are essential. But for an understanding of Wagner, the writings of Nietzsche—insofar as they deal with Nietzsche's own philosophy and not with Wagner himself—are of no importance whatsoever. And, anticipating the discussion of certain aspects of Freud's psychology and metapsychology adumbrated in the writings of Schopenhauer and to be taken up later in the present work, little of fundamental importance bearing on Freud can be found in the writings of Nietzsche that cannot also be found in Schopenhauer.[31]

Ludwig Feuerbach's *The Essence of Christianity* and *Thoughts on Death and Immortality* were, Wagner wrote to Röckel in June, 1853, the two really outstanding works of this "powerful, clear mind." Wagner then asked Röckel, who had received the privately printed version of the *Ring* some time earlier, to give him his opinion of it as soon as possible. Röckel did so, but Wagner was disappointed by the response. Wagner's next letter to Röckel (also written from Zurich) was not forthcoming until January, 1854. In it Wagner makes a number of preliminary remarks that clearly show the influence of Feuerbach's philosophy on the problems raised in the *Ring*. Wagner tells Röckel that the

31. Theodore Dreiser is said to have told H. L. Mencken that Nietzsche was merely "Schopenhauer confused and warmed over." See Robert Penn Warren, *Homage to Theodore Dreiser* (New York, 1971), 146. There is something to be said for this.

essence of reality is eternal change, the eternal round of things from birth to death. If we want to accept life in the fullest sense, we must first learn to accept the necessity of death: "Only what changes is actual (*wirklich*): to be actual, to live, means to be born, to grow, to flourish, to fade and to die; without the necessity of death there is no possibility of life; only that which has no beginning has no end." Now, says Wagner (echoing Mephistopheles' admonition to Faust: *dieses Ganze ist nur für einen Gott gemacht*), we must as human beings give up the search for the "whole" (*dem "Ganzen"*). We must instead seek to comprehend fully, to know in its completeness, the individual phenomenon, for only in this way is the "whole" revealed to us. And how are we to achieve such knowledge? Wagner answers:

Only through love!—everything that I cannot love remains outside of me and I outside of it; here the philosopher can indeed persuade himself that he comprehends, but the genuine human being cannot. Now love in its fullest actuality is possible only between the sexes: only as man and woman can we human beings love in fullest actuality; all other love is only derived from that love, flows from it, relates itself to it, or artificially imitates it.[32]

Love between the sexes—which we recognize here as *erōs* rather than *agapē*—is for Wagner the highest form of love, the paradigm of love. He states that any philosopher who despises love between the sexes as mere animal lust has failed to grasp the real meaning of human love (*menschliche Liebe*). At this point, Wagner again returns to a consideration of human (predominantly male) egoism. Egoism is ultimately unsatisfactory:

We find the ultimate satisfaction of egoism only in its complete relinquishment, and this the human being finds only through love. But the actual human being is man and woman, and it is only through the union of man and woman that the actual human being first comes into existence; only through love, therefore, do a man and a woman become a human being (*Mensch*). Yet today we are so lovelessly stupid as always to think involuntarily only of a man when we speak of a "human being."[33]

Wagner now extends the scope of meaning of this act of recognition —this achievement of true knowledge of what constitutes the real hu-

32. Wagner, *Wagner an Röckel*, 16, 26, 27.
33. *Ibid.*, 28.

man being—to cover all aspects of human life. It becomes an act of recognition that may be eternally repeated. In words that seem to anticipate Martin Buber, Wagner continues:

Egoism truly comes to an end only in the merging of the "I" ("Ich") with the "thou" ("Du"), but the "thou" does not present itself at once when I place myself in conjunction with the whole of the world: "I" and "the world" is nothing more than "I" alone; the world becomes fully actual for me only when it has become for me a "thou," and this it becomes only in the presence of a beloved individual.[34]

What this means is that the only escape from solipsism is through the "I"-"thou" relationship—the achievement of union with a beloved individual of the opposite sex.

Much of what Wagner has said here comes directly from the philosophy of Feuerbach. It will suffice to cite a few passages from Feuerbach's *Fundamentals of the Philosophy of the Future*, a work published in 1843. This title, incidentally, is the source of Wagner's title, *The Art-Work of the Future*. The new philosophy, states Feuerbach (meaning of course his own neo-Hegelianism),

bases itself on the truth of love, the truth of feeling (*Empfindung*). In love, in feeling generally, every human being confesses the truth of the new philosophy. The new philosophy itself is in relation to its basis nothing other than the essence of feeling raised to consciousness. . . . It is the heart brought to understanding. The heart wants no abstract, no metaphysical or theological objects—it wants actual, it wants sensuous objects and beings.[35]

Feuerbach's call for the raising of "feeling" or "heart" to the level of consciousness may well have been echoing in Wagner's inner ear when he himself called for the unconscious (*das Unbewusste*) to be raised to the level of consciousness. (This is not to say that Wagner was merely repeating what he had read in Feuerbach; on the contrary, he had thought it through and added something of his own.) Feuerbach ties love and truth together in much the same way as Wagner: "If the old philosophy said: what is not thought is nothing, then the new philosophy, on the contrary, says: what is not loved, what cannot be loved, is nothing. . . . Where there is no love there is also no truth. And only something that

---

34. *Ibid.*, 29–30.
35. Ludwig Feuerbach, *Sämtliche Werke*, ed. Wilhelm Bolin and Friedrich Jodl (13 vols. in 12; Stuttgart, 1959–64), II, 299.

loves something exists—not to be and not to love is the same thing."
Here Feuerbach has identified *erōs, epistēmē*, and existence; carnal
knowledge in the Biblical sense turns out to be the form of all knowledge. It is not necessary to explore all facets of the intellectual relationship between Wagner and Feuerbach.[36] The above suffices for an understanding of the Feuerbachian explanation of the *Ring* that Wagner will
now give Röckel.

After some four thousand words to Röckel along the above lines,
Wagner turns to his exposition of his "Nibelungen poem." He is not
surprised that Röckel has met with some difficulty in understanding it,
for Röckel is himself creative. A naive reader would grasp his meaning
more easily, although without becoming fully conscious of that meaning; that is, he would understand it through "feeling" rather than intellect. His poem

shows Nature in her undistorted truth, with all of her actual opposites, which,
in their endless and manifold confrontations also contain the mutually repul-
sive. But that Alberich was rejected by the Rhine-daughters—which was
quite natural—is not the deciding source of the disaster. Alberich and his
ring could not have harmed the gods at all had they not already been susceptible to disaster. Now where does the seed of this disaster lie? See the first
scene [in *Das Rheingold*] between Wotan and Fricka—which leads finally to
the scene in the second act of *Die Walküre*. The firm bond uniting the pair,
sprung from love's involuntary error of prolonging itself beyond the point
of necessary change, of guaranteeing itself mutually—this resistance to the
eternal novelty and change of the phenomenal world—brings both partners
to the mutual torture of lovelessness. The course of the whole poem, accordingly, shows the necessity of recognizing and yielding to change, multiplicity
and plurality, to the eternal newness of life and actuality. Wotan raises himself to the tragic height of willing his downfall. This is all we have to learn
from the history of humanity: to will the necessary and to bring it about ourselves. The creative achievement of this highest, self-destroying will is the finally attained fearless, always loving human being: Siegfried. . . . But Siegfried alone (the man alone) is not the perfected "human being" (*der vollkom-
mene "Mensch"*). He is merely the half; only with Brünnhilde does he become the savior. . . . The suffering woman who sacrifices herself becomes in
the end the true knowing savior.[37]

36. *Ibid.*, 299. An extended account is given in Rudolf Lück's *Richard Wagner
und Ludwig Feuerbach: eine Ergänzung der bisherigen Darstellungen der inneren Entwicklung Richard Wagners* (Breslau, 1905).
37. Wagner, *Wagner an Röckel*, 35–37.

Originally, says Wagner, he had put into the mouth of the earth-mother, Erda (when she issued her warning to Wotan to give up the Ni-belung's ring), the words: "A dark day dawns for the gods; your noble race will surely come to a shameful end if you do not give up the ring!" Now he has her tell Wotan: "All that is—ends; a dark day dawns for the gods; I counsel you, shun the ring!" This change may well have puzzled Röckel; it certainly troubled some later commentators. One of them—mentioned by Newman, who could himself offer nothing better —claimed that the second version made no sense at all. The first ver-sion implied that the gods would be saved provided Wotan gave up the ring; the second, that their downfall was inevitable. Hence, Erda's warn-ing (and indeed the whole course of the drama thereafter) was point-less. But if we read the change in the light of Wagner's commitment to Feuerbach's philosophy, it makes sense. Erda's words tell Wotan—and us—that death and change are inevitable; endless power and endless life, symbolized here by the Nibelung's ring, are even beyond the reach of the gods. "We must learn to die, and indeed to die in the fullest sense of the word," Wagner tells Röckel; "fear of the end is the source of all lovelessness, and it arises only where love itself has already withered."[38]

For the rest, says Wagner, his poem shows what actually poisons love in our modern world: the unholy power of gold, torn from nature and misused, symbolized by the Nibelung's ring. The curse will not be lifted until the gold is returned to the Rhine. The power-hungry Wotan learns this truth only at the end of the drama. Yet he was told it by Loge in the beginning, says Wagner. Loge could see that the triumphant gods passing over the rainbow bridge into Valhalla were simply hurrying to their doom. Much else in the poem Wagner tries painstakingly to clarify for his friend. The music would, he says, light up some of the more ob-scure features. But an element of ambiguity would still remain. To Röckel's protest that the *Ring* poem contained too many elements of this kind, Wagner replies:

On the contrary, I believe that I have, in accordance with a rather correct in-stinct, guarded myself against excessive zeal in making things obvious. For it has become clear to my feelings that a too open disclosure of intent quite dis-turbs correct understanding; in drama—as in works of art generally—what

38. *Ibid.*, 35; Newman, *Life*, II, 351.

counts is to produce effects not through the exposition of intent but rather through the exposition of what is spontaneous (*Unwillkürlichen*). Precisely this it is, too, that distinguishes my poetic writings from my political writings which are as yet almost all that is known.[39]

We may disagree with Wagner's notion that his political writings are models of clarity—although it is likely that the novelty of his views rather than the turgidity of his German often makes them unclear to the reader—but less so with his claim that a work of art ought to be ambiguous. To be interesting at all, a work of art must leave something unsaid; to remain interesting, it must contain sufficient ambiguity to allow for an almost endless series of interpretations. The function of ambiguity in works of art is well recognized today, and it was probably no great novelty in Wagner's time. Goethe, for example, protested to those who asked him what idea he had meant to embody in *Faust* that there was no such idea: "I received in my mind impressions . . . and I had, as a poet, nothing more to do than to round off and elaborate artistically such views and impressions, and by means of a lively representation so to bring them forward that others might receive the same impression in hearing or reading my representation of them." Goethe added that, in his opinion, "the more incommensurable, and the more incomprehensible to the understanding, a poetic production is, so much the better it is."[40] Observe that Goethe speaks of "receiving" impressions in his mind: they come to him, he rounds them off, and he trusts that his poetic work will produce similar impressions in the minds of his audience. There is more of spontaneity than there is of deliberate intent. Now this is precisely what Wagner told Röckel. The spontaneous or involuntary element of the artwork—*das Unwillkürliche*, as Wagner calls it—comes from the depths of the artist, and it speaks to the depths of the viewer or auditor. Nevertheless, there were inconsistencies and contradictions of another order in Wagner's poem, and perhaps Röckel had perceived some of them.

Aside from these inconsistencies, one or two of which will be mentioned later, there was another feature of the *Ring* that disturbed Röckel and also—although for quite different reasons—Wagner himself. This

39. Wagner, *Wagner an Röckel*, 37.
40. Johann Peter Eckermann, *Conversations of Goethe with Eckermann*, trans. John Oxenford (London, 1930), 205–206.

feature was the manner of the closing of the *Ring*. As already remarked, some features of the *Ring* can be explained—or at least Wagner thought that they could—along Feuerbachian lines. Feuerbach's materialistic and essentially optimistic outlook was shared by Röckel; and at the time of the letter in question, Wagner thought that he himself was more or less of this persuasion. But even as he was writing to Röckel in January, 1854, Wagner seemed to be troubled by the closing lines of the *Ring*. Yet he was not willing, or able, to admit this until two years later. By that time he had turned away from Feuerbach to the philosophy of Schopenhauer. He was then able to explain to Röckel to his own satisfaction certain features of the poem that had long puzzled him, just as they had puzzled Röckel. But the point is that even in his Feuerbachian period Wagner had begun to see Wotan, rather than Siegfried, as the central figure of the *Ring* and to see Wotan's unconsciously willed self-destruction as the crux of the dramatic action. And this, clearly enough, equates with the "denial of the will"—the crux of Arthur Schopenhauer's chief work.

4. THE PHILOSOPHY OF SCHOPENHAUER AND ITS RECEPTION BY WAGNER

Schopenhauer has been called the philosopher for nonphilosophers, somewhat as Wagner has been called the musician for nonmusicians. Patrick Gardiner has recently pointed out three erroneous notions still abroad: first, that Schopenhauer is essentially an essayist and littérateur; second, that he derives his ideas for the most part from Oriental thought, hence "represents the intrusion into our native intellectual world of a basically alien element"; finally—and this is of course a new misunderstanding—that Schopenhauer, by glorifying the will to power and undermining our belief in the preeminence of reason, became one of the "chief originators of sinister modern ideologies like National Socialism." The first of these notions is true to the extent that Schopenhauer is, among other things, an essayist and belle-lettrist whose literary style is marked by clarity, wit, humor, and an astounding breadth of knowledge. The second is true to the extent that Schopenhauer was aware of Indian, Chinese, and Eastern thought generally and that he admitted certain similarities between his own and Eastern philosophies. The third notion is true to the extent that Schopenhauer recognized the power of the irrational in the human being and in this sense placed "will"—a technical term in his philosophy requiring careful attention—above reason. But the phrase "will to power" is Nietzsche's, not Schopenhauer's. Far from glorifying aggression in any form, Schopenhauer regarded the affirming of one's own will by denying the will of another as the root cause of all evil. Disregard for the rights of other beings—and not only the rights of human beings but those of animals as well—reaches its peak in human egoism, as we see it exhibited in the lives of "tyrants and evildoers, and their world-devastating wars." Napoleon I (admired by Heine and Goethe) was for Schopenhauer merely the leader of a predatory horde of Frenchmen. "Man is a wolf to man," writes Schopenhauer, citing Plautus. For this purpose, of course, some men are more fitted than others, above all the world-conqueror; he sets a few hundred thousand men in opposition and tells them: "To suffer and die is your lot: now start shooting each other with flint and cannon!" And they do it. Wagner expresses a similar opinion regarding the world's Caesars and "great men" in a letter to Mathilde Wesendonck written in 1859. He was happy that he was not one of their company: "Hateful, petty, brutal natures, insatiable—because they have nothing at all within and therefore must forever be gobbling up what is without. Away with these great men! Here I praise the words of Schopenhauer: not the world-conqueror but the world-transcender deserves our admiration! God keep these 'powerful' natures, these Napoleons etc. off my neck."[41]

Although Schopenhauer's first major work, entitled *On the Fourfold Root of the Principle of Sufficient Reason*, appeared in 1813—the year of Wagner's birth, when Schopenhauer himself was twenty-five years old—and *The World as Will and Representation* five years later, he remained little known until the middle of the nineteenth century and at no time became part of the German university academic establishment. Kant was his philosophical starting point. He greatly admired the works of David Hume and Voltaire. The Hegelians, Fichteans, and

41. Patrick Gardiner, *Schopenhauer* (London, 1967), 22–29; Arthur Schopenhauer, *Sämtliche Werke*, ed. Wolfgang Freiherr von Löhneysen (5 vols.; Stuttgart, 1960–65), I, 455; II, 740; Gustav Friedrich Wagner, *Schopenhauer-Register*, ed. Arthur Hübscher (Stuttgart, 1962), 292; Richard Wagner, *Wagner an Mathilde Wesendonck* (Berlin, 1906), 185. From Schopenhauer, *Sämtliche Werke*, I, 524: "The greatest, weightiest and most significant phenomenon that the world has to offer is not the world-conqueror but the world-transcender."

German nature-philosophers excited only his contempt—Hegel, in particular, whose entire work, says Schopenhauer, contained less than could be learned from a single page by David Hume and constituted a "lasting monument to German stupidity."[42] It is perhaps understandable that the second edition of *The World as Will and Representation*, slightly altered and accompanied by a volume of supplementary essays, was again greeted with silence when it appeared in 1844. In 1846, however, Schopenhauer became acquainted with Julius Frauenstädt, a young German Jew who was to become one of the chief promulgators of his philosophy, as well as his literary executor. Frauenstädt helped Schopenhauer find a publisher willing to bring out two additional volumes of essays, the *Parerga* and *Paralipomena*.[43] This was in 1851. But Schopenhauer was still known only to a small group of readers in Germany when he was discovered by John Oxenford in England in 1853.

Oxenford was a drama critic for the London *Times* and the author of several translations from the German, including Goethe's conversations with Eckermann. His detailed account of Schopenhauer's *The World as Will and Representation* was published in 1853. After paying tribute to Schopenhauer's wit and clarity of style, which he finds a refreshing change from the usual output of German metaphysicians, Oxenford makes a remark that has been repeated on innumerable occasions since: Schopenhauer, he says, gives his readers a "theory with which they may agree or not, but which they can hardly fail to understand." Schopenhauer's "discovery" by a book reviewer has a certain element of irony, for he himself remarks, in the preface to the first volume of *The World*, that if the purchaser feels disinclined to read it he can give it to a learned lady friend or, better still, write a review.[44]

Oxenford devotes most of his review to the ethical rather than epistemological conclusions of the "misanthropic sage of Frankfort," as he labels Schopenhauer. What constitutes a *good* human being? For Schopenhauer, writes Oxenford:

42. Arthur Schopenhauer, *The World as Will and Representation*, trans. E. F. J. Payne (2 vols.; New York, 1969), I, 429; II, 582. Further citations will be from von Löhneysen's complete edition of Schopenhauer's works.

43. Schopenhauer, *Sämtliche Werke*, IV, V; see also Arthur Schopenhauer, *Parerga and Paralipomena: Short Philosophical Essays by Arthur Schopenhauer*, trans. E. F. J. Payne (2 vols.; London, 1974).

44. John Oxenford, "Iconoclasm in German Philosophy," *Westminster Review*, April, 1853, pp. 388–407; Schopenhauer, *Sämtliche Werke*, I, 13.

The artist comes in for a large share of his respect, for he, without regard to selfish motives, contemplates the ideas which form the substrata of the world of phenomena, and reproduces them as the beautiful and the sublime. The good man, with his huge sympathy, is another estimable being; but higher still is he, who, convinced of the illusion of the world, is resolved to destroy it, as far as he is concerned, by extinguishing the will to live.

Schopenhauer is not, Oxenford emphasizes, advising us to commit suicide. Still less (it may be added) is he advising us to bring about the equivalent of this act on a global scale. In Schopenhauer's opinion the act of suicide, far from denying the will to live, is a disguised affirmation of the will; it is the reverse side of the same false coin. As Oxenford puts it, suicide merely expresses a "dislike of a particular chain of circumstances . . . and is no alienation of the individual desires from life in general." The extinction or denial of the will called for by Schopenhauer lies on a different plane. What it requires is systematic suppression of the instinctive cravings of the insatiable will; it can be accomplished only by the saint or ascetic. Schopenhauer's message, says Oxenford, is that "freedom of the will is, in a word, annihilation." Schopenhauer denies the existence of freedom of the will in the ordinary sense of the phrase. In the empirical world, human behavior is as strictly determined by causal laws as the fall of a stone. But there is a point (reached by very few) where "freedom of the will" can be achieved in the sense of "freedom *from* the will." And this is a Nirvana point, a "blowing out"—hence an annihilation of the world.[45]

The Schopenhauerian line of argument can be summarized as follows. Schopenhauer repeatedly tells us that his philosophy is no more than the systematic unfolding of a single thought. Its end is contained in its beginning, one may say, and its beginning in its end—rather like a giant Midgard Serpent, tail in mouth—hence Schopenhauer's requirement that his book be read twice. But he was unable to unfold that single thought in anything less than the compass of *The World as Will and Representation*. Further, as he states in the preface to the first volume, he presupposes that the reader has already mastered his opus of 1813, *On the Fourfold Root of the Principle of Sufficient Reason*.

From Schopenhauer's "single thought" flows all that he has to say

---

45. Oxenford, "Iconoclasm in German Philosophy," 406, 407.

on music, dreams, the unconscious forces controlling human beings, death, sexuality, occult or paranormal phenomena, and finally, the affirmation and denial of the will. It is essential that the term *will* (*Wille*) used by Schopenhauer be understood as a technical term, rather than in its ordinary sense. Schopenhauer's "will" is *not* the will of so-called willpower, the will of the subject who says at the conscious level, "I will have it so, and in no other way." In the human being the Schopenhauerian "will," as it comes to the surface level, gives utterance to the inmost core or heart of the human being. The possibility for confusing or interchanging two different meanings of the word *will* is inherent in German as well as in English. Wagner, in a preface written in the 1870s for his essay of 1849, *Art and Revolution*, stated that at the time of his transition from Feuerbach to Schopenhauer he himself had not grasped the distinction. The distinction "has to do with the conceptions of arbitrary choice (*Willkür*) and that which is involuntary (*Unwillkür*), in regard to which, long before my involvement, great confusion had arisen because an adjectivally used 'involuntary' ('*unwillkürlich*') had been elevated to the status of a noun." Those who are acquainted with the philosophy of Schopenhauer know, he continues, "that the misused term 'involuntary' ('*Unwillkür*') in truth should signify 'the will' ('*der Wille*'), whereas 'voluntary' designates the so-called 'rational will' (*Verstandes-Willen*), influenced and led by reflective thought." And, continues Wagner, it is to the pure will—the Schopenhauerian will, that is, "as it becomes aware of itself in the human being as the *thing-in-itself*"—that "truly productive properties" are to be ascribed. The wellsprings of human creativity lie in the realm of the unconscious and the involuntary. William James once remarked (1902) that a certain music teacher was in the habit of telling her pupils after a series of unsuccessful attempts on their part to perform some difficult passage: "Stop trying and it will do it itself." "There is," James added, "thus a conscious and voluntary and involuntary and unconscious way in which mental results may get accomplished."[46]

Schopenhauer's single thought about the nature of the world, if such it may be said to be, acquires a double aspect in his exposition of it: the world as will and the world as representation. The task of the

---

46. Wagner, *Gesammelte Schriften*, III, 3–4; William James, *The Varieties of Religious Experience* (New York, 1958), 169.

reader is to understand the part-aspects and to unite them into a whole. If the connection is not made, Schopenhauer will be misunderstood. To say that the world is representation or idea (*Vorstellung*) directs our attention to the world as we *know* it, from the standpoint of beings-in-the-world. Philosophical discernment dawns on us, says Schopenhauer, when we come to realize that we "know no sun or earth, but only an eye that sees the sun, a hand that feels the earth." The world around us, the world that we at first naively take to be out there as such, is in reality there only as a representation (*Vorstellung*), only with reference to another thing—namely, that which represents (*das Vorstellende*). And "that which represents" is each one of us—each knower, observer, or perceiving subject.[47]

To enter into Schopenhauer's philosophy, it is necessary to get a firm grasp on his starting point. Later on I shall have something to say concerning Schopenhauer's philosophy in relation to phenomenology and logical positivism; here it is worth noting that G. E. M. Anscombe, in her book on Ludwig Wittgenstein, remarks that anyone who is unable to read the opening passage of Schopenhauer's major work without responsiveness will probably be unable to enter into Wittgenstein's thought in the *Tractatus*. Schopenhauer was well aware that this thought had already been expressed (although in his opinion imperfectly) by René Descartes, John Locke, and George Berkeley and by his own avowed mentor, Immanuel Kant. One of the features that distinguishes Schopenhauer from earlier philosophers is his emphasis on the role of the brain and nervous system in the process of "knowing" the world. In his essay of 1813, *On the Fourfold Root of the Principle of Sufficient Reason*, Schopenhauer states that perception is always an intellectual act mediated by a sensory apparatus, nervous system, and brain. The immediate datum of "seeing the world" is an event in the retina taking place, as he puts it, under the skin. In order to construct the ordinary everyday external world of our experience, Schopenhauer points out, we have to invert the two retinal impressions (which are upside down because of the action of the lens of the eye), make a single object out of the two impressions, and then situate this object among other objects in a spatial world of three dimensions. Further, we have

47. Schopenhauer, *Sämtliche Werke*, I, 31.

to maintain the integrity of the object as the retinal impressions, and all else, shift and change in the course of movement and time. Schopenhauer's illustrative comments on the experiences of persons who are born blind and gain sight later are particularly interesting in this connection; so also is his description of the case of Caspar Hauser.[48]

As an indication of the relative novelty of Schopenhauer's neurophysiological approach to the problem of how we actively *know* the world, the English neurophysiologist W. Russell Brain could remark as late as 1951 that with few exceptions—he names Bertrand Russell, Alfred North Whitehead, and Arthur Eddington, but not Arthur Schopenhauer—modern philosophers seem quite unaware of the "importance of the part played by the body in perception and thought." Our knowledge of the external world is derived from "perceptions which depend on the physical structure of the sense-organs and the nervous system," and the philosopher ought to take this into account. For example, says Brain, when we perceive a two-dimensional circle on a sheet of paper, the retinal excitation is directed by way of the optic nerves to the right and left visual cortices of the brain. The two areas of cortical excitation are shaped rather like a long letter *u* with the closed end lying anteriorly. And so, he continues, the brain activity corresponding to the two-dimensional circle is "halved, reduplicated, transposed, inverted, distorted and three-dimensional." Given this limited and symbolic character of the knowledge furnished by brains, nervous systems, and peripheral sensors and given the evidence suggesting that such systems were "evolved to facilitate action" on the external world, how can we believe, asks Brain, that any such system is "capable of providing conceptual symbols for the whole of reality." This is precisely what Schopenhauer says, and for the same reasons, about the commonly held belief that the perceived world has absolute status:

One must be forsaken by all the gods to suppose that the perceived world there outside (*die anschauliche Welt da draussen*), filling space with its three dimensions, moves onward in the strict pitiless course of time, is ruled at every step by the universal laws of causality, but in all these features merely

48. G. E. M. Anscombe, *An Introduction to Wittgenstein's "Tractatus"* (London, 1959), 168; Schopenhauer, *Sämtliche Werke*, III, 67–106. See also Arthur Schopenhauer, *On the Fourfold Root of the Principle of Sufficient Reason*, trans. E. F. J. Payne (La Salle, Illinois, 1974).

follows laws which we can state before all experience with them—that such a world there outside could be completely objective and real (*ganz objektiv-real*) and present without our cooperation, but then, by way of mere sense-impressions, could have gotten into our heads, where it now is once again present just as outside.[49]

So much for Schopenhauer's world-as-representation, which is the world-as-known. If we were to stop at this point, Schopenhauer tells us, we would have arrived at mere Fichtean idealism, where "the 'I' spins out of itself the 'not-I'" or, as Schopenhauer says in *The World*, where the "non-ego result[s] from the ego as the web from the spider."[50] But if solipsism is taken to mean that only the self, the "I," exists, then Schopenhauer is not a solipsist. The world-as-representation is only an abstraction from a whole, the other half of which is the world-as-will. The world-as-will really exists outside of the observer, perceiver, or observing subject. We can pass from Schopenhauer's world-as-representation to his world-as-will by way of his remarks on the fourfold root of the principle of sufficient reason. Three of these "roots" give rise, one may say, to the infinitely branching structure of the tree of knowledge, to the external empirical world of common sense and to science, its refined version. But the fourth root, a taproot as it were, leads deep into the earth, down to the ultimate ground of things. Otherwise stated, it leads us to an understanding of Kantian things-in-themselves; that is, things as they *are*, rather than things as they are *known* (by us and other sentient beings). The world-as-will of Schopenhauer is his answer to the question of the nature of things-in-themselves, an answer that Kant says is forever beyond our grasp.

Schopenhauer begins his study of the principle of sufficient reason with a statement derived from Christian Wolff's *Ontologia*: Nothing is without a reason or ground why it *is* rather than *is not* (*Nihil est sine ratione, cur potius sit quam non sit*, which is translated by Schopenhauer as: *Nichts ist ohne Grund, warum es sei und nicht vielmehr nicht sei*). He then reviews the history of the principle from its first appearance in Plato and Aristotle down through the medieval and modern philosophers, including René Descartes—the "father of modern

49. W. Russell Brain, *Mind, Perception and Science* (Oxford, 1951); Schopenhauer, *Sämtliche Werke*, III, 68.

50. Schopenhauer, *Sämtliche Werke*, I, 70; III, 105.

philosophy"—Baruch Spinoza, Gottfried von Leibniz, Christian Wolff, David Hume, and Immanuel Kant, before beginning his own analysis. The principle is old, but the Schopenhauerian analysis of its fourfold root (*vierfache Wurzel*) is new, even though he himself derived the notion from a Pythagorean oath that he used as an epigraph for his essay. The first of the roots concerns the objects—from chairs to stars—that we find in the everyday, common-sense world. Schopenhauer calls such objects empirical representations; they are re-presented as such, by the knowing subject. These objects undergo constant change in accordance with causal laws. Schopenhauer distinguishes three kinds of cause: the causes operative in physics and chemistry, the stimuli operative in organic life at the vegetative level, and the motives operative in organic life at the higher animal level. Motives, according to Schopenhauer, are to a greater or lesser degree conscious and conditioned by knowledge; but motivation is in the end merely "causality passing through knowledge." Freedom of the will in the ordinary sense of the phrase—that is, the claim that to a given human being, in a given situation, two different actions are possible—is, says Schopenhauer, "absurd."[51] Here he agrees with Hobbes, Spinoza, and Kant; but we must remember that Schopenhauer allows for that transcendental freedom of the will which Oxenford called "annihilation."

The second root has to do with abstract concepts. These are, so to speak, representations of representations. Operative in this sphere are a priori judgments, including the whole corpus of logical laws. The third root has to do with the forms of space and time: the mathematical apprehension of space as position and time as succession. Schopenhauer follows Kant in withdrawing transcendental objectivity from space and time; they are, rather, a priori forms of our *knowing process*. The fourth root of the principle of sufficient reason leads us from the surface world-as-representation into the depths of its foundation, the world-as-will. The "I," or ego, which does the representing, can never itself become an object or representation. But it can become aware of something within itself that wills. "Now the identity of the willing subject and the knowing subject," he writes, "whereby (and indeed necessarily) the word 'I' includes and designates both, is the world-knot and therefore inexpli-

51. *Ibid.*, III, 15–37, 64.

cable." The one leads back into the other. Likewise, it is useless to ask
for proof of the principle of sufficient reason, for whoever does so is
thereby caught in a circle: "He demands a proof of the justification for
demanding a proof." [52]

For Schopenhauer, as for Descartes, there is no such thing as a dis-
embodied thought. Every thought involves a material change in the
brain. But matter is not for Schopenhauer an ultimate category, as it
was for Descartes, or *the* ultimate category, as it is for the naive materi-
alist. Schopenhauer is in no sense a spiritualist. Possibly because there
had been some confusion on that score among those who read the first
volume of *The World*, he was at pains in the second volume to point out
that what he had attempted to demonstrate was "not (as in spiritualism) the independence of the knower from matter, but the dependence
of all matter on the knower"—something "not so easily grasped and so
conveniently handled as spiritualism is, with its two substances." [53]

Schopenhauer has told us that the brain, sitting like a spider in the
center of its ramifying network of nerves and peripheral sensory organs
(a Heraclitean metaphor), does not spin the elaborate structure of the
whole world from a "few miserable sensations" immediately located
under the skin. It is only the world-as-known by each one of us, the
world-as-representation, that is created in this way. Each one of us (and
so also, in accordance with the nature of their perceptual apparatus, all
other sentient beings) maintains a private world-as-representation created anew from microsecond to microsecond, always with its individual peculiarities and special character. That "world" exists only so long
as each one of us is alive and conscious. When we die, it disappears forever and we with it. The "forever," of course, has no meaning for us
after death; in a certain sense, indeed, each one of us has all the time
there is. When we dream, another world of images comes into being,
also constructed by the brain and sometimes so vivid and complete
that we are unsure whether we are in a dreamworld or a real world. Unlike the real world, our dreamworlds really are spun out entirely from
within; they are the work of our inmost core, that which Schopenhauer
calls the "will." It is the parallel of dreamworlds and real worlds that
makes dream theory such an important part of Schopenhauer's philos-

52. *Ibid.*, 38, 171.
53. *Ibid.*, II, 25.

ophy. This is why he constantly refers to the topic of dreams, a topic largely overlooked by other philosophers. To repeat: We begin by taking the world around us to be really "out there" in the commonsense fashion; this is the standpoint of so-called naive realism. It suits us quite well—indeed it is almost indispensable—as a standpoint for fulfilling the needs of everyday life. The human animal, however, eventually begins to investigate the nature of the human body as an instrument for knowing—turning the instrument back on itself and attempting to carry out the impossible task of closing the circle of knowledge. Examination of the structure and function of sensory receptors, nerves, and brain and a more careful analysis of the process of perception soon convince us that naive realism is really a philosophical or metaphysical position—one with obvious deficiencies, which cannot be the whole truth, even though it is not wholly false. But, as critics of Schopenhauer have pointed out, the problem of the nature of the external world becomes even more complicated in the light of our knowledge of neuroanatomy and neurophysiology. It cannot be solved by giving brains a privileged status in the world of otherwise fictitiously real external objects, as Schopenhauer sometimes seems to do. (At this point the reader should be reminded that it is not the purpose of this study to offer a critical analysis of Schopenhauer's philosophy, still less to offer an alternative solution to the problem of our knowledge of the external world, but only to explain Schopenhauer's major ideas, and this only within the context of the themes treated here.)

Granting the truth of Schopenhauer's notion of the world-as-representation, what about the other half, the world-as-will? Schopenhauer, we recall, started from the Kantian standpoint. In Kantian terms the question at issue is: What is the relation of the "phenomenal" world (Schopenhauer's world-as-representation) to the "noumenal" world? Kant's answer is that the noumenal world, although it has to be presupposed as a basis of the phenomenal world, cannot be known as a thing-in-itself, but only as it manifests itself to a knower. And this brings metaphysics to a dead end. Kant's statement is a proclamation of the death of metaphysics, which is why Heine in 1834 called it a proclamation of the death of God, the "January 21st of Deism." But Schopenhauer believed that he had found a path to the thing-in-itself behind the surface world-as-known, behind Kant's phenomenal world. Schopenhauer discovered the world-as-will in the interior Africa of the human heart. He mapped it, described it, and ended by pronouncing it unfit for human habitation.

How was an inner voyage of self-discovery transformed into a metaphysical voyage to the heart of the real world? The answer has already been suggested. We saw that Schopenhauer's fourth root of the principle of sufficient reason takes us to the depths of the world-as-will. At the immediately, indubitably experienced heart or core of the human being, Schopenhauer found "willing," where Descartes had found "thinking." "Willing," Schopenhauer holds, is what is primarily given. No elaborately inferred and mediated world of space, time, and causality is real in comparison with it; *this* is the primary locus of the life of a human being. Having established the locus and nature of concrete indubitable actuality for *human* being, Schopenhauer makes a bold move. He argues that *human* being, as far as *being* is concerned, is no different from the *being* of any other existent in the world, whether animal, plant, or stone. The only privileged status possessed by the human being is a degree of insight into the nature of being. Therefore, says Schopenhauer, what the human being discovers through this insight, namely the inner actuality of "will," is true, if it is true at all, of all other beings in the world. Unless, of course, we believe that human beings have souls (in the spiritualistic sense of the term) different in substance from ordinary matter. And that notion Schopenhauer rejects. To sum up: Objects encountered in the world-as-representation, whether they be human beings, animals, plants, or stones, have a core of real being that is independent of, and other than, the phenomenal being given them by the perceiving subject. That core is given the generic label "will" by Schopenhauer. Schopenhauer's essay *On the Will in Nature* makes it plain that "will" is the equivalent of "drive." Its simplest forms are, according to Schopenhauer, the forces of attraction and repulsion that are the underlying constituents of the physical universe.

Were it not for the very real world-as-will, existing independently of and divorced from the perceiver, the world-as-representation would have no more substance than the world of dreams and waking phantasms. The commonsense world of naive realism is indeed an illusion, a world of Maya, as Schopenhauer sometimes calls it; but it is an illusion that works. Anyone who masters the first half of Schopenhauer's lesson without mastering the second may end up in the position of the man in the Indian fable: "I am God, the creator of my world," he cries, as he sees an elephant bearing down on him in the street; the kindly sage who picks him up after the Juggernaut has trod him down and passed on reminds him that the elephant is "God" too.

Now there is a contradiction, and not merely a verbal one, involved in knowing the unknowable, representing the unrepresentable, or in psychological terms being conscious of the unconscious. Schopenhauer was aware of this. In the second volume of *The World*, he admitted as much. "Strictly speaking," he writes, "we therefore know our own will, too, only as phenomenon, and not according to what it may be in and for itself." Nonetheless, the will remains the only phenomenon whose inner nature is at all accessible to us—the thing-in-itself insofar as it has time, but not space, for its form.[54] Schopenhauer is saying here that, as knowers, we are time-bound. The ultimate thing-in-itself is independent of causal, logical, and mathematical law and wholly divorced from space and time. We, however, can only become aware of its manifestations successively, that is to say, in time. We cannot close the circle of knowledge and see all things at once.

Before taking up Wagner's attempt to explain to Röckel Schopenhauer's philosophy and his own reinterpretation of the *Ring* in the light of that philosophy, a few additional remarks on Schopenhauer's thought in relation to some trends in modern philosophy are worth making. William James's *The Varieties of Religious Experience*, a work that postdates Schopenhauer's earliest writings by nearly a century, has already been mentioned. James, who seems unaware of the relevance of his own ideas to those of Schopenhauer, locates concrete reality exactly where Schopenhauer did. Speaking of "deanthropomorphization of the imagination," James writes:

In spite of the appeal which this impersonality of the scientific attitude makes to a certain magnanimity of temper, I believe it to be shallow, and I can now state my reason in comparatively few words. That reason is that, so long as we deal with the cosmic and the general, we deal only with the symbols of reality, but *as soon as we deal with private and personal phenomena as such, we deal with realities in the completest sense of the term.*

54. *Ibid.*, II, 632.

Any "would-be-existent" that lacked these personal and private features, or something analogous to them, would be a piece of reality only half made up, continues James, for these are what fill up the "measure of our concrete actuality." They may be insignificant, but they are *full* facts of the *kind* to which all realities whatsoever must belong.[55] For support, James cites the physician and philosopher Rudolph Lotze; in the passage cited, however, Lotze was merely paraphrasing Schopenhauer.

In the concluding chapter of the second volume of *The World*, Schopenhauer remarks that he has stood on its head the proposition on which all previous philosophies have been based. He alone, he says, holds that it is more correct to try to understand the world from the standpoint of the human being than the human being from the standpoint of the world. We should try to explain what is indirectly given from what is directly given (self-consciousness) and not the other way around. From the most ancient times the human being has been called a microcosm (*Mikrocosmos*). "I," he writes, "have inverted the proposition, and demonstrated the world as macranthropos (*Makranthropos*)." (In the next chapter we shall find that Schopenhauer's "macranthropos" perhaps bears a Kabbalistic seal.) As Schopenhauer indicates, and as William James reiterates, the main thrust of Western thought has been away from the realm of inner experience in a quest for pure objectivity. The dependence of the objective world on the perceiver is relegated to the background of the world picture. The picture is made to paint itself. "Materialism," Schopenhauer writes, "is the philosophy of the subject who forgets to take account of himself."[56]

That statement is worth comparing with one by a philosopher of the phenomenological school, Maurice Merleau-Ponty: "Objective thought is unaware of the subject of perception." Merleau-Ponty likewise insists that the perceiving subject must be given a central rather than a peripheral—or a nonexistent—place in the structure of the world. He is Schopenhauerian, too, in his claim that the act of perception is not an "event in the world to which the category of causality, for example, can be applied" but rather a "re-creation or re-constitution of the world at every moment." A conceptual field is a "surface in contact with the

55. James, *The Varieties of Religious Experience*, 376–77.
56. Schopenhauer, *Sämtliche Werke*, II, 24–25, 824–25.

world, a permanent rootedness in it." And, says Merleau-Ponty, borrowing a metaphor from Paul Valéry, perception is the "flaw in the great
diamond" of the world. We can never dispose of that flaw; we can never
fill up the gap in the picture of the world—"that gap which we ourselves are, and by which it [the world] comes into existence for someone." Other modern philosophers have taken similar positions. Martin
Heidegger holds that a true account of being can only be derived from a
phenomenological analysis of the concrete immediacy of *human* being,
and in so doing he is a follower of Schopenhauer. Whitehead, not usually
considered a follower of Schopenhauer or a member of the phenomenological school, reveals affinities to both when he tells us that we "finally
construe the world in terms of the types of activities disclosed in our
own experience." G. E. M. Anscombe's comments on Wittgenstein's
Tractatus in relation to Schopenhauer's philosophy have been cited
above. Mario Micheletti has recently dealt at length with the relationship between Schopenhauer and Wittgenstein. He finds that Wittgenstein's path of logical analysis in the *Tractatus* leads to the conclusion
that the limits of language signify the limits of the world and, since
language is always *my* language, the limits of *my* world. This means,
says Micheletti, that "since the propositions of language represent reality, inasmuch as they are one of its images, *the world is my representation.*" This affirmation, he continues, "the same as that with which the
chief work of Schopenhauer opens, is the surprising conclusion of Wittgenstein's logical analysis in the *Tractatus.*" Schopenhauer, William
James, Merleau-Ponty, Heidegger, and Whitehead differ in many ways;
but they share a determination to begin their metaphysical voyages in
discovery of the nature of real being from a starting point of concrete,
immediate, inner human experience. Each in his way, all these philosophers are radical empiricists. Wittgenstein differs in his insistence on
the centrality of language in the world-building process. Schopenhauer
is set apart by the terrifying character of what he finds at the heart of
human being.[57]

According to Wagner himself, Schopenhauer's writings, in particu-

---

57. Maurice Merleau-Ponty, *Phenomenology of Perception,* trans. Colin Smith
(London, 1962), 207; Martin Heidegger, *Sein und Zeit* (Tübingen, 1953), 41–42; Alfred
North Whitehead, *Modes of Thought* (Cambridge, Eng., 1938), 158; Mario Micheletti,
Lo Schopenhauerismo di Wittgenstein (Bologna, 1967), 51.

lar *The World as Will and Representation*, were first brought to his attention in 1854 by Arthur Herwegh. At the time Wagner was living alone in Zurich, his wife Minna being on a visit to Germany. Schopenhauer's public was growing rapidly. One of his Jewish disciples, Julius Frauenstädt, had just published a detailed study of Schopenhauer's philosophy. And thanks to the efforts of another, Ernst Lindner, a German translation of Oxenford's essay in the *Westminster Review* had appeared in a Berlin newspaper, the *Vossische Zeitung*. Lindner was a young German Jew (his English-born wife was the actual translator), who had recently been dismissed on religious grounds from a post in philosophy at the University of Breslau. Subsequently, he had found employment on the editorial staff of the liberal *Vossische Zeitung*. (This newspaper, which had supported the reform movement of 1848, was later to become critical of Bismarck's policies after the foundation of the Second Reich. In 1910 it was taken over by Leopold Ullstein, who was a friend of Rudolf Virchow, another of Bismarck's opponents. When the Nazis came to power, the *Vossische Zeitung*, long stigmatized by the Right as an element of the Jewish press [*Judenpresse*], was at once silenced.) Lindner had become one of Schopenhauer's most active disciples in 1852, and it appears that his attention was drawn to Oxenford's essay by Schopenhauer himself.[58]

Although Wagner's biographers have usually accepted 1854 as the date of his first encounter with Schopenhauer, the fact is that it took place two years earlier in the autumn of 1852, when Herwegh brought the philosopher's writings to the attention of his circle of friends in Zurich. Eliza Wille, a member of the circle, stated later that Wagner had gone into ecstasies at the time. The recollections of Mathilde Wesendonck also confirm this date.[59] Perhaps Wagner's memory played him false later when he dictated his autobiography to his second wife, Cosima (née Liszt); or Wille may have exaggerated the impression made on him by Schopenhauer in 1852. But in any case it is undeniable that

58. Richard Wagner, *Mein Leben* (2 vols.; Munich, 1969), II, 521–22; Julius Frauenstädt, *Briefe über die Schopenhauer'sche Philosophie* (Leipzig, 1854); Wilhelm von Gwinner, *Schopenhauers Leben* (Leipzig, 1910), 348, 352; Werner Becker, "'Demokratie des socialen Rechts': Die politische Haltung der Frankfurter Zeitung, der Vossischen Zeitung und des Berliner Tageblattes" (Doctoral dissertation, Munich, Ludwig Maximilian University, 1965).

59. Edouard Sans, *Richard Wagner et la pensée schopenhauerienne* (Paris, 1969), 17–21.

Wagner was not entirely unaware of Schopenhauer when, in the summer of 1853, he composed the opening bars of *Das Rheingold*—a point, as we shall see, of some interest.

Early in 1855 Wagner sent Röckel (who was, throughout their correspondence, a political prisoner at Waldheim) a copy of Schopenhauer's *World* and informed him that he himself had reached a stage of life where only the philosophy of Schopenhauer could satisfy his needs. "Although he has marked out for me a course rather different from my earlier one," continues Wagner, "nevertheless this turning was the only one corresponding to my deeply felt intuition of the nature of the world." Wagner was at the time in London, reluctantly earning money by conducting a concert series and living meanwhile at 22 Portland Terrace, near the North Gate of Regent's Park. London, incidentally, made a powerful impression on Wagner's mind. In 1877 he would call the monstrous, brooding, smoky town "Alberich's dream . . . Nibelheim, world-dominion, work, activity, everywhere the press of steam and fog."[60]

Röckel, apparently, resisted the new idea of the world that Wagner was attempting to thrust on him. Later in 1855 Wagner wrote a long letter to his friend, less, as he said, for the purpose of converting him from Feuerbachian optimism to Schopenhauerian pessimism than for the purpose of putting the meaning of Schopenhauer's philosophy into his own words. Nevertheless, he calls Röckel an "obstinate optimist"; he himself, with the aid of Schopenhauer, has expelled "that last Jewish superstition . . . that last despotic delusion." The process has been painful, but now that it is complete he feels at last "free." Schopenhauer's philosophy, Wagner explains, is based on Kant's distinction between phenomena as we know them and things-in-themselves, independent of knowers. The full realization of the ideal character of time, space, and causality is "so sublime a process" that it can take place only in a "peculiar state of arousal":

But if this happens then all the delusions that had formerly burdened our judgment disappear as if by a stroke of magic; suddenly language itself fails us for intelligible communication, since our language was formed in the service

---

60. Wagner, *Wagner an Röckel*, 51–52; Newman, *Life*, II, 472; Carl Glasenapp, *Das Leben Richard Wagners* (6 vols.; Leipzig, 1904–12), V, 358. This passage is cited in Herbert Knust's informative study of T. S. Eliot's literary debt to Wagner: *Wagner, the King and "The Waste Land"* (University Park, Pa., 1967).

of a kind of cognition very different from that which we have newly gained. The difficulty now is to communicate in that atrociously limited language of pictures without arousing misunderstandings at every turn.[61]

What Schopenhauer—and others who have followed his path—accomplishes by reasoning Wagner seems to reach by mystical insight. He arrives in a realm that lies beyond the limits of the spoken word—beyond Schopenhauer's world-as-representation or Wittgenstein's world-as-language. But how to communicate one's findings in this world? The activity of "knowing," says Wagner, is ordinarily entirely at the service of our inmost being, that which Schopenhauer designates the "will":

The normal human being has all organs and specifically the brain, the organ of cognition, solely at the service of the will. Dissociation of cognition from the service of the will is, on the other hand, an abnormal act, and occurs only in abnormally organized beings (as a monstrosity, so to speak). In this abnormal state, as we apprehend it at its highest potency in genius, cognition becomes aware, in this possible case, of precisely what the normal state of affairs is, thus recognizing that the organ—freed now in the genius—is everywhere else solely in the service of the will, and now asks what this all-forming and all-dominating will has so far shown itself to be, up to the point where it —in the abnormal state where cognition has been set free—falls silent?[62]

The will is said by Wagner to fall silent. The phrase is apt, for Schopenhauer had seen the will as constantly uttering itself in the form of the world-as-representation. And this world is Wittgenstein's language-world. Now that the will is silenced for the moment, the intellect turns the light of reason on her master. What does she find? Says Wagner:

With shame we see then that it wills nothing more than to continue living, i.e. to feed (by destroying others) and to reproduce itself. As those who are really active, we cannot become aware of anything at all beyond. In the already abnormal state in which we become aware of this, we must now ask ourselves whether it is not a highly questionable matter to serve a will so constituted, and we push further into the disclosure of this phenomenon. Then we find that the same will is present in all perceptible phenomena as one and the same thing, that all individual phenomena are, in consequence, only those of our apperception, in accordance with the basic forms of perceiving; they are precisely the recognizable individualizations of that same will,

61. Wagner, *Wagner an Röckel*, 54–64.
62. *Ibid.*, 56.

of a will, therefore, that perpetually consumes itself in order perpetually to reproduce itself, hence of a being that is in constant conflict, in eternal contradiction with itself, and, as the solely visible outcome of this contradiction, shows us only pain and suffering. In the best case, to what height are we impelled by this will? To just where we now stand, to the possibility (precisely in the abnormal case) of setting free one of its organs, the organ of cognition, and also to the recognition of the nature of the will.[63]

It remains for us to make a moral decision on the basis of our newly found understanding of the human predicament:

What do we feel then—in this highest case—by virtue of our knowledge? Obviously indeed only the weight, the horror, of just that will,—and thereby at last compassion (*Mitleiden*), sympathy—characteristically, we are not familiar with the word "Mitfreude" in this connection. And so knowledge acquires here its moral significance, up to then unrecognized. In the highest and happiest stage we achieve sympathy with all living things, with all things found in the unknowing service to the will; here is the source of all sublime virtue, of all salvation, of perfect union with all things separated by the illusion of individuation.[64]

All religions, according to Wagner, have started from this point; that is, the recognition of the essential unity of a group of apparently diverse beings (even if that of only a very small group of such beings). Once the whole world of beings has been enfolded by the spirit of compassion, once we recognize that the sufferings of all beings are sufferings of our own being, how is our new understanding to manifest itself?

In a concern, perhaps, for making things somewhat more pleasing, for softening the everlasting conflict of the will with itself, its frightful and perpetual devouring and reproduction of itself, through more humane arrangements, etc.? Whoever would believe and hope for this would indeed have achieved nothing at all of just that kind of knowledge in question; his knowledge would in fact still be fully in servitude to the will, which—through the fraud of individuation—still continues to deceive our captured knowledge about its nature. Therefore, to that highest outcome of knowing, to compassion, there remains only one possible salvation: conscious denial of the will, i.e. awareness

63. *Ibid.*, 56–57.
64. *Ibid.*, 57. Wagner's point here is that our compassion is excited only by the *suffering* of another person; hence, we can experience only *Mitleid* and not really *Mitfreude* (or, to coin a word, *compleasure*). On this subject see Schopenhauer, *Sämtliche Werke*, III, 742–43. The noun *Mitfreude* is not included in many German dictionaries, although Grimm's *Wörterbuch* cites instances of its use as far back as the fourteenth century.

of its reprehensible character and refusal to share in it; this is primarily and solely conceivable and feasible for us as the compassionate renunciation of the individual will. But this is in fact precisely a denial of the will in general, its annihilation.[65]

The idea of annihilation, which had preoccupied Wagner's thoughts for so many years and which had first been voiced by his goddess of revolution in 1848, has now received its Schopenhauerian form. As we shall see, this required Wagner to rethink the closing of the *Ring*.

5. WAGNER, ANTI-SEMITISM, AND RACISM

Why did Wagner call his own former, and Röckel's persisting, optimism a Jewish superstition? The answer is that he had learned from Schopenhauer to regard the two Semitic religions, Judaism and Islam, as this-worldly religions, in contrast to the other-worldliness of Buddhism, Brahmanism, and Christianity—not that of the established Church, of course, but undiluted, "true" Christianity. Affirmation of the will to live, he tells Röckel, affirmation at *any* price, is inherent in Judaism; this is the reason why the Jews of Europe are becoming so powerful now that they have been released from their former bondage. The true source of Christianity lies in the sacred books of the East (of which Europe only began to become aware at the end of the eighteenth century). Wagner points out to Röckel:

The latest scientific investigations also have established beyond question that the original idea of Christianity had its home in India. The enormous difficulty, indeed the impossibility of grafting this idea—pure, world-despising and completely turned away from the will to live—onto the barren trunk of Judaism is the sole cause of the contradictions that have so sadly distorted Christianity down to the present day and made it almost unrecognizable. Once again, the real core of Judaism is that heartless and unspiritual optimism for which everything is quite all right if only belly and purse can be kept well filled. . . . How god-like, on the other hand, is the open confession of the nullity of the world in early Christian thought, how glorious are the teachings of the Buddha, which make us one with all living things through compassion![66]

For Wagner, clearly, Judaism is now seen as the incarnation of the worldly spirit of nineteenth-century Europe, which he (along with

65. Wagner, *Wagner an Röckel*, 58.
66. *Ibid.*, 60–61.

Heine, Carlyle, and Marx) so deeply feared and despised. Schopenhauer's ideas had confirmed Wagner's own experience with Judaism; that is, with the tiny group of Jews whom he—together with Goethe, Heine, Disraeli, and others—regarded as the hidden manipulators of the press, art, and finance of Europe.

After what we have seen happen to the Jews of Europe at the hands of the Nazis—and before that to blacks and "colored" races generally in the hands of Europeans and Americans—most of us have become so hypersensitive to issues involving race and religion that we are unable to distinguish positions taken against principles from those taken against persons—but not under all circumstances. We feel free to reject, for example, the "police mentality" or the "military mentality"— to look forward to a society free of both—without considering ourselves committed to the physical extermination of policemen and soldiers or to the position that the "mentality" in question is found in *all* policemen and soldiers and *only* in them. The same appears to have applied to anti-Semitism, in one of its aspects, in Europe. So it was that Schopenhauer and Wagner could speak as they did and yet have Jewish friends and disciples. The young Schopenhauer, for example, supplied "his Israelitic friend"—as Johanna, Schopenhauer's mother, called Joseph Gans, a companion of Schopenhauer's youth—with books, clothes, and even a room in his mother's house. Schopenhauer's Jewish disciples, Frauenstädt and Lindner, have already been mentioned. In fact, aside from Karl Bähr, the only "active disciples"—as Schopenhauer called those who accepted and promulgated his philosophy—mentioned in Schopenhauer's will were three Jews, Frauenstädt, Lindner, and David Asher. In 1857 Asher, who carried on an extensive correspondence with Schopenhauer, called his attention to the eleventh-century Jewish philosopher and Kabbalist Avicebron (ibn Gabirol), whose *Fons vitae* (*Source of Life*) had just been edited in Paris. Asher suggested that Avicebron had anticipated Schopenhauer's doctrine of the primacy of the will over the intellect (in the unregenerated human being). Schopenhauer appears to have found a measure of truth in Asher's remark. "Had Schopenhauer followed this trail further," commented Gwinner in this connection, "he might perhaps have corrected his prejudices against the philosophy and theology of ancient Judaism." Asher, incidentally, wrote a study of Schopenhauer's philosophy in relation to

Goethe's *Faust*. He closed it with a pertinent anecdote from the Talmud: a rabbinical dispute as to whether it was better not to be born into a world such as this was concluded in the affirmative, with the proviso that, since we have no choice in the matter, it behooves us to make the best of a bad lot—a thoroughly Schopenhauerian assessment of the human situation.[67]

The matter is far from simple. Hermann Levi, the son of a rabbi and the conductor of the first performance of *Parsifal*, wrote to his father in 1882 that Wagner would one day be recognized as a great man as well as a great artist. "The fight that he leads against what he calls Judaism in modern music and literature," Levi informed his father, "proceeds from elevated motives, and his attitude toward me, toward Joseph Rubinstein [a pianist who was part of Wagner's household at Triebschen and Bayreuth] and, in the past, [Carl] Tausig, shows that he has nothing of the small-spiritedness of a country squire or of a sanctimonious Protestant."[68] Since the subject is one more likely to attract the efforts of propagandists than scholars, the history of the background and development of the anti-Judaistic idea in its theological, philosophical, cultural, social, and political dimensions during the nineteenth century remains to be written. The meaning of the rejection of the Jewish idea will in each instance require separate analysis. The anti-Semitism of Karl Marx, for example, plainly rests on his erroneous identification of the Jewish idea with the spirit of modern European capitalism. When Marx says that "Christendom" has become completely "Judaized"—a statement that could equally well have come from Wagner—he means that money-power, and all that it signifies in the realm of human relationships, rules Europe, *not* that "ethnic" Jews are in control, the power of Rothschild and other Jewish bankers notwithstanding. The same would apply, more or less, to Heinrich Heine. It is worth noting that neither Marx nor Heine thought it necessary to emphasize that they were speaking of ideas rather than individuals. At the time, physical persecution of the Jews seemed entirely out of place in the enlightened present. No doubt an emancipated Central European Jew could then accept a verbal attack on Judaism with much the same equanimity that a

---

67. Gwinner, *Schopenhauers Leben*, 93–94, 370, 398–99; David Asher, *Arthur Schopenhauer als Interpret des Goethe'schen Faust* (Leipzig, 1859).
68. Sans, *Richard Wagner et la pensée Schopenhauerienne*, 248.

physician now might show in the face of an attack on the medical pro-
fession. The physician, or Jew, might even agree that some of the charges
were justified.

A book that sheds some light on the character of Wagner's anti-
Semitism and that is, in any case, one of the most revealing documents
of its time is Otto Weininger's *Geschlecht und Charakter* (*Sex and
Character*). This double-pronged attack on "Woman" and "Jew" was
first published in 1903, only a few months before the suicide of its ex-
traordinarily talented twenty-three-year-old author, a Viennese Jew who
had become a Protestant convert a year earlier. The book is of particular interest for what it has to say about Wagner—whom Weininger
calls "the most profound of anti-Semites"—and about that frequently
overlooked aspect of anti-Semitism to which the attention of the reader
is invited.[69]

Unlike Marx sixty years earlier, Weininger—whose book was written in the midst of the Dreyfus scandal in France and not long after the
pogroms in Russia following the assassination of Alexander II in 1881
—felt it necessary to define the character of his own anti-Judaism with
great care. Judaism (*das Judenthum*), he writes, has "for me, nothing to
do with a race, a people, or a legally recognized creed. Judaism must be
understood as a spiritual orientation, a psychological constitution existing as a possibility for all human beings, which has, in historical
Judaism, simply found its most grandiose actualization." And, he adds:

Although it should be self-evident, I emphasize once again that, in spite of
my derogatory estimate of the true Jew, nothing is further from my mind
than to lend a helping hand to the theoretical, still less to the practical, persecution of the Jews with these or the following remarks. I speak of Judaism as
a Platonic idea—an absolute Jew no more exists than does an absolute Christian—I speak not of individual Jews, to so many of whom I would have done
harm most unwillingly, to whom a great and bitter injustice would occur, if
what I have said were to be turned against them.[70]

We can no more blame Weininger—or Wagner—for failing to foresee
the Nazi Third Reich than Fedor Dostoevsky (the vociferously anti-

69. Otto Weininger, *Geschlecht und Charakter* (21st ed.; Vienna, 1926), 404. The
authorized English translation, *Sex and Character* (London, 1906), is incomplete and at
times inaccurate.
70. Weininger, *Geschlecht und Charakter*, 414. Compare this with Chap. I, note
47 and text.

Jewish Dostoevsky of *The Diary of a Writer*) for failing to foresee the pogroms in Russia.

Judaism, then, is for Weininger a state of the soul, a psychological or spiritual rather than an ethnic or racial category. Hence, there exist "Aryans who are more Jewish than many Jews, and actual Jews who are more Aryan than certain Aryans." The amount of Jewishness is directly proportional to the degree to which the individual human being concerned *"participates in the Platonic idea of Judaism."* What is the essence of Weininger's Platonic idea of Judaism? Weininger, like Wagner, sees Judaism as a celebration of the crudest kind of materialism. The Platonic idea of Judaism is distinguished, according to Weininger, by its ethical inferiority. In the Old Testament we are told how "Jakob the patriarch lies to his dying father Isaac, takes in Esau his brother, and cheats his father-in-law Laban." For anyone who participates fully in the Jewish idea, blind submission to the patriarchal power-God of the Old Testament is the sole requirement. The Semitic ethic, based on total submission, is entirely devoid of autonomous character. It is law imposed from without: "From his servile nature springs his heteronomous ethic, the Decalogue, the world's most immoral book of laws, which offers the prospect of happiness on *earth*, and the promise of the conquest of the world." Such, Weininger tells us, is the idol worshipped by Carlylean heroes, by the "men of action" of this world. The greatest of them—Alexander, Caesar, Cromwell, and Napoleon (all "Platonic" Jews)—are ready to lie, cheat, steal, and murder in order to gain their ends.[71]

Our time, says Weininger—the time of capitalism and Marxism, the time in which history has been reduced to economics and science reduced to technology, the time in which sexuality is affirmed as coitus —is "not only the most Jewish but the most womanish of all times."

71. *Ibid.*, 293, 404–405, 409–10, 416. The Viennese writer Karl Kraus, during the Great War, argued that the "new German and the ancient Hebraic drive for conquest" were of similar character. Asked by "the optimist" whether anyone else had ever thought of comparing Paul von Hindenburg to Joshua, Kraus, "the carping critic" (*der Nörgler*), replies: "Schopenhauer, who equated the institution of a separate god who gives away or 'promises' neighboring lands, into the possession of which one then has to come through robbery and murder, with that of a national god to whom the earthly possessions of other peoples must be sacrificed." Karl Kraus, *Die letzten Tage der Menschheit*, in *Werke*, ed. H. Fischer (14 vols.; Munich, 1952–67), IV, 353–54.

Weininger's recipe for moral regeneration has a flavor of Schopenhauer, Wagner, and Marx (plus something of the Tolstoy of the *Kreutzer Sonata*). Jews, ethnic Jews in particular, must learn to understand themselves in order to overcome themselves, in order to "conquer their inner Judaism." Only then, he adds, will they be ripe for Zionism.[72] Weininger, like Marx and Wagner, equates Jewish emancipation with emancipation *from* Judaism. And as does Wagner in *Parsifal*—"the most profound poem in the world's literature"—he finds that the "emancipation of woman from woman" is called for as well. Kundry and Ahasuerus alike must disavow their old selves. Weininger adds: "Christ spoke in this sense (without the later palliation for the sex found by Paul and Luther), according to the Church Father Clement: Death will prevail as long as women bear, and the truth will not be seen until out of the two one, out of man and woman a third self, neither man nor woman, comes into being."[73]

Weininger's admiration for Wagner approached idolatry. As he saw it, Wagner, like Christ (although with a lesser measure of success), had been obliged to struggle with the "Jewishness" within him. Christ's forty days in the wilderness ended in complete triumph over the spirit of this world. But as for Wagner, it could not be denied that both his work and personality retained strongly "Jewish" characteristics:

No one is an anti-Semite for nothing. Just as Wagner's aversion for grand opera and the theater derives from the strong attraction that he himself felt toward them, an attraction still distinctly recognizable in *Lohengrin*, so also his music, in its individual motif-thoughts the world's most powerful, cannot be absolved from something of the obtrusive, loud and unrefined. Wagner's pains with the external instrumentation of his work stand in this connection. Further, we cannot fail to recognize that Wagner's music makes its strongest impression on Jewish anti-Semites, who have not entirely freed themselves from Judaism, and Indo-Germanic anti-Semites, who are afraid of succumbing to Judaism.

Weininger, who was familiar with the work of Sigmund Freud, Josef Breuer, and Pierre Janet, understood hate and love as projection phe-

72. It is not clear whether he meant Theodor Herzl's political Zionism. Given his other views, this is perhaps unlikely.
73. Weininger, *Geschlecht und Charakter*, 414, 440–41, 455–56, 457. As with the proletariat and the Jews, so with women: the full emancipation of women involves the self-abolition of "woman." See Chap. I, note 33.

nomena. Hence, his remark that "true" Jews and "true" Aryans are alike incapable of anti-Semitism.[74]

In 1930 the German-Jewish philosopher Theodor Lessing formulated (three years before he was assassinated in Marienbad by the Nazis) the concept of "Jewish self-hatred" (*jüdischer Selbsthass*). This concept has since been applied in retrospect to explain the behavior and writings of Wagner's Jewish associates—Herman Levi and Joseph Rubinstein, for example—and of Otto Weininger, Karl Kraus, and other so-called "anti-Semitic Semites." Whatever the general worth of the concept, it is most often used to close off discussion by shifting attention from the meaning and validity of a writer's statements to his or her presumed psychological grounds for making them. The disclosure of their ideological basis is supposed to make further discussion unnecessary. But this is to fall victim to the genetic fallacy. Weininger's suicide (like that of Joseph Rubinstein) has been ascribed, retrospectively, to Jewish self-hatred by both Jews and (Nazi) Germans. One can only say that, in the case of Weininger at least, the idea did not occur to Weininger's father or to his biographer. But to what extent can Weininger's predominantly nonracial, "Platonic" anti-Semitism be equated with Wagner's anti-Semitism? A full discussion of this subject would take us too far afield. On the basis of the scanty evidence available, Weininger appears to have placed both under the same rubric. Weininger's biographer, Emil Lucka, it is true, contrasts the "racial anti-Semitism" of Houston Stewart Chamberlain, whom he calls its "most distinguished proponent," with the "spiritual anti-Judaism" (*geistigen anti-Judaismus*) of Weininger; but he states that the two forms have much in common. We are probably safe in equating Chamberlain's views on the subject with those of Wagner, his father-in-law. The ethnic idea is definitely a component of Wagner's anti-Semitism. But so it is also for Weininger, insofar as he holds that the ethnic Jew, by and large, participates most fully in the Platonic idea of Judaism. To a full "racial" anti-Semite, a Jew can no more be converted to Christianity than a black skin to white. We find Wagner, however, fruitlessly attempting to persuade

---

74. *Ibid.*, 317, 402–404. Additional comments on Wagner's music-dramas may be found in the posthumously published work, Otto Weininger, *Dr. Otto Weininger über die letzten Dinge* (6th ed.; Vienna & Leipzig, 1920).

Hermann Levi to undergo baptism. (Later, in the case of Gustav Mahler, Cosima Wagner was more successful.)[75]

Since World War II, Wagner's anti-Semitism has been depicted in a much harsher light, especially in the United States. Citation is hardly necessary, for Wagner, in the popular mind at least, seems almost to have become identified with Nazism. And not only in the popular mind. In 1950 Leon Stein accused Wagner of "virulent anti-Semitism," "distorted anti-Christian thinking," and in general, the "grossest social immorality." Stein claimed that Wagner's innate anti-Semitism had been strengthened by his study of Schopenhauer, for Schopenhauer too was guilty of "virulent anti-Semitism," based on his claim that Judaism accords no rights to animals.[76]

This last claim is an interesting one, worth further comment. It is true that Schopenhauer, a friend of animals and an opponent of vivisection, held that compassion for animals—we might even say a decent regard for "animal rights"—was implicit in Buddhism, Christianity, and Hinduism but absent from the religion of the Jews. Spinoza, for example, was a very great man, but in one respect he could not free himself from Judaism: he regarded animals with contempt as "mere things for our use, and devoid of rights."[77] Although Wagner's sentiments regarding the mistreatment of animals antedate his acquaintance with Schopenhauer's writings, he did no doubt acquire an ethical basis for these sentiments from the philosopher, who remains to this day the only philosopher to ground ethics on compassion. This appears in an open letter to Ernst von Weber in 1879, in support of Weber's newly founded antivivisection society. Wagner states here that his objections to the mistreatment of animals are not based on the premise that ani-

75. *Encyclopaedia Judaica* (16 vols.; Jerusalem, 1971–72), XI, 50. Emil Lucka, *Otto Weininger: Sein Werk und seine Persönlichkeit* (Vienna & Leipzig, 1905), 62–63. The book includes an appendix contributed by Weininger's father. No support for the idea can be found in Dr. Moriz Rappaport's biographical foreword in Weininger, *Dr. Otto Weininger*, v–xxiv. Newman, *Life*, IV, 635.

76. Leon Stein, *The Racial Thinking of Richard Wagner* (New York, 1950), 34, 229.

77. Schopenhauer, *Sämtliche Werke*, II, 828. Schopenhauer cites Spinoza's *Ethics*, IV, Chap. 27, Appendix. I can find nothing there to the point. But in IV, xxxvii, Scholium I, Spinoza does sharply limit the rights of animals; it is our privilege, he says, to make free use of animals and to treat them as is most convenient for our purposes. See Baruch Spinoza, *Benedicti de Spinoza opera quotquot reperta sunt*, ed. J. van Vloten and J. P. N. Land (4 vols.; The Hague, 1914), IV, 209.

mal experimentation is useless or that the mistreatment of domestic animals is uneconomic. They are not based on any utilitarian principle whatsoever, but instead on the Schopenhauerian claim that the "sole, true foundation of all morality" is compassion (*Mitleid*), extending to animals as well as human beings. The "curse of our civilization" is that we have forgotten this. In ancient times animals had been looked on as sacred. But man has become transformed into a "rending predatory animal." And today "the Old Testament has triumphed; the rending predatory animal has become a 'reckoning' predatory animal (*aus dem reissenden ist das 'rechnende' Raubthier geworden*)."[78] This is, admittedly, anti-Judaism of a (Weiningerian) sort. Stein's comment is that Wagner's compassion was "limited only to man's relationship to animals—certainly it would not apply to Catholics, Jews and other composers."[79]

In 1880 Wagner refused to sign an anti-Semitic petition to the German parliament (drawn up by Bernhard Förster, who was later to marry Nietzsche's sister). Stein attributed Wagner's unwillingness to commit his prestige on this occasion to the failure of Weber's campaign against vivisection. Drawing the contrast between "good" Germans and "bad" Germans that was fashionable in the 1930s, Stein opposed the "cosmopolitan humanitarianism" of Schiller, Goethe, and Lessing to the "autocratic chauvinism" of Hegel, Fichte, Wagner, Bismarck, Chamberlain, Wilhelm II, Ludendorff, and Hitler. Again, this is an oversimplification. It was Goethe who vehemently opposed the new laws permitting Christians to marry Jews. The "virulently anti-Semitic" Schopenhauer, on the other hand, favored such marriages, arguing (as Frauenstädt tells

---

78. Wagner, *Gesammelte Schriften*, X, 194–97, 202. Wagner adds here that our understanding of the unity of all animal life has come to us too late to ward off the curse mankind has called down on itself by resorting to eating flesh. He suggests that the migration of an originally peaceful, frugivorous and herbivorous species into the harsh climate of the north had resulted in its transformation into a predatory race of meat-eaters. Wagner was unaware that the most far-reaching tradition of a primal state of vegetarianism is to be found in the Old Testament, as interpreted by rabbinical commentators. According to one (the eleventh-century rabbi Solomon ben Isaac [Rashi]), the true significance of Genesis 1:29 ("every herb bearing seed . . . [and] the fruit of a tree yielding seed; to you it shall be for meat") is that not only Adam and Eve but *all* animals were vegetarian before the Fall. Adopted by John Milton (probably from Rashi), this view is set forth in *Paradise Lost*, Book X. See Harris F. Fletcher, *Milton's Rabbinical Readings* (Urbana, Ill., 1930), 179–81. For a post–World War II, Jungian interpretation, see Robert Eisler, *Man into Wolf* (London, n.d.).

79. Stein, *The Racial Thinking of Richard Wagner*, 34.

us) that any character defects such as might be found in European Jews were not racial but the result of the "long and unjust pressure under which they had labored."[80] To Wagner and Schopenhauer, the Caesars and Napoleons of this world were criminal monsters; Goethe, on the other hand, was an admirer of Napoleon. And it was Chamberlain who first branded as absurd the belief in the surpassing virtues of "pure" races.

A great distance lies between Disraeli's claim that "all is race" and his dream of a world ruled by the two great races—or by the progeny of the Nordic Tancred and the Jewish Eva—and Stein's claim, one hundred years later, that there *is* no such thing as race—Jewish, English, French, German, or whatever. Perhaps this is a measure of what we have learned in the interim. But the lesson was hard to learn. Until the Nazi takeover, the idea of racial purity had at least as many Jewish as "Aryan" proponents. Writing in 1916, Rabbi Max Eichler argued that the Jews had survived as a people only because they had remained obedient to laws that had "rendered the Jewish race immune from disease and destruction" by forbidding "any practice that might vitiate the purity of the race." Abraham had refused Eleazar's offer of his daughter to Isaac with the words: "Thou art cursed, and my son is blessed, and it does not behoove the cursed to mate with the blessed, and thus deteriorate the quality of the race." The rabbinical fathers, says Eichler, had "discouraged any kind of intermarriage, even with proselytes" in their zeal to preserve a Jewish race "pure and undefiled, devoid of any admixture of inferior protoplasm." When King David was asked to pass judgment on the desirability of marriages between the children of Israel and the Gibeonites, he spoke against it on the ground that the Gibeonites were lacking in "sympathy, modesty and philanthropy." Further, says Eichler, the rabbis of old had favored breeding out of the Jewish race a number of undesirable psychological characteristics. Eichler's comments reveal the deeply rooted nature of the belief that heredity is all—which is simply a rephrasal of Disraeli's "race is all." With it goes an

---

80. *Ibid.*, 34. See Chap. IV, note 50 for Wagner's rejection of anti-Semites in Berlin. Julius Frauenstädt, *Schopenhauer-Lexikon* (2 vols. in 1; Leipzig, 1871), I, 381. For Wagner's views on a wide variety of subjects, assembled from his writings, see Richard Wagner,*Wagner-Encyclopädie*, ed. Carl Fr. Glasenapp (Leipzig, 1891); and Richard Wagner, *Wagner-Lexikon*, comp. Carl Fr. Glasenapp and Heinrich von Stein (Stuttgart, 1883).

unwillingness to admit the flexibility of human behavior in response to social conditioning. The chances that the offspring of an Israelite-Gibeonite union would exhibit inherited "Gibeonite" behavior are remote. But the chances that such behavior would be thrust upon the child and then assigned to a "Gibeonite" heritage are not.[81]

Eugenic ideas of this kind drew new strength in the nineteenth century from Darwinism and its bastard offshoot, social Darwinism. A pseudoscience of human eugenics came into being. Nowhere was it more cultivated than in the United States. The movement reached its height just before World War I, and it is no accident that Western imperialism and Western racism peaked at about the same time. In 1913 a German writer could actually point to the United States as the teacher of Europe on the subject. Sir Francis Galton's dream that "race-hygiene would become the religion of the future proceeds towards its realization in America," wrote its author approvingly, "where the average Yankee not infrequently sees in everyone who does not belong to the northern European race an inferior being. . . . A drop of negro blood brands the bearer a black before the law and his fellows." Thirty-two of the North American states punished sexual intercourse (marital or extramarital) between blacks and whites, or between whites and Chinese, as a criminal offense. In the Kansas Territory a law of 1855 called for the castration of blacks who attempted to entice white women into marriage.[82]

Eugenic sterilization, for which the Nazis were arraigned at Nuremberg, was first practiced on a large scale in the United States. Sixteen of the states had enacted laws for sterilizing the hereditarily unfit by 1917; by 1931 such laws were on the books of thirty-one states. By 1935 nearly 10,000 sterilization procedures are said to have been performed in California alone. The proponents of race-hygiene helped bring about the passage of the Immigration Restriction Act of 1924, for they saw the rising tide of emigrants from southern and eastern Europe as a threat to Nordic supremacy. Orientals had already been excluded by earlier restrictive measures. Lest it be supposed that the eugenics movement

81. Stein, *The Racial Thinking of Richard Wagner*, 10; Max Eichler, "Jewish Eugenics" (New York, 1916), 1–2, 9, 12, 59.

82. Kenneth Ludmerer, *Genetics and American Society: A Historical Appraisal* (Baltimore, 1972); Géza von Hoffmann, *Die Rassenhygiene in den Vereinigten Staaten von Nordamerika* (Munich, 1913), 17, 67–68. A bibliography of some nine hundred books and articles on race-hygiene, chiefly written in the United States, is included.

was supported only by a fringe group of fanatics and unqualified biologists, consider the following statement by Henry Fairfield Osborn, an acknowledged leader in the fields of paleontology and anthropology two generations ago. "The greatest danger which threatens the American republic today," he wrote in 1916, "is the gradual dying out of those hereditary traits through which the principles of our religious, political and social foundations were laid down, and their insidious replacement by traits of less noble character."[83]

6. THE CLOSING OF THE "RING"

We recall that at the close of Wagner's sketch of 1848 for his Nibelung drama the gods, including Wotan, are triumphant—redeemed by Siegfried's death and Brünnhilde's return of the ring to the Rhine—and the Nibelungs, including Alberich, are released from their servitude to the ring. To make the happy ending complete, Brünnhilde and Siegfried are reunited in Valhalla. Only Hagen is not saved; he makes a futile last attempt to seize the ring and is drawn into the depths of the Rhine by the three water-women (the Rhine maidens of the music-drama). The preliminary drama *Siegfried's Death*, written shortly thereafter, differs from the sketch in that Alberich, too, goes under with Hagen. And Brünnhilde's horse, Grane, shares in the general salvation. Before plunging into Siegfried's funeral pyre on Grane's back, Brünnhilde cries out: *"Freue dich, Grane: bald sind wir frei!"* (Rejoice, O Grane: soon we shall be free!). It is quite possible that the notion of "animal salvation" was not explicitly present in Wagner's mind at this time. Later, after he had read in Schopenhauer's *World* the following lines by Angelus Silesius, this is less likely to have been the case: *"Mensch! Alles liebet dich; um dich ist sehr Gedrange/Es lauffet all's zu dir, dass es zu Gott gelange"* (O human being! Everything loves and crowds about you, so that it may reach God). Still more pertinent is the remark Schopenhauer makes after citing the above lines. In Buddhism too, he says, we meet with a similar idea. When Buddha—while still Bodhisattva and not yet having attained perfect knowledge—saddles his horse for the last time,

---

83. Ludmerer, *Genetics and American Society*, 87, 95–96; *Collected Papers on Eugenic Sterilization in California: A Critical Study of the Results in 6000 Cases* (Pasadena, Calif., 1930); Madison Grant, *The Passing of the Great Race; or, The Racial Basis of European History* (4th ed.; New York, 1922), ix.

he addresses it as follows: "O Kantanka, bear me away from here only this time again, and when I have attained the law (have become Buddha), I shall not forget you."[84]

The failure of Hagen and Alberich to achieve salvation by rejecting the Nibelung's ring and their subsequent plunge into the depths can be read as Wagner's warning of the fate in store for humanity as a whole if this is not done. Wotan and Alberich are doubles, counterparts, as Wagner tells us when he calls the one a light-elf (*Lichtalbe*) and the other a dark-elf (*Schwarzalbe*) in *Das Rheingold*. Siegfried and Hagen, their heroic half-human issue, are likewise doubles. A significant parallelism is evident between the close of *Siegfried's Death* and the close of Wagner's essay *Judaism in Music*, which was written two years later. In the essay Wagner remarks that a "very gifted Jewish writer," Heinrich Heine, has been engaged in exposing the insipidity and hypocrisy of the art and music of the time, including the work of his fellow Jews. Heine is "the conscience of Judaism, just as Judaism is the bad conscience of our modern civilization." But Heine's utter cynicism bars him from salvation. Another Jew, the writer Ludwig Börne (Loeb Baruch, a member of the Young Germany group), has succeeded where Heine has failed. But the task is not an easy one: "To become a human being together with us means, however, first and foremost so much as—to cease being a Jew. Börne achieved this. But precisely Börne teaches us, too, that this salvation (*Erlösung*) cannot be arrived at in comfort and cold, indifferent ease, but rather that it costs, as it does for us, sweat, distress, anxieties and a fill of suffering and pain." Then, addressing the Jews, Wagner concludes *Judaism in Music* with the following words: "Share ruthlessly in this work of salvation, regenerating through self-destruction, and we are one and without difference! But remember that your salvation from the curse resting on you can be one thing only: the salvation of Ahasuerus—the end!" (*der Untergang*: literally, a "going-under").[85] Whether Wagner himself was consciously aware of the paral-

---

84. Wagner, *Gesammelte Schriften*, II, 227; Schopenhauer, *Sämtliche Werke*, I, 518.

85. Richard Wagner, *Gesammelte Schriften*, ed. Julius Kapp (14 vols. in 5; Leipzig, 1914), XIII, 29. As an appendix to *On Judaism in Music*, this edition includes a letter to Frau Marie Muchanoff (Countess Nesselrode) dated 1869. In it Wagner accounts for the widespread hostility of the press to him in Germany, England, and France as the result of an implacable hatred aroused among Jews by his essay. Wagner says that he is under

lel is a question that cannot be answered. It is pertinent to mention here that another Ahasuerus avatar, Wagner's Flying Dutchman, achieves salvation at the same time he is swallowed up by the waves.

Wagner's final solution, if we are to call it such, of the Jewish problem requires careful attention if it is to be understood. Like Schopenhauer, he opts for assimilation; like Marx, he says that the Jew must cease to be a Jew; like Weininger, he says that everyone, Jew or Gentile, must cease to be a (Platonic) Jew. And in *Judaism in Music* Wagner does not say to the Jews: Become one of us *or* you will be destroyed. He says: Become one of us *and* you will no longer be a Jew, for in your case as in ours salvation demands self-destruction. Whether we are Jews or Gentiles, we may feel inclined to doubt Wagner's assumption that Nordic light-elves are closer to salvation than Jewish dark-elves. But before engaging in polemics, we should know what we are talking about. It is nonsense to claim that Wagner's words in *Judaism in Music* "pointed irrevocably in one direction: to Hitler, the laws of Nuremberg . . . the ovens of Auschwitz" or that the word *Untergang* implies the physical "annihilation" or "total destruction" of the Jews.[86]

Several years lay between the writing of *Siegfried's Death* and the completion of the four dramas constituting *The Ring of the Nibelung* that Wagner sent to his friends in 1853. We have already seen how he attempted to explain the meaning of the completed *Ring* cycle to Röckel in 1854. The *Ring* closes with Valhalla in flames, with the downfall of the gods and heroes alike. The motive of the redemption of the Nibelungs has disappeared altogether. Newman's opinion is that sometime in 1851 Wagner decided to combine the Siegfried myth with the myth of the twilight of the gods, that is, of the *Götterdämmerung* or Rag-

---

some constraint in discussing the matter "because of a careful regard for the devoted and truly sympathetic friends whom fate brought to me from the same national-religious element." But he is encouraged to speak because these Jewish friends "stand . . . on exactly the same ground" with him and, moreover, suffer more than he does "under the completely paralyzing pressure of the dominant Jewish group." See XIII, 29–52, especially p. 30.

86. Stein, *The Racial Thinking of Richard Wagner*, 86, 176. Adorno, who makes a similar claim, attempts (to my mind, quite unsuccessfully) to dissociate what he calls Marx's views on the "emancipation" of the Jews from Wagner's on the "extermination" (*Vernichtung*) of the Jews. See Theodor Adorno, *Versuch über Wagner* (Berlin, 1952), 28. The anathema pronounced on Wagner's anti-Semitism by Adorno in this essay must be understood in the context of the time and persons involved.

narök.[87] This may well be the case, but it should be obvious by now that the idea of self-destruction had long been one of Wagner's preoccupations. The circle of destruction is widening, however; and the light-elves as well as the dark-elves now fall within its scope. We recall Wagner's remark to Liszt (in 1853) that the *Ring* poem contained "the beginning and the end (*der Untergang*) of the world." At that time Wagner seems to have meant by "world" simply the world of nineteenth-century European capitalism and power politics. The influence of Feuerbachian ideas on Wagner is evident when he has Alberich forswear love in order to win the gold of the Rhine. It is also evident in some words uttered by Brünnhilde just before her immolation—words that Wagner later struck out:

> Not goods, not gold—nor god-like pomp;
> Not house, not court—nor lordly show;
> Not the deceiving bond of clouded compacts,
> Nor the hard law of hypocritical custom:
> Love alone leaves us happy in both joy and sorrow!

That these words had been greatly relished by Princess Caroline von Wittgenstein was the only comment on the content of the *Ring* poem received by Wagner from Liszt.[88] Wagner's reason for striking them from the final version was that they were tendentious; that is, too explicitly stated for inclusion in a necessarily ambiguous work of art. Further, his understanding of love had been faulty prior to making contact with Schopenhauer's philosophy.

Brünnhilde's words are little more than a standard nineteenth-century protest, voiced then as now by social revolutionaries of an anarchist bent, against a life based on material possessions and entrammeled by the network of compromise, tacit agreement, and social hypocrisy that makes escape from such a life so difficult. Combined with the protest that things are in the saddle and rule mankind is the familiar claim that love is all we need. Wagner's artistic instincts were sound in rejecting this all too explicit message, the more so because Brünnhilde's sentiments regarding love are at variance with the course of the dramatic action in the *Ring*. There, as in the medieval *Nibelungenlied*,

87. Newman, *Life*, II, 356; see II, 325–62, "Difficulties in the Rounding of the 'Ring,'" for a complete discussion.
88. *Ibid.*, 366.

in the story of Tristan and Iseult, and in the Arthurian cycle, uncontrolled love leads to disaster. No matter how sublimated and transformed, the fruits of erōs are apt to be poisonous in the extreme. Further, it may reasonably be argued that the desire for material possessions is simply another manifestation of love as erōs. Wagner told Röckel in 1854 that love in the Feuerbachian sense would enable humanity to unite male and female principles and to understand the secret of birth, life, and death. He stated that love in its fullest actuality was possible only between the sexes. The union of heart and mind, of prakriti and purusha, of the hitherto separated female and male principles would yield the complete human being of the future. But these Feuerbachian ideas were not only in contradiction with the new understanding of love in its highest form as sympathy, compassion, Mitleiden and agapē —love free of desire, purged of erōs—that he had found in Schopenhauer, but also with his own earlier analysis of the Oedipus myth. For there he had said that Antigone's love was neither sexual, parental, nor filial, but "purely human" and that the realization of this form of love involved "self-destruction through sympathy."

All this comes out in Wagner's letter of August 23, 1856, to Röckel. He would, he tells Röckel, no longer dispute with him about the proper closing for the Ring or attempt further explanations of its inconsistencies. In the end what counts is intuitive rather than conceptual understanding. A work of art produced by an artist can be understood by another person intuitively, if at all, just as the innermost aspect of human nature itself is in the end accessible only to the intuitive understanding. And even the artist-creator often fails to reach a proper understanding or does so only after a long time and with great difficulty. Continues Wagner:

I am able to speak about this because it is precisely here that I have made the most surprising discoveries. Seldom indeed has a human being gone so marvelously astray in his intuitions and concepts, and been so estranged from himself, as I, who must confess that only now, with the help of another— who supplied my intuitions with completely compatible concepts—have I really understood, that is, grasped conceptually and made plain to my reason, my own works of art.[89]

89. Wagner, Wagner an Röckel, 65–72.

Wagner had in mind here not only the *Ring* but his earlier works as well. The point at which he had begun to create from his inner intuition (*inneren Anschauung*) was marked, he tells Röckel, by *The Flying Dutchman* (1840–1841), after which came *Tannhäuser* (1841–1845) and *Lohengrin* (1841–1847). If there was a common feature of these three operas, it was the "high tragedy of renunciation" and the necessary (and solely redeeming) denial of the will. These features alone consecrated his music and poetry. Although as an artist he had been working in the full security of an intuitive understanding of his creative impulses, as a philosopher he had been attempting to reach an entirely opposed explanation of his work. And so, to his own amazement and despite his efforts, those explanations had been again and again overturned by his "involuntary, purely objective, artistic intuition" (*unwillkürlichen, rein objectiven, künstlerlichen Anschauung*). He continues:

> The most extraordinary thing in this connection I had to undergo at last with my Nibelung poem: I gave it shape at a time when I had, with my concepts alone, built up a Hellenistic-optimistic world the realization of which I held to be quite possible as soon as and if only human beings desired it. Doing so I rather ingeniously sought to help myself over the problem of why they did not in fact really want it.

Wagner then passes over the complicated explanation of the *Ring* on Feuerbachian principles that he had given Röckel in 1854 to say that his first intent in dramatizing the Nibelung myth had been to point out the original injustice—that is to say, the loveless egoism and the desire for power and gold—on which "a whole world of injustice" had been so insecurely founded from the first that it must inevitably crash into ruins. The drama aimed "to teach us how to recognize the injustice, root it out, and found a just world in its place."[90]

It had escaped his attention entirely that, while engaged in carrying out his plan along these lines at the conceptual level, he had "unconsciously followed a quite different and much deeper intuitive understanding" of the matter in hand. Conceptually, he had wanted to show how one phase in the development of society had come to an end—the phase represented by a society based on gold, power, and hypocrisy— but intuitively he had "seen and recognized in its nothingness (*Nichtig-*

90. Ibid., 66–67.

keit) the nature of the world itself in all conceivable phases of its development instead of in one alone."[91] Annihilation no longer meant for him the mere destruction of a surface world but the annihilation of the roots of all possible worlds—an annihilation possible only after a conscious denial of the unconscious strivings of the Schopenhauerian will. And this meant that the renunciation of greed for power and gain was not enough—love, too, love as *erōs* that is, must be renounced in favor of love as *agapē*: the disinherited, unattached, unselfish love that desires nothing. Obviously, love between the sexes could no longer be the paradigm for the supreme form of love that Wagner now had in mind.

Wagner admits that he had been unhappy all along with the "tendentious closing phrase" directed at the audience by Brünnhilde just before her immolation. That phrase—"Love alone leaves us happy in both joy and sorrow"—referred to his earlier conception of love between the sexes as the supreme expression of love: "I recall that I finally brought my intent to expression by main force . . . in the tendentious closing phrase which . . . points away from the objectionableness of possession toward love as the sole source of bliss without (regrettably!) really having myself come into the clear with regard to this 'love' that we, in the course of the myth, actually saw appear as something downright devastating." Wagner assures Röckel that he has now deleted the tendentious closing phrase (*tendenziösen Schlussphrase*) and has put words in Brünnhilde's mouth that constitute an "appropriate keystone" for the whole dramatic structure.[92]

According to Newman, the new ending was jotted down on the final page of Wagner's copy of the privately printed version (1853) of the *Ring*. But the new ending also proved too tendentious. The words were never set to music, and they survive only as a footnote in certain printed editions of the poem:

> If now I no longer
> Fare to Valhalla's fastness,
> Know you whither I fare?
> From the home of desire I depart,
> Flee forever the home of illusion;
> Behind me I lock
> The open gates

91. *Ibid.*, 67.
92. *Ibid.*, 67–68.

Of eternal change:
She who knows now proceeds
Toward the most holy chosen land,
Toward world-wandering's goal,
Void of illusion and desire,
Released from rebirth.
The blessed end
Of all eternity,
Know you how I won it?
Deepest sorrow
Of love's suffering
Opened my eyes:
I saw the world end.[93]

Here, says Newman, Wagner was expressing his "artistic conviction that the right ending for the drama was the destruction of the world."[94] We may add that in Wagner's drama destruction of the world is equivalent to destruction of the self. For the self, as he has learned from Schopenhauer, is the creator and upholder of its world. Brünnhilde has become "she who knows" (die Wissende); her eyes have been opened by love's suffering, and she has at last achieved full consciousness. She is now a Buddha, *one who is fully awake.* And so she departs from the Maya-world, brings the cycle of birth and rebirth to an end, and departs for the Grail homeland, whether in Monsalvat or the distant East. Brünnhilde is also a fully developed goddess of revolution, an Antigone. Still to be destroyed is the old Adam (or the God of the Old Testament)—the arbitrary, grasping, possessive, egoistic male principle operative within every human being. But there is no longer the intention of replacing one deluded self (or social order) by another, equally deluded.

Such were Wagner's views on political revolution in 1856, and such they remained to the end of his life. In an essay published in the *North American Review* in 1879, Wagner describes the genesis of his doubts as to the ultimate value of political revolution of any kind. With reference to the aborted revolution of 1848, he writes: "After a brief consideration of its methods, a feeling of doubt began to trouble me, as to

93. Newman, *Life,* II, 356; Wagner, *Gesammelte Schriften,* ed. J. Kapp, IV, 286, note.
94. Newman, *Life,* II, 356.

whether the purely human element that was at the foundation of the revolution would not be lost sight of amid the prevailing disputes of parties as to the value of different forms of government—the difference between which was, after all, only a matter of preference." Wagner wanted a new kind of human being, not merely a new form of government, to come into existence:

It seemed to me that from this basis of general human interests a new civilization might spring which would make men truly free, and which might reach its noblest heights in that pure and humanizing art which would be its natural outgrowth. The only element in history which had always attracted and inspired me had been this effort of the race to mutiny against the tyranny of a traditional and legalized formalism; and I could see no triumph of this impulse of the natural man in the mere victory of one party over another. When I saw that this idea of mine, as to what should be the essential motive of a revolution, was utterly misunderstood by the politicians, whose efforts were limited to the temporary interests of the moment only, I once more turned my back on the realities of things, and sought my ideal world again.[95]

Wagner had no real faith in the goals and leadership of Bismarck's Second Reich, which appeared on the scene in 1871 and briefly competed with Great Britain for world dominion. Further, he had no faith in the future of the Germans (die Deutschen) of Germany. In his essay of 1879 he states that the "true strength and greatness" of the German race manifested itself only outside of Germany—long ago in England, Normandy, Lombardy, and Andalusia (the Angles, Normans, Lombards, and Vandals), and more recently in North America. That part of the Nordic or Germanic race bearing the "special distinctive name of Germans" had, says Wagner, always represented the peculiar type of German Philistine—petty, pusillanimous, and wretched, continually bickering with neighbors of much the same character. The communal strength of the Germanic spirit had been revealed only on the international scene. In Germany proper it had shown itself chiefly in "the line of mighty German poets and musicians."[96]

Wagner's doctrine of salvation by art seems to conflict with Brünnhilde's (subsequently deleted) Nirvana message at the close of the Ring. Nor is it quite in keeping with the close of The World as Will and Rep-

95. Richard Wagner, "The Work and Mission of My Life," North American Review, September, 1879, pp. 241–42.
96. Ibid., August, 1879, pp. 110–11.

resentation. Schopenhauer says that, when the will has at last been abolished, the dream of life (*Lebenstraum*)—a life of never-ending and never-satisfied desires in which the human being still in servitude to the will is caught—comes to an end. And on the countenance of one who has awakened is visible that "unshakeable confidence and serenity depicted by Raphael and Correggio":

> In this way, therefore, by contemplation of the lives and deeds of holy ones— to meet with whom first-hand is, admittedly, seldom granted to us, but which is brought before our eyes by their recorded histories and, with the stamp of inner truth, by art—we are to banish the dark impression of nothingness that hovers behind all virtue and holiness as a last boundary, which we fear as children fear the dark, instead of evading it by means of myths and empty words, such as the Hindu's resorption into Brahma, or the Buddhist's Nirvana. Instead we freely admit that what remains behind after the complete abolition of the will is, for all who are still filled with will, indeed nothing. But on the other hand, to those in whom the will has turned and denied itself, this our so very real world, with all its suns and galaxies, is—nothing.[97]

The conflict vanishes when we regard the matter from another standpoint. Wagner's quest for the Grail eventually brought him to Bayreuth. There his music-drama would unite eye and ear, concept and intuition, male principle and female principle, for the benefit of all who were ready for it. This was his salvation, and he offered it to others. And Schopenhauer's philosophy is itself really a work of art, one in which Schopenhauer found his salvation. Like the narrator in Marcel Proust's *In Search of Lost Time*, Schopenhauer rises above life, time, and death; and in the one case as in the other, when we have reached the end, we are brought back to the beginning.

97. Schopenhauer, *Sämtliche Werke*, II, 558.

Chapter III
MUSIC, DREAMS, AND THE UNCONSCIOUS

1. ORIGINS OF THE IDEA OF THE UNCONSCIOUS

We recall that in 1851 Wagner saw in the Oedipus myth a depiction of the social history of humanity from its first beginnings to the downfall of the state. Sophocles' Antigone—his own goddess of revolution—was a perfected human being, a whole human being who had reached this stage by becoming "conscious of the unconscious" and by obeying the "unconscious compelling necessity of self-destruction through sympathy." We saw also that "self-destruction through sympathy" meant for Wagner the destruction of the selfish, predominantly male ego. The newly perfected male-female or female-male human being would then stand under the sign of selfless love (agapē, Mitleid, Sympathie). It is worth emphasizing that Wagner thereby locates in the unconscious a self-destructive tendency; this makes its way to the surface and becomes a conscious moral imperative. Such a dialectical and apparently paradoxical course of development is in the best Hegelian tradition. Wagner may have been the first to formulate the task confronting European humanity of the present age as *the making conscious of the unconscious*. In so doing he anticipated Eduard von Hartmann's use of the same words in 1868 (with reference to a philosophical and social task) and Freud's use of them in 1896 (with reference to a psychological task). Wagner's use of the Oedipus myth to point up a present political necessity may also be without precedent. Even Bachofen's interpretation of the Oedipus myth, which came ten years later, has reference to a *past* stage in the development of humanity; that is, from pure "mother-right" to pure "father-right," from a matriarchal to a patriarchal culture.

Before discussing Schopenhauer's theory of dreams and musical creativity and Wagner's elaboration of Schopenhauer's line of thought, we pause to examine the development of the idea of the unconscious in nineteenth-century Europe. According to Hartmann and all other nineteenth-century students of the subject, it was Leibniz who first took cognizance of "unconscious" ideas. Leibniz's *petites perceptions* —perceptions lying on the fringe of or below the threshold of awareness—were accepted as the equivalent of unconscious ideas. Hartmann (who was writing at a time when "unconscious thinking" had been hypostasized) stated that Leibniz had failed to recognize the full significance of "the Unconscious as a province opposed to Consciousness." After Kant had located the "essence of sexual love" in the realm of the unconscious, the next step had been taken at the close of the eighteenth century by Friedrich Schelling. That nature-philosopher had derived from Fichtean absolute idealism a "conception of the Unconscious in its full purity, clearness and depth." The idea of the unconscious had then been variously exploited by philosophers, physicians, psychologists, and writers generally, some of whom Hartmann lists.[1]

It is worth noting that the geographical or topographical metaphors increasingly employed by early nineteenth-century students of unconscious mentation originated with Kant. Kant speaks of an immense field of perceptions and emotions lying beyond the reach of our waking consciousness. He tells us that our innermost being is shrouded in darkness. "On the great map of our heart (*Gemüt*)," he writes, "only a few places are lit up." The conscious "I" or ego occupies a small lighted clearing in the midst of a vast unknown realm. At the close of the eighteenth century, Friedrich Schelling added to the Fichtean absolute ego a hidden realm called the unconscious. Schelling (who may have been the first to use the term as a substantive) writes:

This eternal unconscious which, like the eternal sun in the realm of spirits, conceals itself behind its own clear light and, although it never becomes an object, nevertheless impresses its identity on all free actions, is at once the

1. Eduard von Hartmann, *Philosophy of the Unconscious*, I, 16–42.

same for all intelligences, the invisible root, of which all intelligences are only potencies, and the eternal mediator between the self-determining subjective in us and the objective or intuited—at once the ground of conformity to law in freedom and of freedom in conformity to law of that which is objective.

And Jean Paul, one of Schelling's contemporaries and the author of many philosophical novels and fantasies, claims that "we make far too small or narrow a survey of the broad territories of the 'I' (*das Ich*) when we leave out the huge realm of the unconscious (*das Unbewusste*), that real inner Africa."[2]

Preoccupation with the idea of the unconscious was largely confined to German thinkers until 1836, when Sir William Hamilton turned his attention to the subject. Born in the same year as Schopenhauer, Hamilton was more fortunate academically. In 1836 he became professor of logic and metaphysics at Edinburgh; in his inaugural lecture he asked whether an "unconscious action or passion of the mind" was theoretically conceivable and whether such unconscious mentation in fact took place. Pointing out that both questions had already been answered in the affirmative by German philosophers—although they had been dismissed as absurd in France and Great Britain—Hamilton traces the idea of unconscious mentation back to Leibniz in the usual way. Leibniz, he says, had supplied some strong arguments in favor of the occurrence of unconscious mentation but had been unhappy in his choice of terms. To speak of "obscure ideas" and *petites perceptions*, says Hamilton, "violated the universal usage of language," for the very notion of an idea or a perception involves the notion of consciousness. Hamilton illustrates the actual occurrence of unconscious mental processes from his own experience. While thinking one day of Ben Lomond, he found himself at the next moment thinking, rather to his surprise, of the Prussian system of education. The two thoughts seemed without a connecting link, but after some reflection he recalled that he had once encountered a German traveler on the summit of Ben Lomond. The missing links in the chain of associations were, he says, the product of unconscious mentation. Although Hamilton never speaks of *the*

2. Immanuel Kant, *Werke* (6 vols.; Frankfurt, 1956–64), VI, 418; Friedrich Schelling, *Sämmtliche Werke* (14 vols.; Stuttgart, 1856–61), Pt. 1, III, 600; Jean Paul [Johann Paul Richter], *Werke* (7 vols.; Munich, 1960–), VI, 1183.

unconscious, but only of unconscious mentation, he does use a geographical or spatial metaphor at one point: the evidence requires us to conclude that "the sphere of our conscious modifications is only a small circle in the center of a far wider sphere of action and passion, of which we are only conscious through its effects." Hamilton's terminology was rejected by J. S. Mill. Granting the existence of the phenomena ascribed by Hamilton to unconscious mental modifications, Mill argues that they should be ascribed instead to "unconscious modifications of the nerves." For, says Mill, our "mental feelings" have as "their physical antecedents particular states of the nerves."[3]

Hamilton's argument that the existence of potentially discoverable missing links in chains of associated ideas pointed to the occurrence of unconscious mental processes was advanced a little later by William B. Carpenter, an English professor of physiology. Carpenter, too, comments on the difficulty of finding "an appropriate designation for this class of operations." Not only do the words "unconscious reasoning" involve a contradiction, but they fail to take into account certain "subterranean" changes in our feelings and emotions, changes of which we become aware only after their occurrence. Like Mill, he suggests that "unconscious cerebration" is preferable. In a later work Carpenter concludes that it makes little difference whether the facts of the matter are set forth in "metaphysical" or "psychological" terms. Meanwhile, another English physician, Henry Maudsley, had looked into the subject from a slightly different point of view. After tracing the idea of unconscious mentation (which he equates with unconscious brain activity) back to Leibniz, Maudsley uses it to account for the phenomenon of *déjà vu*—"that occasional sudden consciousness ... of having been before in exactly the same circumstances as those which are then happening"—and to explain certain aspects of dreams and artistic creativity. Speaking of the latter, Maudsley says that not only can ideas be associated and blended below the level of consciousness, but they can even be initially *assimilated* at that level; that is, without any conscious awareness on the part of the subject. Then, after a suitable lapse of time, the "results of the mind's unconscious workings flow, as it

---

3. William Hamilton, *Lectures on Metaphysics* (2 vols.; Boston, 1859–64), I, 235, 242–45, 251; John Stuart Mill, *An Examination of Sir William Hamilton's Philosophy* (London, 1867), 334–41.

were, from unknown depths into consciousness." And so it is that "great writers or great artists . . . have been truly astonished at their own productions and cannot conceive how they contrived to produce them." The secret of artistic and scientific creativity, according to Maudsley, is that the wellspring of creativity is an unconscious transforming process taking place in the depths of the creator's mind—whatever is culturally in the air at the time being assimilated and creatively transformed. Further, the artistic creative process and the dream process are essentially the same. On this topic Maudsley cites a pertinent admonition to writers by Jean Paul: "The character must appear living before you, and you must hear it, not merely see it; it must, as takes place in dreams, dictate to you, and not you to it."[4]

Among the men in Germany mentioned by Hartmann in connection with the development of early nineteenth-century thought on the idea of the unconscious, perhaps the most important is Carl Gustav Carus (1789–1869), anatomist, psychologist, and for a time court physician at Dresden. Given Wagner's intellectual interests and his association with the court as assistant *Kapellmeister*, it is hard to see how he could possibly have overlooked Carus' book of 1846 on the psychology of the unconscious. But Carus is mentioned nowhere in Wagner's writings. As for Wagner's small personal library at Dresden—thought by Newman to have been dispersed after Wagner fled the town—it contained neither *Psyche* (1846) nor the *Lectures on Psychology* (1831), the two books by Carus that come into question. Although the ideas set forth by Wagner in 1851 are not to be found in Carus, the two books are important landmarks in the history of the idea of the unconscious. Carus states that the conscious mind can be understood only in the light of the unconscious; further, that the content of the unconscious mind is accessible by way of analysis of the conscious mind. In his own words, "the key to knowledge of the nature of conscious psychic life lies in the region of the unconscious (*in der Region des Unbewusstseins*)"; and contrariwise, we can achieve an "understanding of the unconscious (*des Unbewussten*) through that which is conscious (*das Bewusstsein*)."

4. William B. Carpenter, *Principles of Human Physiology* (Philadelphia, 1853), 784–85, 791–93; William B. Carpenter, *Principles of Mental Physiology* (New York, 1875), XIII, "Of Unconscious Cerebration"; Henry Maudsley, *The Physiology and Pathology of Mind* (New York, 1897), 1–37.

We are told by Carus that it is possible to reconstruct the content of the unconscious by working back from the known to the unknown (*unser Dasein geistig zu rekonstruieren von dem bewussten Sein ins Unbewusste*), but the technique is not spelled out.[5]

Carus' circle in Dresden included the dramatic soprano Wilhelmine Schroeder-Devrient and the tenor Joseph Tichatschek, two artists closely associated with Wagner, but not Wagner himself. The pianist Clara Wieck, who was later to marry Robert Schumann and to engage in a prolonged liaison with Johannes Brahms, was a young member of the circle. Although Carus wrote on music and the arts generally, he has little to say of Wagner. Only in his memoirs do we find anything of interest. Commenting on the Dresden uprising of 1849, Carus remarks that music, too, was under attack at the same time, specifically from second *Kapellmeister* Richard Wagner, who seemed to want "to reform music from top to bottom."[6]

The omission of Wagner's name from any of the numerous editions of the *Philosophy of the Unconscious* may well have been deliberate, since Hartmann and the followers of Schopenhauer seem to have had an aversion for each other. In view of Hartmann's use of Wagner's words, the omission is rather startling. We have seen that Hartmann's "third illusion" would, when transcended, be followed by the end of all things. And, says Hartmann, this would involve making "ends of the Unconscious ends of our own consciousness." Even the much narrower task facing the historian of philosophy is defined by Hartmann in the same terms: philosophers heretofore have been half unconsciously developing an idea or set of ideas welling up from the "depths of the Unconscious," and the task now is the *"bringing to consciousness of the Unconscious relations between different philosophies"* (Hartmann's emphasis). He calls the transformation of the goal of the unconscious into a

5. Newman, *Life*, I, 377, II, 50–51; Curt von Westernhagen, *Richard Wagners Dresdener Bibliothek 1842–1849* (Wiesbaden, 1966), 84–113; Carl Gustav Carus, *Psyche*, ed. Ludwig Klages from the 2nd ed. (1860) (Jena, 1926), 1–3; Carl Gustav Carus, *Vorlesungen über Psychologie* (Darmstadt, 1958). In 1854 Dostoevsky made plans to translate *Psyche*, according to Konstantin Mochulsky, *Dostoevsky: His Life and Work*, trans. Michael A. Minihan (Princeton, N.J., 1967), 157.

6. Sophie Gräfin von Arnim, *Carl Gustav Carus: Sein Leben und Wirken* (Dresden, n.d.), 68; Carl Gustav Carus, *Gedanken über grosse Kunst* (Leipzig, 1944); Carl Gustav Carus, *Lebenserinnerungen und Denkwürdigkeiten* (4 vols. in 2; Leipzig, 1865–66), III, 212.

conscious goal a "principle of practical philosophy." The goal—which is nothing less than redemption from the misery of eternal willing and striving—has been present in the unconscious, apparently as an urge to negate itself, from the beginning. Consciousness then adopts this goal as its own. The end of all things is not conceived of as a fiery, catastrophic last judgment or *dies irae*; it is rather (precisely as in Schopenhauer) a blowing-out of the flame of existence—Nirvana, in short. There is an ominous note in Hartmann's statement that our conscious mind, now having made "the goal of the world-redemption from the misery of volition its own goal," has the "persuasion of the all-wisdom of the Unconscious, in consequence of which it recognizes all the means made use of by the Unconscious as the most suitable possible, even if in the special case it should be inclined to harbour doubts thereon."[7] The destruction of the *physical* world, as a last resort?

The third man to adopt the notion of transforming the unconscious into the conscious was Sigmund Freud. In 1893 when the first of his papers on psychoanalysis appeared, Freud was thirty-seven years old and an established neurologist and neuroanatomist. The paper of 1893 contains no reference to the unconscious. By 1896 Freud had reached the conclusion that in his hands psychoanalysis was a method, in fact the only method, for "making conscious what was previously unconscious." In 1904 after calling attention to Pierre Janet's belief that an "unconscious *idée fixe*" was the cause of hysterical symptoms, Freud stated that patients with hysteria could be cured by the "transformation of this unconscious material . . . into conscious material." Again in 1904, he postulated that the goal of the psychoanalytic method was to make the unconscious accessible to consciousness. The first hint of the coming importance of the Oedipus complex in Freudian psychodynamics appeared in 1897 in a letter to Wilhelm Fliess. Freud states in the letter that the power of Sophocles' *Oedipus Rex* derives from "a compulsion which everyone recognizes because he has found traces of it in himself." In 1900 Freud analyzed Sophocles' *Oedipus Rex* in more detail and observed that Shakespeare's *Hamlet*, too, had its roots in the Oedipal soil, namely in an infantile wish to oust the father and possess the mother. The resemblance, which can hardly be called superficial,

7. Hartmann, *Philosophy of the Unconscious*, II, 7; III, 133.

between Freud's therapeutic goal and Wagner's "ontic-political" goal and the importance accorded by both men to the Oedipus myth in Sophocles seem to have escaped the attention of Freud and his followers.[8]

Freud, a busy practicing psychotherapist, was not seriously concerned with intellectual history, even as it impinged on his chosen field of activity. A case in point is the doctrine of repression, that "cornerstone on which the whole structure of psycho-analysis rests." He had thought it entirely his own until Otto Rank called attention to a passage in Schopenhauer fitting his conception of repression so completely that, says Freud, "once again I owe the chance of making a discovery to my not being well read." For this reason he had also avoided reading Nietzsche. He was quite prepared "to forego all claim to priority in the many instances in which laborious psycho-analytical investigation can merely confirm the truths that the philosopher had already recognized intuitively." Rank's paper, published in 1910 in a journal edited by Freud, contains a passage from *The World as Will and Representation* in which Schopenhauer argues that if the resistance and opposition of the will to the assimilation of some piece of knowledge reaches a degree such that the assimilation is not entirely carried through, madness will occur. There is no reason to doubt Freud's statement that he had not read Schopenhauer in his youth. But as Maudsley remarked in 1867, assimilation of ideas by creative minds often goes on far below the level of conscious awareness. And before Maudsley, Schopenhauer claimed that the most fundamental aspect of thinking usually occurs at a subterranean level. "The rumination of material taken in from the outside, whereby it is worked over into thoughts," he wrote in 1846, "usually takes place in the dark depths of the mind . . . almost as unconsciously as the transformation of nourishment in the humors and substance of the body."[9]

8. Sigmund Freud, *Collected Papers* (5 vols.; New York, 1959), I, 157, 263, 269; Sigmund Freud, *Sigmund Freud: The Origins of Psychoanalysis; Letters to Wilhelm Fliess, Drafts and Notes, 1887–1902,* trans. Eric Mosbacher and James Strachey (New York, 1954), 223–24; Sigmund Freud, *Standard Edition of the Complete Psychological Works,* ed. James Strachey (23 vols.; London, 1953–74), IV, 260–66. Otto Rank used a passage from Wagner's essay on the Oedipus myth as an epigraph for one of the chapters in his study of the incest motif in literature and legend. See Otto Rank, *Das Inzest-Motiv in Dichtung und Sage: Grundzüge einer Psychologie des dichterischen Schaffens* (2nd ed.; Leipzig, 1926).
9. Sigmund Freud, *Gesammelte Werke* (17 vols.; London, 1941–49), X, 53. In

In 1913 Freud, whose ideas on the topography of the unconscious had undergone considerable development during the intervening years, adopted a term used by Georg Groddeck to designate the impersonal drives of the unconscious. The term *das Es* (the "it") appears in English translations of Freud's writings as the Latin word *id*. The new word is needed, says Freud, because of his recent discovery that there is "something in the ego itself which is also unconscious, which behaves exactly like the repressed." Groddeck had borrowed the word from Nietzsche, who had used it as a grammatical term for "whatever in our nature is impersonal." The revised version of Freud's psychoanalytic imperative now became, "Where id was, there shall ego be" ("Wo Es war; soll Ich werden")—a cultural task equivalent to draining the Zuyder Zee. The lines of relationship connecting Freud's id, Nietzsche's "it," and Schopenhauer's "will" should have been clear enough. When Egon Friedell called attention to the resemblance between Freud's id and Kant's thing-in-itself in 1931, however, he failed to mention Schopenhauer, although Schopenhauer himself had plainly stated that his "will" was the supposedly forever unknowable thing-in-itself of Kant. But in 1937 Thomas Mann stated that Freud's description of id and ego was to a hair the equivalent of Schopenhauer's description of will and intellect. And in 1938, after again equating Schopenhauer's "dark realm of the will" with the id, Mann called Schopenhauer the father of all modern psychology.[10]

2. *SCHOPENHAUER ON DREAMS, THE OCCULT, WIT*

To the waking consciousness of eighteenth-century Europe, preoccupied as it was with the rational and scientific world view that had been

---

Freud's *Collected Papers*, I, 297, the passage is mistranslated as "this philosopher," as if only Nietzsche were meant. Otto Rank, "Schopenhauer über den Wahnsinn," *Zentralblatt für Psychoanalyse*, I (1910), 69–71; Schopenhauer, *Sämtliche Werke*, II, 175, 516.

10. Freud, *Standard Edition*, XIX, 23; Georg Groddeck, *Das Buch vom Es* (2nd ed.; Leipzig, 1926); Sigmund Freud, *New Introductory Lectures on Psycho-Analysis* (New York, 1933), 112; Egon Friedell, *Kulturgeschichte der Neuzeit* (3 vols.; Munich, 1927–32), III, 586–87; Thomas Mann, *Freud, Goethe, Wagner* (New York, 1937), 3–45; Thomas Mann, "Schopenhauer," in *Adel des Geistes* (Stockholm, 1948), 329–387. As in classical Greek, the existence of a neuter form of the definite article (*das*) in German makes it easy to use participles as substantives and thus to reify activities or processes. Further, the word *es* in German, unlike the word *it* in English, at times indicates an indefinite, indescribable "something" and imparts a weird, ghostly impression. The Latin word *id* was therefore a brilliant solution to the problem of translating Freud's *Es* into English.

cultivated since the beginning of the seventeenth century, dreams and the occult were of relatively little moment. Together with myth and fable, dreams and occult occurrences seemed, to children of the age of reason, topics that had been taken seriously only in the childhood of the race. Dreams could be brushed aside in the bright light of day as mere irrational by-products of the sleeping mind, devoid of all significance. Occult or paranormal phenomena could be dismissed entirely or exposed as fraud. Toward the end of the eighteenth century, however, part of Europe began to turn away from the dominant rationalism. The view of the world that we now call romanticism began to assert itself, and nowhere in Europe was the romantic movement stronger than in the German-speaking lands. Nineteenth-century nature-philosophy (*Naturphilosophie*) is romantic science par excellence. And its strongly marked speculative bent was matched or exceeded by the work of philosophers whose interest lay elsewhere than in the problems of natural science. The romantic imagination was most evident in German writers and poets, such as Jean Paul, Novalis, E. T. A. Hoffmann, and Heinrich von Kleist. France was at this time as rationalistic as ever; witness the further efforts of Heine to explain German thought to the French in his essay "The Romantic School." Later in the century the "night-side" of human existence began to manifest itself even in France, in the work of Gerard de Nerval, Victor Hugo, Charles Baudelaire, Stéphane Mallarmé, Arthur Rimbaud, and Marcel Proust.[11] Schopenhauer reached intellectual maturity during the high tide of the romantic movement in Germany. But his was a rational eighteenth-century mind—he was born in 1788—and part of his impressive philosophical achievement consists in the rationalizing of the irrational.

Schopenhauer's most illuminating insights into the nature of the dream process and the significance of dream life for waking life are presented in a collection of his essays published in 1851. The first of the two essays to be discussed here, "Transcendent Speculation on the Apparent Deliberateness in the Fate of the Individual," has an epigraph drawn from Plotinus: "Chance has no place in life; harmony and order

11. Heine, *Werke*, VII–IX, 163–278. This essay, "Die romantische Schule," was first published in French translation in *L'Europe littéraire*, March, April, and May, 1833. Albert Béguin, *L'Âme romantique et le rêve: essai sur le romantisme allemand et la poésie française* (Paris, 1946).

alone rule." The gist of Schopenhauer's argument is that even our waking lives have a dreamlike structure. Just as the apparently random course of events in our dreams is directed by a hidden stage manager—who is our hidden self—so also the apparently chance course of events in our waking lives is secretly given shape within by the same agency. Not only have such poets as William Shakespeare and Pedro Calderón long since recognized this veiled correspondence, says Schopenhauer, but even the transcendental idealism of Kant himself can be read as an explicit "presentation of this dream-like structure of our conscious existence." He continues: "And indeed it is this analogy with the dream that lets us see, if only in the misty distance, how the secret power that controls and directs the external circumstances affecting us with an eye to its own ends could nevertheless have its roots in the depths of our own unfathomable nature."[12]

As we look back on our lives, we seem to see that some hidden power has impressed a pattern on everything—even the most trivial events—that has happened to us. This power has of course traditionally been externalized as the power of fate or destiny. Schopenhauer internalizes it and locates its seat in the realm of the (unconscious) will. It is the same power that shapes the structure of our dream lives:

For in dreams also the circumstances that furnish the motives for our actions are encountered as external, accidental and independent of ourselves, even as abhorrent. But there is nonetheless a hidden and purposeful connection between them. A concealed power, obeyed by all contingencies in the dream, guides and arranges these circumstances too; indeed it alone brings them in relation to us. The most extraordinary thing here is that this power can in the end be nothing other than our own will, but from a standpoint that does not fall within our dream consciousness. So it is that the events of the dream quite often unfold in a manner entirely opposed to our desires, and transport us into astonishment, distress, even into terror and fear of death, without fate —which we ourselves nevertheless secretly control—coming to our rescue.[13]

What Schopenhauer says here is crucial for his (and the later psychoanalytical) interpretation of dreams. A dream is entirely controlled

12. Schopenhauer, *Sämtliche Werke*, IV, 264. For the first complete translation of the essays into English, see Schopenhauer, *Parerga and Paralipomena*, translated by E. F. J. Payne.

13. Schopenhauer, *Sämtliche Werke*, IV, 264–65.

from within—from the subjective standpoint, by the many-faceted personality of the dreamer; from the objective standpoint, by whatever factors determine cerebral activity in the sleeping brain. There can no longer be any question of "spiritualistic" influences on dreams. Not only are all the personalities in the dream mere fragments split off from the dreamer, but the whole course of dream events is the expression of the dreamer's secret self. Schopenhauer states that the dreamer is the hidden director of the dream theater: fate and the dreamer are one and the same. In the dream the statement "character is destiny" is *literally* true. But to what extent is it true in waking life? Schopenhauer now makes his most striking claim. Our waking life, too, obeys a hidden controlling power that operates below our superficially placed waking consciousness:

Let us look back from here at the chief result of my whole philosophy, namely that the *will* presents and supports the phenomenon of the world, a will that lives and strives in every individual being. And at the same time let us recall the widely recognized resemblance between dreams and life. Then, taking all that has been said into consideration, we can in general regard it as quite possible that just as everyone is the hidden director of his dream theater, so also, by analogy, the fate that rules the actual course of our lives ultimately stems in some way from our own *will*, which at this point, where it appears as fate, works from a region that lies far beyond our individual representing consciousness. Consciousness, on the other hand, furnishes us with motives that direct our empirically knowable individual will—which as a result often has to fight bitterly against the *will* that presents itself to us as fate, as our directing genius.[14]

Finding this conclusion both "daring" and "surprising," Schopenhauer lends it history and respectability by bringing it into relation with certain views of the ninth-century theologian and philosopher Scotus Erigena on the divine ignorance (*divina ignorantia*) of God. The God of Scotus Erigena is, says Schopenhauer, equivalent to the will-to-live of his own philosophy: both alike are the invisible basis of all things; both alike do not know what they will do until they have done it. Possibly Schopenhauer's philosophy owed something else to Scotus; just as Schopenhauer's "will" corresponds to Scotus' "God," so also Schopenhauer's "intellect" may correspond to Scotus' "Logos."[15]

14. *Ibid.*, 266–67.
15. Victor White, *God and the Unconscious* (London, 1952).

In the second and longer of Schopenhauer's two essays, "Essay on Spirit Seeing and Everything Connected Therewith," the subject of dreams and paranormal phenomena is dealt with from the neurological as well as the psychological (or metaphysical) point of view. From the neurophysiological standpoint, according to Schopenhauer, dreams are a state or form of activity characteristic of the sleeping brain. Brain, nervous system, and peripheral receptors are, in this state, turned inward, directed toward the microcosm rather than the macrocosm. The brain, or that part of it involved in the dream process, continues to do with inward impressions precisely what it does during waking life with impressions derived from the external world. It makes them into three-dimensional pictures and sets them in motion in accordance with the form of time and category of causality inherent in its manner of working:

Just as the stomach makes chyme out of all it can handle, and the intestines prepare chyle from this, the original stuff of which we do not see, so also the brain reacts to all stimuli reaching it by carrying out its own special function. This consists primarily in the projection of pictures in all three dimensions of space, according to its mode of perceptions, next in moving these pictures in time, along the guiding thread of causality. . . . For it will always speak only in its own tongue.[16]

To this Schopenhauer adds that dream content is in no way explained by pointing out initiating stimuli and further, that the nature of the accompanying brain process remains a mystery. He suggests, however, that the parts of the brain concerned with memory and judgment are in abeyance during dreaming.

In dreams, as in waking life, all that appears to us as a phenomenon does so under the sign of causality, says Schopenhauer. It follows then that in our dreams "all that takes place, takes place of necessity." There are no random events. Dreams are expressions of the unconscious will; and if we study the cast of characters and the stage management of a dream, we may attain access to the realm of the will. But a twofold difficulty presents itself when the attempt is made. First, the will can express itself only in the categories of the intellect; second, the dream that we recall immediately after waking usually lies at one remove from

16. Schopenhauer, *Sämtliche Werke*, IV, 286.

the original dream. In some instances, it is true, the sleeper awakes with a direct representation of the dream in mind. Following the terminology of Artemidorus, Schopenhauer calls dreams of this character *theorematic*. But what more often happens, especially in the case of dreams whose deeper meaning concerns us, is that we awake with a transformed version of the original dream in mind. The content of the original *theorematic* dream is translated into the content of an *allegorical* dream. This is because the original dream takes place in the depths of sleep at a stage of "somnambulistic clairvoyance," a deep stage from which no immediate recollection is accessible to the waking mind. The only way in which the dreamer can retain any contact with the original *theorematic* dream is by the "translation of its content into allegory, in the clothing of which the original prophetic dream now reaches the waking consciousness." In consequence, the allegorical dream requires careful interpretation and exposition before its meaning can be understood. The traditional method of dream interpretation was to ascribe to the characters and events the fixed symbolic meanings given in traditional dream books. To Schopenhauer that method, resting as it did on the false proposition that the events and characters of allegorical dreams always had the same symbolic meanings, was inacceptable: "The allegory is, rather, solely and individually adapted to the actual object and subject of the theorematic dream underlying the allegorical dream. Exposition of allegorical, fatidic dreams is for the most part so difficult that as a rule we understand them only after their message has been fulfilled; we then must marvel at the peculiar, demonic slyness of wit, otherwise quite foreign to the dreamer, with which the allegory has been laid down and carried out."[17]

How we are to get at the meaning of dreams is not dealt with further in this essay. In the chapter "On the Association of Ideas" in the second volume of *The World as Will and Representation*, Schopenhauer remarks in passing that the association of ideas may furnish us with a thread to draw the original content of a dream back into our consciousness. But, as he says above, we must always reckon with the demonic slyness of wit (*dämonische Schalkhaftigkeit des Witzes*) displayed by the unconscious will, the stage manager of the dream, when

17. *Ibid.*, 308.

it communicates with the waking consciousness of the dreamer. If we take into account Schopenhauer's definition of wit as the arbitrary identification of two different objects, ideas, or perceptions by means of a concept embracing both at once, we obtain a clue to ways in which the dream message becomes distorted. The will identifies opposites, ignores incongruities, treats one person as another, and behaves in general like a comedian or trickster in spinning out the fabric of our dreams. Even in waking life, flashes of wit (sinnreiche Einfälle) are tentatively related to unconscious (unbewussten) reminiscences by Schopenhauer.[18]

In the dream world the unconscious will is free to manipulate events, persons, and things at its pleasure. It is omnipotent. In the real world, however, it is only one of many manifestations of the will. Yet even when subjected to the constraints of the real world, it has enormous power to shape the course of events in our lives. It is the secret agent, the hidden stage manager, the invisible ruler of our lives, working quietly behind the surface facade. Throughout our lives we pick and choose in accordance with a pattern or schema, the very existence of which is unknown to us. The outlines of the pattern become clearer as our lives proceed. At last it is revealed as the pattern of our (self-created) fate—a pattern formed by events but in a certain sense independent of them, a pattern like that of iron filings on a surface beneath which a powerful, intricately configured magnet exercises an invisible yet compelling force. Much of what we do in our waking lives merely masquerades as conscious and rational action and is in reality fully or partially determined at an unconscious level. We are sleepwalkers. Schopenhauer says that many of our actions resemble Marshall Hall's "reflex actions" (Reflexbewegungen); we are like newly hatched turtles, who make their way unerringly to water that they have never seen and do not know is their goal.[19]

Somnambulism, clairvoyance, telepathy, and other paranormal or occult phenomena were in the air throughout the nineteenth century. Schopenhauer's attitude was one of caution. He comments that believers and skeptics have for thousands of years debated the reality of such phenomena and are now no closer to agreement than when they began. But he reminds us that there are more things in heaven and earth than

18. Ibid., I, 105; II, 73, 173.
19. Ibid., IV, 251.

are dreamt of in our philosophy.[20] Perhaps we should not turn away from occult phenomena merely because they have been exploited by quacks, frauds, and impostors, nor even because they seem inexplicable and irrational and therefore have no place in a world ruled by reason. Perhaps there *is* a way of "dreaming" about them in our philosophy.

Schopenhauer's attempt to rationalize occult phenomena is as follows. The "real" reality of the world—its noumenal (in the Kantian sense) reality—is the impersonal, universal, timeless, spaceless will. The noumenal reality of all individual beings in the world, including human beings, is an individual manifestation in each of those beings of the universal will. The phenomenal or perceived world of human beings, on the other hand, is a continuing creation of the human brain; the forms of space and time and the category of causality governing all events in the world-as-known apply to that world alone. None of these forms apply to the noumenal world, the world of the will. Clairvoyance, telepathy, animal magnetism, and sympathetic cures—to the extent that they actually take place and are not the result of fraud—represent points at which the noumenal and phenomenal worlds intersect. The occurrence of these manifestations indicates that we have access, by way of the unconscious will at the core of our real being, to a world behind (or below) the surface world. And in that world the differences between the near and the far, between the past, the present, and the future, vanish.[21] Putting Schopenhauer's metaphysical explanation into more familiar psychological terms, he is saying that the events in question are at home in the world of the unconscious; they appear as strange and inexplicable to the world of the waking mind only because they are incompatible with its working categories. They are dreamlike, but they are dreams of a deeper reality than that presented by our waking world.

Paranormal phenomena, then, are in a sense more real than normal phenomena. They occur where the timeless, spaceless, acausal world of the will breaks through the facade of the world of the intellect—and the latter world is, according to Schopenhauer, largely an a priori construct by the perceiver. Given such a constitution of the world of phenomena—that is, given that the forms of space and time and the cate-

20. *Ibid.*, 270, 372.
21. *Ibid.*, 318.

gory of causality constitutive of the phenomenal world are inherent in the mind of the perceiver—how far, asks Schopenhauer, is it possible to go in understanding the entire phenomenal world on an a priori basis? Although unimpressed by the attempts of Schelling and his school along this line, Schopenhauer states that conceivably a genial mind may some day successfully "derive laws of nature from mere laws of space and time," making use of mathematical philosophy as a vehicle. Schopenhauer is in this way also able to rationalize a fund of esoteric knowledge that had long been of interest to Western thinkers. Thus he suggests that an "obscure discernment" of the possibility of so constructing a world had been responsible for the "origin of the Kabbala and of the mathematical philosophy of the Pythagoreans."[22]

3. SCHOPENHAUER ON SEX AND DEATH

Schopenhauer may have found in Kant the cue for his own treatment of sexuality. We saw that Kant situates the source of sexual love in the unlighted reaches of the human heart. Kant also comments on the thin veil thrown by wit "from time immemorial" over the topic of sexual love. But Schopenhauer goes much further than Kant in according importance to sexuality in the scheme of things, macrocosmic and microcosmic. Schopenhauer admits that he has few if any precursors in this respect and that the devotees of the sublime and ethereal will find his view of sexuality far too physical. Sex, he says, is half of what life is about. The "jest of the world" is the fact that this "invisible central point of all action and conduct . . . the cause of war, the aim and object of peace, the basis of the serious and the aim of the joke, the inexhaustible source of all wit, the key to all hints and illusions . . . the daily thought of the young and very often of the old as well" is ostensibly ignored but hotly pursued in secret. Now why, asks Schopenhauer, all this uproar over what, to express it politely, is merely a matter of every Jill finding a Jack? Why so much rage over a missing penny? The answer, of course, is that at issue is nature's sole aim, the perpetuation of the species. From the individual standpoint the driving urge of the will is to survive; this urge is most clearly expressed orally. From the standpoint of the species—the standpoint of nature—the driving urge to sur-

22. *Ibid.*, I, 214.

vive is expressed sexually, and the organs concerned are not left under our control. The sexual urge is the primary manifestation of the will to live. Schopenhauer claims that the sexual impulse is the very "kernel of the will to live"; the human body is "concrete sexual impulse," the objective counterpart of a metaphysical drive; the desire of all desires is the "act of copulation."[23] The actors and actresses on the stage of life are cued in by an off-scene director.

If sex constitutes half of what life is really about, death constitutes the other half, says Schopenhauer. The two are inseparable. Their inseparability appears most plainly when we consider what affirmation of the will means. Affirmation of the will is a stance taken by the intellect *after* the true nature of the goal of the will has been raised to the level of consciousness, a stance possible for human beings alone among animals. In affirming the will, the intellect makes the goal of the will its own goal; thereafter, thinking is concerned largely with the choice of means for attaining that goal. Since the human body is simply the objective form of the will (that is, the phenomenal reflection of the thing-in-itself), affirmation of the will necessarily amounts to affirmation of the body. The body is the objective expression of the hunger and sex drives of the will. And since the circumstances of life on this planet are such that there is not enough of everything to go around, conflict is inevitable. When the will is aroused in one individual, the affirmation of the existence of that individual by the intellect, acting in the service of the will, often involves the denial or suppression of the existence of other individuals. Here we have Schopenhauer's dark vision of the self-devouring, cannibalistic will at the heart of all life.[24]

There is a more pleasant side to the picture. Considered from another point of view, all that takes place in life is a cheerful game with no real losers, presided over by nature. The stands are always full, the players are always there, and the sun is always shining. The game continues with new players who are, in a sense, the same; the dying losers fall back into the lap of nature, which does not grieve (*natura non contristatur*). Death and birth are like the "forces of attraction and repulsion, through whose antagonism matter persists." For, says Schopen-

23. Kant, *Werke*, VI, 419–20; Schopenhauer, *Sämtliche Werke*, II, 651–60, 678–718, *passim*.
24. Schopenhauer, *Sämtliche Werke*, I, 447–53.

hauer, quoting Aristotle on Empedocles, "if strife did not rule, all would be one." Death and birth are equally part of life; the "wisest of all mythologies, the Indian, expresses this by giving as an attribute to the very god who symbolizes destruction and death . . . to Shiva himself a necklace of skulls and, at the same time, a lingam, the symbol of generation."[25]

The game goes on in an everlasting present. There is no real reason for us to fear the coming of night and death. But, says Schopenhauer, some of us may come to feel that we no longer like the game.[26] And this is what denial of the will to live means; it is a new, rebellious stance taken by the intellect after the goal of the will has been brought to full consciousness. The intellect then refuses to affirm the goal any longer. Like Ivan Karamazov, the intellect refuses to accept life on the terms offered; it returns the ticket. This does not mean, as some of Schopenhauer's readers appear to have thought, that he is advising anyone to commit suicide. On the contrary, Schopenhauer regards suicide as a disguised affirmation of the will; it is failure to *achieve* the goal of the will that drives the suicide to death. Denial of the will to live, rather, means the acceptance of a new moral imperative telling us how we must live from then on. Schopenhauer holds that all evil in the world flows from the conflict of individual beings who struggle to survive and reproduce themselves at all costs. Among animals in a state of nature the results are horrifying enough. But the human condition is even worse. There, where "hatred and wickedness" are intensified and given new force by an intellect wholly committed to the service of the will, a new dimension of evil has come into being. In denying the will, the intellect turns away from life and shudders at the pleasures in which it formerly rejoiced. It becomes the "pacifier" of the will. And since the body is the will objectified—the will as it appears in the phenomenal world—denial of the will to live is equivalent to denial of the body. Our guide to life is no longer *erōs*, which enslaves us to our own egoistic cravings, but *agapē, caritas, Mitleid*, universal love and sympathy.

4. KABBALISTIC AND SCHOPENHAUERIAN ANTHROPOLOGY

Already mentioned above, the sole overt reference to the Kabbala in

25. *Ibid.*, I, 218, 381–82; II, 654.
26. *Ibid.*, II, 612.

Schopenhauer's writings bears on the possibility of devising an a priori mathematical physical cosmology. We may suppose that Schopenhauer had in mind the combinatorial procedure presented in the *Book of Creation* (*Sefer Yetsirah*).[27] But one can argue with some degree of plausibility that covert references are present in Schopenhauer's microcosmology—his anthropology, that is. In any event, it cannot be denied that similar metaphors occur in Schopenhauer's symbolic description of the human being and in the Kabbalistic account of Adam Kadmon.

A plant, says Schopenhauer, can be regarded as a symbolic picture (*Sinnbild*) of consciousness. A plant has two poles, the root and the crown. The crown strives upward into the realm of brightness, dryness, and warmth; the root reaches downward into darkness, moisture, and cold. The root (*Wurzel*) is essentially perennial and primary, whereas the crown (*Krone*) is secondary, transient, and dependent on the root for its continued life. Now, continues Schopenhauer, we can regard the root as representative of the will and the crown as representative of the intellect. The point at which root and crown meet, the rootstalk or stem (*Wurzelstock*), corresponds to the "I" (*das Ich*) or ego, the transient "subject" of human knowing and willing.[28] This much is true, speaking inwardly or psychologically (*psychologisch*), he adds; but outwardly or physiologically speaking, the genitals represent the root, and the head the crown.

Schopenhauer's symbolism here may well be neither originally nor purely Kabbalistic. Root and flower imagery occurs in many contexts, ranging from the sacred to the profane, in different lands and cultures. But Schopenhauer's analogy does look somewhat as if it had been drawn from the *Zohar* and then altered in accordance with his own needs. In the *Zohar* the primary, invisible, and perfect *en soph* is said to send forth ten *sephiroth*, ten emanations that constitute the structure of both macrocosm and microcosm. The microcosm is Adam Kadmon, the archetypal man. When the *sephiroth* are pictured on the tree of life, the crown (*kether*) of the tree corresponds to the head of Adam Kadmon, in which wisdom and intelligence are united. The foundation

27. For the possible influence of this procedure in another connection, see L. J. Rather, "Alchemistry, the Kabbala, the Analogy of the 'Creative Word,' and the Origins of Molecular Biology," *Episteme*, VI (1972), 83–103.
28. Schopenhauer, *Sämtliche Werke*, II, 261.

(*yesod*) of Adam Kadmon is constituted by the ninth *sephira*, called "foundation" because it is the source and basis of all things, the generative principle itself, represented in the body by the genital organs. "All marrow, all sap and all power are congregated in this spot. . . . All powers which exist originate through the genital organs," says the *Zohar*.[29]

When the Schopenhauerian will has turned and denied itself, what is left, Schopenhauer has told us, is "nothing." This "nothing" would seem to be the equivalent of the *en soph* in the Kabbala—that invisible, illimitable, and perfectly unknown realm (of which the ten *sephiroth* are manifestations) lying beyond the confines of Adam Kadmon. Schopenhauer's denial of the will is, in religious terms, a denial of the whole of creation, a denial of the will of Jahweh. The God of the Jews in the Old Testament looked on his work and pronounced it good. Schopenhauer looks on it and pronounces the judgment of Mephistopheles in Goethe's *Faust*: it is not good; it merits destruction; it should never have been created in the first place:

> *Und das mit Recht: denn alles, was entsteht,*
> *Ist wert, dass es zugrunde geht.*
> *Drum besser wär's, dass nichts entstünde.*
> (And rightly so, for everything that arises
> deserves to perish; it would therefore be
> better for nothing to arise.)[30]

Schopenhauer, like Martin Luther, sees this world as the devil's work, or at least as a world given over entirely to the devil's power. Hence he ranks the "optimistic" religions of Judaism and Islam (he is harder on Islam than on Judaism) far below the "pessimistic" religions of Buddhism, Christianity, and the religion of the Hindus.[31] To Schopenhauer the whole of Jewish myth, religion, and philosophy is a continuing affirmation of the will to live—an endless paean in praise of life as it is, combined with Job-like submission to the will of the power-God of things as they are. Schopenhauer aims, it is true, to provide a higher

29. *Ibid.*, 652; Christian D. Ginzburg, *The Kabbalah* (1863; reprint ed., London, 1970), 97–102.

30. Gershom Scholem, *Ursprung und Anfänge der Kabbala* (Berlin, 1962), 381–91: "En-soph, Urwille und Uridee"; Johann Wolfgang Goethe, *Faust*, ed. Wolfgang Herwig (4 vols.; Zurich, 1965–), I, ll. 1339–41; cited by Schopenhauer, *Sämtliche Werke*, II, 735.

31. Schopenhauer, *Sämtliche Werke*, II, 569. Islam is here called a "variety" of Judaism.

moral law for the conduct of life, as long as live we must—rather like the rabbis in David Asher's anecdote from the Talmud. Seen from the negative side, however, Schopenhauer is calling for the destruction of Adam Kadmon—and this to be accomplished by turning crown (intellect) against root (sexuality), *kether* against *yesod*.

5. THE VOICE OF THE UNCONSCIOUS: SCHOPENHAUER ON MUSIC

If the arts conceal a mystery, surely the heart of that mystery lies in the art of music. The plastic and pictorial arts are part of the light-world, the world of the surface. Works of art composed of words fall into the same category: their aesthetic effect depends largely on the meaning of the words. And the world of meanings is coextensive with the world as known; Wittgenstein's verbal world is, as we have seen, structurally identical with Schopenhauer's world-as-representation. In the mythical sense the word is creative, but it creates a known world rather than an ontically founded world. When no logical or discursive meaning is conveyed by the human voice, the speaker is transformed into a singer, a musician. If something that cannot otherwise be designated than as "meaning" is conveyed to the listener by musical tones, the meaning must lie beyond or below the world of logic and rationality. A simpler way of dealing with the question of the meaning of music is to deny that music has any meaning at all; it merely gives the ear pleasure or does not, exactly as would a bit of food on the tongue. From this point of view, the composer of music is a cook of sorts, concerned with the pleasures of the ear rather than those of the palate. But if this is so, why has music always been venerated and musicians cultivated or even worshipped? Why do certain kinds of music seem to touch at once on the heights of sublimity and the depths of significance?

In the seventeenth century, Leibniz gave a Pythagorean answer to the question of musical meaning. Musical beauty, he says, is constituted by the harmony of numbers, unconsciously apprehended by the human mind. The whole charm of music lies in the apprehension of these numbers. Schopenhauer, citing Leibniz's definition of music as "an occult exercise of arithmetic by a mind unaware that it is counting" (*exercitium arithmeticae occultum nescientis se numerare animi*), remarks that it is correct as far as it goes. Yet it fails to explain why music is capable of moving us so profoundly. Leibniz is quite right insofar as the external, empirical aspect of music is concerned, for music does indeed offer us the possibility of "grasping, immediately and in the concrete, very large numbers and complex numerical relations, which we can otherwise know only indirectly by conceptual comprehension." Music is, so to speak, a philosophy of numbers translated from an abstract into a concrete world. Just as a mathematical genius might be able to construct an abstract model of the world-as-representation using only the forms of space and time and the category of causality, so a musician of genius is actually able to construct a concrete model of another world. But what kind of world? Schopenhauer gives the answer we might expect. Music, he says, speaks to us in a "universal language" and utters the meaning of the "inmost being of the world and of our own self." Unlike the plastic and pictorial arts, unlike the verbal arts, music bypasses the world-as-representation and speaks directly from and to the world-as-will. It is the voice of that world, the voice of the will. Since the world-as-representation is the objective manifestation of the world-as-will, the structure of the two worlds is identical. Hence, says Schopenhauer, if we were ever to succeed in working out a "perfectly accurate and complete explanation of music . . . this would also be at once a sufficient repetition and explanation of the world in concepts." Consequently, the definition of music offered by Leibniz ought to be reformulated as follows: "Music is an unconscious exercise in metaphysics in which the mind does not know that it is philosophizing."[32]

Schopenhauer recognizes that his explanation of the nature of music is not only insusceptible of proof but obscure and even paradoxical in the light of his philosophy. For the explanation seeks to establish music as a representation of the unrepresentable. He is face to face again with the paradox that had arisen in the course of his attempt to probe into the will when he had tried to show how the intellect, momentarily free from servitude, could turn inward and grasp the true nature of its master. Reconsidering the matter, he admits later in his life that we can, strictly speaking, know our inmost will only as representation. It remains nonetheless the only representation or phenomenon whose inner nature is at all accessible to us, the closest we can come to grips

32. *Ibid.*, I, 357, 369–70.

with the elusive thing-in-itself. As for his explanation of music, Schopenhauer freely admits that his account of musical meaning lacks true philosophical rigor. For him it sufficed, and for his readers it will stand or fall to the extent that they find his "single thought" valid or invalid.[33]

A corollary to Schopenhauer's explanation may have suggested itself to the reader. Does it not imply that music is a preeminently Jewish art? That music, which "seems to speak to us of worlds other and better than our own," can in fact do no more than "flatter the will to live" is, says Schopenhauer, a paradox. Music is incapable of denying the will because it is the expression of the will.[34] Music is, we may add, the song of the unconscious will, forever celebrating the very world that Schopenhauer himself finds deserving of annihilation. The suspicion that music might, after all, be unworthy of the high position he had accorded to it seems to have come to Schopenhauer as an afterthought, and it cannot be said that he sets the mind of the reader at rest with respect to the matter.

Does Schopenhauer really say anything about music that had not been said by others long before him? Does not Schopenhauer himself cite Plato's remark that the movement of melody somehow suggests the movement of a mind aroused by passion, and does he not recall Aristotle's question as to how it is that sounds, in the form of melody and rhythm, can so resemble states of the soul? And is it not a philosophical commonplace, as Schopenhauer himself admits, that music is the language of feeling and passion, just as the word is the language of reason? In answer to these questions it can be said that Schopenhauer succeeds in clearly articulating the important distinctions between the logical, rational, mathematical *structure* of music and its alogical, arational *meaning*. The structure of a musical composition, in whole or part, is susceptible of rational analysis. We can talk about it. But the *meaning* of music can only be felt. And the meaning of music is what music is all about. The structure is only a vehicle or garment to carry or clothe the meaning. The structure of music is articulated by the intellect, but the meaning is given by the will. The distinction is like that drawn between the world-as-representation and the world-as-will, the one governed by the forms of space and time and the category of

33. *Ibid.*, I, 358, 359; II, 632.
34. *Ibid.*, II, 586.

causality—a logically structured world—and the other free of those restraints, but free at the price of formlessness. The unique feature of music is that it functions to channelize meaning from the nether realm to the upper world.

There are two passages in *The World as Will and Representation* so deeply evocative of Wagner's music that they deserve quotation in full. The first will perhaps call *Tristan and Isolde* to mind:

Now the nature of human beings is such that the will strives, becomes satisfied, and strives anew, and so on indefinitely; indeed happiness and well-being consist only in that the transition from wish to satisfaction, and from this to a new wish, takes place rapidly (since the absence of satisfaction is suffering and the empty longing for a new wish is boredom and languor). Correspondingly, the essence of melody is a perpetual deviation and divergence from the tonic along a thousand paths, not only to the harmonic intervals, the third and the dominant but also to every tone, to the dissonant seventh and to the extreme intervals; yet a return to the tonic always follows. In all these ways the melody expresses the manifold striving of the will and, through the eventual rediscovery of a harmonic interval or, even more so, of the tonic, its satisfaction. The invention of melody, the disclosure in it of all the deepest secrets of human willing and feeling, is the work of genius. . . . The composer reveals the inmost essence of the world and expresses the deepest wisdom in a language that his reason does not understand; in the same way a magnetic somnambulist gives information about things that she has no idea of when awake.[35]

The second passage is even more remarkable. It amounts to a musical cosmology:

In the lowest harmonic tones I recognize the lowest stages of the objectivation of the will: the mass of the planet, inorganic nature. As is well known, all the higher tones, moving easily and dying away more rapidly, are considered to arise from secondary vibrations of the fundamental bass tone; when it sounds they always sound gently along with it. A law of harmony requires that a bass note be accompanied only by the higher tones that are already of themselves sounding with it, due to secondary vibrations. These are its *sons harmoniques* or overtones. Now this is analogous to the necessary origin, by stepwise development, of the totality of bodies and organizations in nature from the mass of the planet, which is their support and source. The higher tones have a similar relation to their ground bass.[36]

35. *Ibid.*, I, 363.
36. *Ibid.*, 360. This is strictly true only for the Pythagorean scale, in which all tones are derived from the interval of the pure fifth; in the well-tempered scale the spiral of fifths is made into a circle by deviating from the pure interval.

Bearing in mind Wagner's previously cited statement to Liszt in 1853 that the *Ring* poem embraced "the beginning and the end of the world," it is difficult to escape the conclusion that the above lines inspired the opening bars of *The Rhinegold*. A prolonged E-flat, sounded in the lowest orchestral register, is first heard. It rises an interval of a fifth to the nearest overtone, B-flat, the dominant of the scale, then to E-flat one octave higher, then to G. Other instruments gradually join in, and the notes of the E-flat major triad are repeated in succession, over and over again, until a full orchestral crescendo is reached. A sudden break in the music then occurs. It is followed by the voice of a Rhine maiden, coming in on the supertonic, the "dominant of the dominant" as it has been called. The score was completed in January, 1854. But in his autobiography, we recall, Wagner stated that it was not until the summer of 1854 that he became acquainted with Schopenhauer's writings.[37]

Perhaps a buried remembrance of what Wagner had merely glanced at in passing helped fertilize the soil in which the opening of *The Rhinegold* germinated and reached fruition. Wagner's account of his mental state when the musical inspiration came to him is itself interesting, especially in the light of Schopenhauer's theory of music. In September, 1853, he had set out alone for Italy. He traveled from Zurich to Geneva, reached Turin on a mailcoach that passed over Mount Cenis, and hurried on to Genoa. From there he took a steamer to Spezia. Depressed, restless, ill from a combination of dysentery and seasickness, he lay on his hard bed in a noisy hotel. Then, he tells us, he fell into "a kind of somnambulistic state" (*eine Art von somnambulem Zustand*)—not a "somnolent state," as the authorized translation has it:

I suddenly experienced a feeling as if I were sinking in swiftly flowing water. Its rustling noise soon presented itself as the musical sound of the E-flat major chord ceaselessly rocking away in broken figures; these broken figures showed themselves as melodic passages of increasing movement, but the pure E-flat major triad never changed and seemed to wish to give the element

37. Wagner, *Mein Leben*, II, Chap. 2, note 93; Wagner, *Richard Wagners Briefe*, IX, Pt. 1, p. 209, Pt. 2, pp. 3, 42. Strictly true only for the Pythagorean scale: see Percy Goetschius, *The Material Used in Musical Composition* (New York, 1913), 3–6, 131–33. For the thematic musical structure of the *Ring*, see Curt von Westernhagen, *The Forging of the "Ring": Richard Wagner's Composition Sketches for "Der Ring des Nibelungen,"* trans. Arnold and Mary Whittall (Cambridge, Eng., 1976). For a similar account of *The Rhinegold* prelude, see Paul Bekker, *The Story of the Orchestra* (New York, 1936), 181–83.

in which I sank an infinite significance. With the feeling that the waves were now foaming high over me, I awoke in sudden terror from my half-sleep. I recognized at once that the overture to *The Rhinegold*, which I had been carrying about, although I had been unable to find it exactly, had risen up within me; and I quickly comprehended also what relevance it had generally: not from the outside but only from within would the stream of life flow to me.

This event was the miracle for which Wagner's "subconscious mind" had been crying out for so many weary months."[38]

6. WAGNER'S THEORY OF MUSIC

Wagner's major contribution to the philosophy of musical meaning appeared in 1870 on the occasion of the centennial celebration of Beethoven's birth. A considerable part of this unique essay deals with Beethoven's crucial position, both as man and musician, in the history of music. Wagner's account is based on Schopenhauer's theory of musical meaning, as well as on his own ideas concerning revolutionary breakthroughs in general. By bringing Schopenhauer's theory of musical meaning into a more intimate relationship with his theory of dreams, Wagner anticipated the Freudian explanations of musical meaning that were to be forthcoming some sixty years later.[39]

Wagner begins his explanation where Schopenhauer stopped. Schopenhauer had said that a part of the brain remained active during dream-filled sleep to receive and work up impressions originating within the dreamer's body, just as another part of the brain dealt (in the course of waking life) with impressions derived from the external world. Schopenhauer had also explained why the pictures created by our dream-organ (*Traumorgan*) required interpretation before they could be understood, why the message of the unconscious will could be delivered only in "allegorical" form:

The dream message conceived by this inner organ could be delivered only by way of a second dream, immediately prior to waking; this dream could transmit the true content of the first dream in allegorical form only; for at this point, in the course of the full awakening of the brain to the outside world be-

38. Wagner, *Mein Leben*, II, 511–12; Richard Wagner, *My Life* (2 vols.; New York, 1911), II, 602–603; Newman, *Life*, II, 388–90.

39. Wagner, *Gesammelte Schriften*, IX, 61–126. Willy Bardas, "Zur Problematik der Musik," *Imago*, V (1917), 364–71, and Frieda Teller, "Musikgenuss und Phantasie," *Imago*, V (1917), 8–15. Teller mentions Wagner's essay briefly.

ing readied and at last taking place, it became necessary to apply the forms of our knowledge of the phenomenal world in accordance with space and time; a picture concordant throughout with everyday life-experience had thus to be constructed.

But, adds Wagner, it is not only the internal world that reaches us at second remove; the external world, too, first presents itself as a mere show or play of pictures (*Schauspiel*). And did not Faust cry out for something more? To this cry, music responds with the utmost confidence:

The external world speaks to us here with such matchless clarity because, by means of the effect of sound on our ears, it communicates precisely that which we ourselves, from the most profound depths of our inner being, call out to the world. Without conceptual mediation of any kind, we understand the utterance of the cry of help, woe or joy received and answer it at once, in the corresponding sense.[40]

In the sound-world any doubt on our part that the fundamental being of the external world differs from our own being—that is, the internal world—has no place. The gulf present in the light-world does not exist. The art of music makes us immediately aware of the essential unity of inner and outer being. In words that call to mind Tristan's response to Kurwenal in the third act of *Tristan and Isolde*, Wagner says that, when the individual will *sees*, it looks into a world beyond space and time:

What it sees there cannot be communicated in any spoken language. Just as dreams in the state of deepest sleep can pass over into the waking consciousness only when they are translated, immediately before waking, into the language of a second (allegorical) dream, so also the will creates a second organ of communication for the immediate depiction of its vision of itself. While one side of this organ is turned toward the inner vision, the other, through the uniquely immediate and sympathetic heralding of tone, makes contact with the external world, which again presents itself on waking. The will calls out, and in the answering call it recognizes itself. Call and answering call thus become a consoling and, in the end, enchanting form of play of the will with itself.[41]

To clarify his meaning, Wagner offers two brief anecdotes. Once,

40. Wagner, *Gesammelte Schriften*, IX, 71, 108–109; Wagner cites Goethe, *Faust*, I, ll. 454–55.
41. Wagner, *Gesammelte Schriften*, IX, 73–74.

during a sleepless night in Venice, he had stepped out on the balcony of his room over the Grand Canal. The silence covering the sleeping city was suddenly broken by the rough, plaintive call of a gondolier. Echoing through the labyrinth of canals, that call evoked a succession of counter calls from fellow gondoliers. At last Wagner recognized the "immemorially ancient melodic phrase to which the familiar verses of Tasso had been set in his time . . . one surely as old as the canals of Venice and their inhabitants." The dialogue grew livelier and the voices seemed to merge into unison; at last sleep again brought silence over the city. What, asks Wagner, could waking Venice utter that would bear comparison in depth and immediacy with this "night-dream of tones?" The second story is of a similar experience in the canton of Uri. Wagner had once been present when Swiss herdsmen were calling back and forth across the vast silences of the Alpine valleys; he had been affected exactly as in Venice. Of these near mystical experiences, Wagner writes:

Just so the child wakes from the night of the mother's womb with a cry of longing, answered by the soothing caress of the mother; just so the passionate youth understands the mating call of the forest bird; so, too, speak the plaintive calls of animals and winds and the howl of the hurricane to the meditating man—over whom then comes that dream-like state in which he understands through the ear what his sight, by the fraud of distraction (*in der Täuschung der Zerstreutheit*), had kept from him, namely that his inmost being is one with the inmost being of all that he perceives and that only with this understanding does the being of things external really become known to him.[42]

Wagner compares the birth of music to the birth of a child; the voice issuing from the unconscious will is like the primal scream of an infant in transit from the dark night of the womb to the bright, hateful light of day. Throughout our lives such calls well up from the depths. The musician transforms the inchoate, infantile cry into a coherent structure of sound. By virtue of its nature and origin, then, music carries an almost unbearable weight of meaning, no less heavy because it is—like the mystical experience itself—ineffable. Wagner's Schopenhauerian metaphysics gives depth to his vision of the world. The meaning of music is *reality*. The world of the eye—the light-world, the world of

---

42. *Ibid.*, 74–75. Appropriate lines from William Wordsworth or Lord Byron will occur to the reader. See Schopenhauer, *Sämtliche Werke*, I, 260, for Byron.

the idea or intellect, the world as phenomenon or representation—is seen as a world of illusory appearances, a falsely or at least superficially discriminated surface world overlying a deep unity. As Schopenhauer often repeats, *tat tvam asi*, "that art thou." In crying out to its God, the soul is crying out to itself. The world we know is a fraud, most of us would agree, in many senses. But what Wagner means is that the visible world (which is also the world of words) is a *transcendental* fraud, a fraud in the Kantian sense. This revelation is brought home to us by the art of tones.

7. THE MEANING OF BEETHOVEN

Before turning to Wagner's assessment of Beethoven's music, some comments of Schopenhauer on musicians are worth noting. In the first volume of *The World*, Schopenhauer is loudest in praise of Gioacchino Rossini: his music "speaks its own language, so distinctly and purely that it needs no words at all." Imitative or onomatopoetic music, as well as music that relies on words, meets with Schopenhauer's disapproval. For this reason he censures certain passages in Haydn; Beethoven, too, was at times guilty of writing imitative music; Rossini (and Mozart) never. But in the second volume of *The World*—the first volume antedated Beethoven's death by eight years, the second postdated it by seventeen—the great composer comes into his own. Schopenhauer has now recognized the peculiar force of Beethoven's music. Beethoven's symphonies give voice to the whole range of human passions: "joy, grief, love, hate, fear, hope and so on." More than this, the symphonies offer us a "true and complete image of the world, rolling on in the boundless whirl of illimitable forms, and maintaining itself through perpetual destruction."[43] From the special attention given Beethoven's music by Schopenhauer in the volume of 1844, we may infer that he found it the best exemplification of his own philosophy of music.

In the case of Wagner there is no room for doubt. Beethoven was for him the supreme musician of the present age, just as Giovanni Palestrina and Johann Sebastian Bach had been supreme in theirs. Beethoven, as Wagner saw it, had freed music from the chains of formality in order to express the world's inner turmoil and expose the driving unconscious *will* as the ontic foundation of the world. But—as will ap-

---

43. Schopenhauer, *Sämtliche Werke*, I, 365; II, 577; V, 507.

pear in Wagner's discussion of the C-sharp Minor String Quartet—after having unleashed these terrific forces, Beethoven was still able to master them. In so doing Beethoven accomplished something analogous to the Schopenhauerian denial of the will; the forces released were in the end quieted. Beethoven the man was, says Wagner, one with Beethoven the musician. For he had led a life that openly denied the will to power still dominant in the crumbling structure of Europe. Unlike Mozart and Haydn, Beethoven was no musician-lackey whose task was to supply entertainment to a display-loving aristocracy. Mozart remained "true to his emperor," says Wagner, and his reward was a pauper's death. Beethoven, on the other hand, remained a free spirit: a few well-disposed aristocrats "pledged themselves to keep Beethoven free, as he desired."[44]

To Wagner, Beethoven's very deafness makes him the prototype of the musician as seer. A blind painter is hardly conceivable, says Wagner, reverting again to the Oedipus story: "But we recognize the blind seer (*Seher*) Tiresias, to whom the world of appearance was closed, and who became aware, in return, of the ground of all appearance with his inner eye. He has his counterpart in the deaf musician who, undisturbed now by the world's clamor, listens henceforth to his inner harmonies alone. To that world, which has nothing more to say to him, he still speaks—but only from the depths."[45] The blind seer reports in words what he sees with his inner eye; the deaf musician-seer reports in tones what he hears with his inner ear.

Wagner then turns to Beethoven's C-sharp Minor String Quartet. His words are well known but nevertheless worth presenting here in context:

The rather long introductory Adagio—surely the most melancholy thing that has ever been expressed in tones—I would characterize as an awakening on the morning of a day "which in its long course will not fulfill a single wish, not one!"[46] Yet it is at the same time a prayer of repentance, a counsel with God, in the belief of eternal goodness. Here the inward directed eye perceives a consolatory appearance recognizable to it alone (Allegro 6/8), in which the longing becomes a mournfully pleasing play with itself: the inmost dream picture awakens as the loveliest of recollections. And now (with the short transitional Allegro moderato) it is as if the Master, aware of his craft, has put

44. Wagner, *Gesammelte Schriften*, IX, 88, 91.
45. *Ibid.*, 92.
46. Goethe, *Faust*, I, l. 1556.

himself to rights in his work of magic; he now exercises (Andante 2/4) the renewed power of the magic that is his alone to summon up a charming figure, the blissful witness of inmost innocence, in order to enrapture himself without end over the ever new and unheard of changes brought about by the prismatic breakup of the eternal light that he throws over it. We believe that we now see him casting an unspeakable exhilarated glance at the outer world, deeply happy from within (Presto 2/2). Once again the world stands before him as it did in the Pastoral Symphony. All is illuminated by inner joy; it is as if he were hearing the very tones of airy, yet solid appearances moving before him in a rhythmic dance. He looks on life and seems to consider how to go about striking up a dance tune for life itself (short Adagio 3/4): a short but clouded meditation, as if he were plunging into the deep dream of his soul. A glance has again shown him the inner side of the world; he wakes, and now he strikes the strings in dance music such as the world has never heard (Allegro finale). This is the dance of the world itself: mad pleasure, painful lament, love's ecstasy, highest bliss, misery, rage, lust and sorrow. Lightning strikes and the storm thunders. And above all is the monstrous minstrel who conjures up and controls all that he proudly and securely conducts from whirlpool to vortex to abyss: he smiles to himself, for to him this conjuring is but play. So night beckons. His day is done.[47]

Schopenhauer might have found this too psychologically oriented for his taste. But he would not have quarreled with the close, where the musician, after having conjured up a vision of all the passion and torment of the world, dismisses the whole show of things as mere play— in the manner of Shakespeare bringing *The Tempest* to an end.

Wagner was perhaps trying to extract from the C-sharp Minor String Quartet the musical equivalent of Schopenhauer's philosophy of life. And since the ethical imperative of that philosophy was the denial of the will to live, what did the quartet mean in that respect? Wagner did not pose the question. But it is plain that for him Beethoven is a Tiresias of music who has recognized and depicted the true "inner nature" of the world, who has conjured up from his own depths the driving tones equivalent to the nearly insane turmoil assailing his inner ear. The musician-creator Beethoven ends by dismissing the show of things as a mere dream of passion. That world is Maya. While we are left uncertain whether the will has been denied, we are fairly sure that it has not been affirmed. Wagner's closing words suggest a mood of detached irony.

It was Beethoven's Ninth Symphony that carried the heaviest load

47. Wagner, *Gesammelte Schriften*, IX, 96–97.

of meaning for Wagner, and it was with this symphony that he strug-
gled to come to terms throughout his entire life. As a youth of seventeen (at a time, according to Newman, when the Ninth Symphony and
the last quartets of Beethoven were virtually unplayable for many per-
formers and misunderstood even by musicians of the caliber of Hector
Berlioz), Wagner made a piano arrangement, still extant, of the Ninth.
The Ninth Symphony was still almost an unknown quantity when
Wagner conducted it in Dresden on Palm Sunday, 1846. And it was the
Ninth Symphony that Wagner, as Royal *Kapellmeister*, chose to conduct at Dresden on Palm Sunday, 1849—six weeks before he became a
fugitive from the police of Saxony because of his participation in the
aborted revolution. When he had concluded the symphony, so Wagner
wrote in the 1860s, the giant anarchist Michael Bakunin came up to
congratulate him, calling out "in a loud voice that if all music should
be lost in the expected world-conflagration, we should bind ourselves
to guarantee its preservation, even at the risk of our lives."[48]

Central to the story of Wagner's perennial concern with the meaning
of the Ninth Symphony are his two interpretations of Beethoven's introduction, in the fourth movement, of words into the heretofore purely
tonal fabric of the symphony. The words were taken from Schiller's
"Ode to Joy" (*An die Freude*), that memento of late eighteenth-century
optimism. They sing of the brotherhood of humanity that is to come
after the stifling bonds of convention (*Mode*) have been thrown off.
Wagner's two interpretations—the one Feuerbachian, the other Schopenhauerian—lie twenty years apart. We shall see that in these interpretations Wagner assimilates musical, psychological, and social organization, the structure of one mirroring the structure of the others.

In "The Art-Work of the Future" (1850), Wagner tells us that Beethoven's goal, in the long musical journey from the First to the Ninth
Symphony, was the discovery of a new land, "the land of the human
beings of the future":

On a giant ship, strongly built, and tightly joined, he set forth on this stormy
voyage; with a sure hand he gripped the mighty helm; he knew the goal of the
journey. . . . He wanted to measure the boundaries of the ocean and find the

48. Newman, *Life*, I, 128–33, II, 633; Wagner, *Mein Leben*, I, 397–98.

land that must lie beyond the watery wastes. Thus the Master forced his way through the most unheard of possibilities of absolute tonal language . . . to the point where the mariner begins to measure the sea's depths with his plumb line . . . where he must decide whether to cast anchor in the new harbor or turn back to the bottomless ocean. But it was not raw sea fever that had driven the Master on so far a voyage; he must and would land in the new world, for only in search of it had he undertaken the voyage. Boldly he dropped anchor, and the anchor was the *word*. . . . This word was: joy! (*Freude*)[49]

Freude, the first word of Schiller's "Ode to Joy," is also the first word heard in the Ninth Symphony; it is then repeated by several voices, as if they were calling back and forth to each other, before the subsequent words of the poem are heard. Earlier in the essay, Wagner has told us that, where pure tonal expression reaches its limit, speech makes its appearance. The goal of Beethoven's voyage might be stated, in terms of Wagner's program of a few years later, as a breakthrough from the unconscious to the conscious or as a transformation of the unconscious into the conscious. Wagner's metaphor recalls Goethe's *Faust*: the dikes that Faust has built will, he hopes, allow the conversion of the swampy wastes of the lowlands into a "land of paradise" (*paradiesisch Land*) in which a "boldly active" people will dwell. And the metaphor appears again in 1923 when Freud compares the task of transforming id into ego with that of draining the Zuyder Zee.[50]

The Ninth Symphony, as Wagner understands it in 1850, is the gospel of the artwork of the future; and it is linked to the coming transformation of humanity. For this transformation to become possible, a revolutionary breakthrough must take place: music must deny its very essence.[51] And the essence of music is its sole reliance on the expressive power of pure tone:

Beethoven's last symphony represents the saving release (*Erlösung*) of music from its own most characteristic feature, i.e. reliance on pure tone, so that it becomes a universal art. This symphony is the *human* gospel ("*menschliches*" *Evangelium*) of the art of the future. Beyond it no progress, i.e. purely musical progress, is possible, for after it only the perfected art-work of the future, the

49. Wagner, *Gesammelte Schriften*, III, 95–96.
50. *Ibid.*, 63–64; Goethe, *Faust*, II, ll. 11563–69.
51. I have taken the term *breakthrough* (*Durchbruch*) from Mann's discussion of the fictional symphonic cantata, "The Lament of Doctor Faustus" (*Doktor Fausti Weheklag*), composed by Adrian Leverkühn as a negative image of the Ninth Symphony. See Thomas Mann, *Doktor Faustus* (Stockholm, 1951), 723.

universalized drama to which Beethoven has forged for us the key, can follow.[52]

Music alone of the Muses has broken through the bonds of outworn convention; in a gesture of "magnanimous and loving self-sacrifice," she has denied herself and extended a "saving hand" to her sisters.[53] We see that for the Wagner of 1850, music is already the Antigone of the Muses, defying the rules laid down by Creon. Likewise, Beethoven is already the Siegfried of the *Ring*, shattering Wotan's spear with its rune-engraved conventions.

When we turn from the Wagner of 1850 to the Wagner of 1870, two questions present themselves. What changes will be necessitated in the interpretation of the Ninth Symphony by his shift from a Feuerbachian to a Schopenhauerian standpoint? And which of these will he recognize? Since the Schopenhauerian view gives precedence to tonal language over verbal language, he cannot, it would seem, say that the cry *Freude*! heralds the discovery of land in the "watery wastes." He cannot exalt a breakthrough from the inarticulate depths of the will to the discursive realm of the intellect. Schopenhauer has taught him that the surface world is Maya, the mere show of things. Nor can he, if consistent, find in the Ninth Symphony a life-affirming, this-worldly, *politically* meliorative message of human brotherhood. He can, however, still accept Schiller's message, but with a difference. In accordance with Schopenhauer's thought, the bond of union—no longer *Freude* (joy), but *Mitleid* (sympathy)—must unite not only human beings but *all* living things. And the mood of union becomes one of renunciation rather than jubilation.

The Ninth Symphony, Wagner tells us in 1870, begins with a depiction of the "idea of the world in its most horrifying light." Rage and despair are expressed in turn by the music until the fourth movement, with its verbal interjection, arrives. Then, says Wagner, it is as if Beethoven calls out—to someone "awakening from a frightful dream with a cry of anguish"—"Yet the human being *is* good!" Beethoven, after depicting or rather expressing the torment of the world, has made a "leap of desperation" and reached a "new world of light." On the soil of this new world, the "long sought-for and divinely sweet melody of human-

52. Wagner, *Gesammelte Schriften*, III, 96.
53. *Ibid.*, 96–97.

ity, pure and free of guilt, blossomed forth." The saving message is now carried by Beethoven's *tones* rather than Schiller's *words*: "It is quite obvious that Schiller's words are subsumed under the leading melody in a makeshift way, indeed with little care; for that melody, carried by the orchestral instruments alone, was previously unfolded in its full breadth, and it filled us then with a nameless feeling of joy over the paradise regained."[54]

In Wagner's new interpretation of the Ninth Symphony, only the breakthrough that he had envisioned in 1850 is negated. The message of hope still remains valid.[55] Music is now the supreme art, triumphing over the word. But in view of Schopenhauer's admission that music could not but flatter the will even when it seemed to speak of worlds better than our own, a difficulty presents itself. If the good news is uttered by Beethoven's music rather than by Schiller's words, may this not mean that the paradise of which the music speaks is another fraud, a "flattering" message? Wagner passed over the difficulty. Otherwise he would have been forced to conclude that music, the supreme art, was life affirming in its essence and "Jewish" or "Hellenic" in spirit.

Wagner was as convinced in 1870 as he had been twenty years earlier that European civilization, corrupt to the core, was moving toward a terrible catastrophe. In his early years he had believed that rational reform of the social order along communal lines would be sufficient to usher in the new world, and this was the message he found in the Ninth Symphony. The triumph of reaction after 1849 convinced him that this was not to be. Acquaintance with the thought of Schopenhauer helped persuade him that it was not even to be desired. A reform of the kind he had hoped for in the 1840s—any such reform, in fact—would merely divert, and in no way check or abolish, the aggressive drives of an egoistic, selfish European civilization. A kingdom of this world would not suffice. The salvation of Europe lay in a revival of the spirit of music, a necessary preliminary for which was the release of music from the bonds of mode, fashion, or convention.

The centennial celebration of Beethoven's birth coincided with the outbreak of the Franco-Prussian War. Identifying the French world with

54. *Ibid.*, 69–71.
55. Leverkühn, in Mann's *Doktor Faustus*, aims to "retract" the Ninth Symphony in his own composition. The humane (*das Menschliche*) is *not to be*, he says (p. 712).

mode and the German with freedom, Wagner saw the penetration of France by German arms as a symbol of the previous penetration of a congealed civilization by the liberating spirit of Beethoven's music:

There, at the original seat of "insolent mode" where our weapons now are penetrating, his genius had already initiated the noblest conquest of all. What our philosophers and poets touched on with vague, laboriously transmitted and half-understood words, Beethoven's symphony had already stirred to the very depths: the new religion, the world-redeeming gospel of sublimest innocence, was already understood there as with us. So let us honor the great pathbreaker in the wilderness of the degenerated paradise! But let us honor him as he deserves—no less deserving than the triumph of German valor. For the world-benefactor ranks even before the world-conqueror![56]

The phrase "insolent mode" (*freche Mode*) in the above citation has a curious history, recounted by Wagner. In Schiller's poem the word *strict* (*streng*) is used to characterize the mode, custom, or convention that has hitherto isolated the members of various strata of society. Beethoven found the word too weak and substituted *insolent* (*frech*). Do we not, asks Wagner, see Luther standing in front of us, inveighing against the pope? But then some misguided soul replaced *insolent* with *strict* in the collected edition of Beethoven's works published by Härtel. In any case, says Wagner, the moribund civilization of Europe can be revived only by "the spirit of our music, the music that Beethoven freed from the bonds of mode." And the task of introducing the "new religion" to the "new, more spiritual civilization" that it will shape is a German task.[57] Wagner may remind some of us of the Indian idealist who confronted an elephant: confronted by the Juggernaut of destruction approaching to crush Europe, Wagner offers to strike up a tune.

What else can be said of the musical bond that will unite in brotherhood the human beings who have been freed from the bonds of outworn custom to participate in the religion of the future? Something that is perhaps disquieting, for Wagner tells us that Beethoven's dissolution of mode will lead to a strictly determined style:

For the most important determining factor in Beethoven's music with respect to the history of art is this, that here every technical artistic detail, through which the artist is placed in a conventional relationship to the world in order

56. Wagner, *Gesammelte Schriften*, IX, 125–26.
57. *Ibid.*, 122–23.

to be understood, is raised to the highest importance as an immediate expression. As I have said elsewhere, here there is no ornamentation or framing of the melody; instead all becomes melody, every voice in the accompaniment, every note, even the pauses themselves.

The quirks of the dialectic of freedom, then, are such that Beethoven, the man who freed music, placed it under absolutely binding constraints. Not even the silences are free, much less the tones.[58]

The difference between the Wagner of 1850 and the Wagner of 1870 is most evident in his denial that the new kingdom will be of this world. Just as Christianity once broke through the crumbling facade of the Roman world, so in our time music offers us the hope of salvation from the ''chaos'' of the modern world. But it is only a hope. For if ''social communism'' succeeds in ''mastering the modern world in the sense of a practical religion,'' then we shall indeed be confronted by a kingdom of this world.[59] Twenty years earlier Wagner would have looked on this possibility with some favor. But now, under the influence of Schopenhauer, ''social communism'' is for him merely a variant form of egoism, one in which the group replaces the individual ego. We might call it ''social egoism'': the tyrant *will* remains in control and ruthlessly continues to pursue its ends.

To what kind of paradise had Beethoven pointed the way? Wagner answers that it is a lost paradise:

If we want to picture for ourselves a true paradise of human spiritual productivity, we have to put ourselves back in the times before the discovery of letters and their registry on parchment or paper. We must find that here the whole of cultural life was born, a life that now is maintained only as an object of study or purposeful application. Poesy too was at that time nothing other than the actual invention of myths, of ideal models, that is, in which human life, in keeping with its various features, was mirrored as objective reality, as immediate apparitions of the mind. We see that every nobly consti-

---

58. *Ibid.*, 87. See Leverkühn on the dialectics of musical freedom in Mann's *Doktor Faustus*. The ''emancipation of dissonance'' brought about by freedom from convention inevitably leads to ''forced order'' (289–91). Mann borrowed the idea from Theodor Adorno, who held that in our time music had fallen victim to historical dialectics: Schoenberg's twelve-tone technique ''puts music in chains, even as it sets it free'' (*fesselt die Musik, indem sie sie befreit*). See Theodor Adorno, *Philosophie der neuen Musik* (Tübingen, 1949), 44. In this essay Adorno's debt to Wagner's ''sociology'' of music, the music of Beethoven in particular, is everywhere evident but nowhere acknowledged.

59. Wagner, *Gesammelte Schriften*, IX, 119–20.

tuted folk has this native ability, down to the point in time when the use of letters arrives. From that time on its poetic power dwindles; language, which was until then taking shape, as if it were alive, in a steady process of natural development, deteriorates and stiffens in a process of crystallization; the poetic art becomes the art of decking out the old myths, now no longer to be invented anew, and ends as rhetoric and dialectic.[60]

We continued to make do, as best we could, with the legacy accumulated before the living word crystallized into frozen, dead conventional forms. But even this was not the end. Writing gave way to print, and print gave birth to journalism. Wagner continues to trace the decline and fall of Calliope from Muse of poetry to public prostitute:

Let us picture now the leap from letters to the printing of books. The head of the household read to his family and guests from a precious handwritten tome, but now everyone reads silently to himself from the printed book, and the writer now writes for the reader. One must recall the religious sects of Reformation times, with their disputations and petty tracts, to gain an idea of the madness of unreason that took power over the heads of men possessed by print. We may suppose that only Luther's glorious chorale rescued the healthy spirit of the Reformation, as it brought hearts into tune and thus healed brains of print-disease. Yet the genius of a people could still reach an understanding with the printer of books, deplorable as the association with him might be. But with the invention of newspapers, and the full bloom of journalism, this good spirit of the people had to withdraw from life entirely. For now only opinions still rule, "public," to be sure, and to be had for money, like public prostitutes. . . . If we now compare the transformation of the poetic world into the literary journalistic world with that which the world has undergone in form and color we find that exactly the same thing has taken place.[61]

This is the "degenerated paradise" in which we live and out of which Beethoven has pointed the way. Wagner is calling for the restoration of artistic creativity to the lives of the Nibelungs who inhabit that "paradise." A beautiful dream! It tells us that Wagner was too much the artist to choose between affirmation and denial of the world. What he chose instead was affirmation of the world as art.

60. *Ibid.*, 115–16.
61. *Ibid.*, 116.

Chapter IV

WHAT WENT WRONG

> Only then, when life turns back
> to its origin, can the world be saved.
> In symbolic form this is represented
> by the return of the ring (life) to its
> original home, out of which it was taken.
> Sabina Spielrein (1912)

1. HOW SHAW FISHED THE GOLD FROM THE RHINE

Two years after Wagner's death in Venice at the Palazzo
Vendramin-Calergi in 1883, George Bernard Shaw was to be found in
the Reading Room of the British Museum dividing his attention alter-
nately between Marx and Wagner. Although not aware of it, the twenty-
nine-year-old Shaw was soon to begin work on his first play, *Widowers'
Houses*. Here he would stamp a permanent impress of his own on the
legend of the treasure of the Rhine. *Widowers' Houses*, however, was
not finished and performed until 1892. In the preface (1893) Shaw included a long excerpt from an already published note by William Archer
that purported to give an account of the genesis of the play. Archer, a
daily frequenter of the Reading Room, stated in the note that in 1885
he had become aware of a "young man of tawny complexion and attire"
who was to be seen there day after day, assiduously studying the score
of *Tristan and Isolde* and the text (in French translation) of *Das Kapi-
tal*. Making his acquaintance soon after, Archer learned from Shaw
that he was the author of several unpublished masterpieces of fiction.
The two agreed to collaborate in writing plays. Archer was to furnish
plots; Shaw, dialogue. Archer's note continues:

So said, so done. I drew out, scene by scene, the scheme of a twaddling cup-and-saucer comedy vaguely suggested by Augier's *Ceinture Dorée*. The details I forget, but I know it was to be called Rhinegold, was to open, as *Widowers' Houses* actually does, in a hotel garden on the Rhine, and was to have two heroines, a sentimental and a comic one, according to the accepted Robertson-Byron-Carton formula. I fancy the hero was to propose to the sentimental heroine, believing her to be the poor niece instead of the rich daughter of the sweater, or slum landlord, or whatever he may have been, and was ultimately to succeed in throwing the tainted treasure of his father-in-law, metaphorically speaking, into the Rhine.[1]

After about six weeks Shaw informed him, continues Archer, that he had run out of plot but not finished the play. Archer told Shaw, in turn, that his plot was a "rounded and perfect whole" and that Shaw had failed to make proper use of it. The two men were unable to reach agreement, and their collaboration came to a speedy end. Shaw went on to say (in the preface to *Widowers' Houses*) that he had in fact taken Archer's plot as given, but that he himself could not accept the "renunciation" of the treasure as a suitable ending. Since Archer had been unwilling to supply a new one, he had to "fish up the tainted treasure out of the Rhine, so to speak, and make it last out another act and a half."[2]

Archer says in the note that his plot was only "vaguely suggested" by Emile Augier's *Ceinture Dorée*. Actually, the resemblance is very close. Augier's play was first produced in 1855. It is the story of an idealistic young man, Trélan, who has fallen in love with the daughter, Caliste, of a sharp financial practitioner by the name of Roussel. Some of Roussel's money is derived from slum rentals. In addition he had been responsible for the financial ruin of Trélan's father. Learning of all this, Trélan is no longer willing to marry Caliste, and he informs Roussel that his tainted fortune flows from a poisoned source (*source empoisonnée*). The repentant father is on the point of giving his money to the poor when war breaks out and he is ruined. Trélan and Caliste are reconciled, and the play ends.[3]

Why did Archer transfer the scene from Paris to the banks of the Rhine, making the metaphorical river into a real one? The likely ex-

1. William Archer, "*Widowers' Houses*," *World*, December 14, 1892, pp. 14–15.
2. George Bernard Shaw, *The Complete Prefaces of Bernard Shaw* (London, 1965), 699–700.
3. Emile Augier, *Théâtre Complet* (6 vols.; Paris, 1885–86), III, 291–425.

planation is that he was parodying Brünnhilde's disposal of the Nibe-lung's ring.[4] Archer could well have been struck by the curious resem-blance between one of the characters in Augier's play (who does not figure in *Widowers' Houses*) and Wagner himself. Landara, a musician and an unsuccessful suitor of Caliste, calls himself a member of the "ideological school" and believes that the time is ripe for music to take over the role of language as the chief instrument of thought. Gluck, Mozart, Gretry, and Rossini had musical genius, says Landara, but "they were not thinkers." Landara himself has written a "philosophical sym-phony" entitled "The Golden Calf." He explains to Roussel that noth-ing personal is meant. He is a moralist, not a satirist; he attacks vice, not the vicious (Roussel is offended nonetheless). Whether Augier ac-tually had Wagner in mind is questionable. Work on the *Ring* was, how-ever, well under way by 1855, and Wagner had announced his plans publicly as early as 1851. Something of Wagner's ideas on the nature of music-drama and on the evils of money may have been known to those with whom he had associated during his stays in Paris in 1839 and 1849.

Shaw, in *Widowers' Houses*, metaphorically fishes the tainted trea-sure out of the Rhine in a typically Shavian fashion. Sartorius, the slum landlord, points out to his daughter's idealistic young suitor, Dr. Harry Trench, that Trench's unearned income (the source of which Trench has never troubled to look into) is derived from a mortgage on Sartorius' own slum properties. Says Sartorius: "When I, to use your own words, screw, and bully and drive these people to pay me what they have freely undertaken to pay me, I cannot touch one penny of the money they give me until I have first paid you your seven hundred a year out of it." Seeing the error and impracticality of his ways, Harry joins hands in business with Sartorius and Lickcheese (Sartorius' for-mer hireling, who has branched out on his own) and takes up relations again with Sartorius' daughter, Blanche—or rather she, a typical Shavian woman, chooses to take up relations again with him.[5]

In an open letter dated December 19, 1892 (also excerpted in the pref-ace to *Widowers' Houses*), Shaw comments that Sartorius, his "house-

---

4. Archer's note in the *World* gives no explanation. For his comments on Wagner, see William Archer, *About the Theater: Essays and Studies* (London, 1886).

5. George Bernard Shaw, *The Bodley Head Bernard Shaw: Collected Plays and Prefaces*, ed. Dan H. Laurence (7 vols.; London, 1970–74), I, 47–121; see p. 93.

knacking widower," has been denounced by critics as a "monstrous libel on the middle and upper class, because he remorselessly grinds his money out of the poor." On the contrary, says Shaw, Sartorius is simply acting as he *has* to act, given the social system in which he finds himself. He is, in fact, a rather favorable member of his class. "I might have made him," writes Shaw, "a shareholder in a match factory where avoidable 'phossy jaw' is not avoided." And what of his critics? They live, Shaw answers, in "comfortable homes full of furniture made by 'slaughtered' (i.e. extra-sweated) cabinet-makers, and go to church on Sunday in shirts sewn by women who can only bring their wages up to subsistence by prostitution." And yet, he continues, they are "naïvely astonished and revolted at the spectacle of a man on the stage acting as we are all acting perforce every day." As for Dr. Harry Trench, "the highly connected young gentleman naturally straightforward and easygoing, who bursts into genuine indignation at the suffering of the poor, and, on being shown that he cannot help them, becomes honestly cynical and throws off all responsibility whatsoever, that is nothing but the reality of the everyday process known as disillusion." In a postscript added to the preface of *Widowers' Houses* in 1933, Shaw pointed out that the play had not become dated. Tenements and cellar dwellings in London were as overcrowded and bad as ever; one-family houses were now being partitioned, while their gardens and backyards were remodeled into so-called studios.[6]

2. SHAW AND WAGNER

Shaw made an appearance as Wagner's advocate in 1895 in response to Max Nordau's charge that Wagner, Henrik Ibsen, Leo Tolstoy, and William Morris, among others, were men with the "degenerate's incapacity for self-adaptation" and "deep, devouring discontent with existing facts." Shaw's essay entitled "A Degenerate's View of Nordau" appeared in the American anarchist periodical *Liberty* and is worth reading if only as evidence of Shaw's grasp of Wagner's strict style; that is, the "system, order, logic, symmetry, and syntax" of Wagner's compositional technique. In 1898 appeared the first edition of Shaw's *The Per-*

6. Shaw, *The Complete Prefaces*, 709–10, 714–15. The *Bodley Head Shaw* does not include Shaw's open letter and postscript.

fect Wagnerite: A Commentary on the Ring of the Niblungs. Shaw's involvement with the theme of Wagner's *Ring* over the next forty or more years can best be characterized in his own words as a continuing attempt to "fish up the tainted treasure out of the Rhine."[7]

Shaw remarks in the preface to the first edition of *The Perfect Wagnerite* that, as one who had learned in his youth more about music than anything else and sown his "political wild oats subsequently in the revolutionary school," he is well equipped to guide the reader through the intricacies of Wagner's *Ring*. Unfortunately, there are also reasons why Shaw is not always a reliable guide. Shaw's heroes are often men whose forte is getting things done—and, at times, never mind how. His heroines, also, are nothing if not effective. The Caesars and Napoleons of the world exerted, all too frequently, an irresistible command over Shaw's admiration. The "Shavian emphasis on effectiveness," says Alfred Turco, was responsible for Shaw's "flirtation, during the 1920s and 1930s, with dictators and fascists." In the heat of World War II, Sidney Hook was outspoken in his condemnation of Shaw's earlier remarks in favor of Stalin, Mussolini, and Hitler: Shaw, he charged in 1944, would not object to "efficient Hitlerism without heroics or race-nonsense."[8] This charge is not so shocking as it at first sight appears. Hitlerism was certainly not lacking in heroics or race-nonsense; and its boasted efficiency, other than in genocide, turned out to be more theatrical than real. Hook was merely saying, in his own fashion, that Shaw wanted society to be efficient at almost all costs and might be willing to accept dictatorial control at the top to ensure it. But for Shaw efficiency was not an end in itself. The everyday work of the world had to be carried out in one

7. George Bernard Shaw, "A Degenerate's View of Nordau," *Liberty*, July 27, 1895, pp. 2–10; published separately as *The Sanity of Art: An Exposure of the Current Nonsense About Artists Being Degenerates* (London, 1908). Shaw's *Major Critical Essays* (London, 1948) includes a version of *The Sanity of Art* and the fourth edition of *The Perfect Wagnerite*. George Bernard Shaw, *The Perfect Wagnerite: A Commentary on "The Ring of the Niblungs"* (London, 1898). The mistranslated title of the music-drama was corrected in the third and fourth editions.

8. George Bernard Shaw, *The Perfect Wagnerite: A Commentary on "The Ring of the Niblungs"* (Chicago & New York, 1899), vi. Alfred Turco, *Shaw's Moral Vision: The Self and Salvation* (Ithaca, N.Y., 1976), 11, 87. Freud may be included among those who "flirted" with Stalin and Mussolini in the 1930s. See Paul Roazen, *Freud and His Followers* (New York, 1971), 534. Sidney Hook, Review of Eric Russell Bentley's *A Century of Hero-Worship*, *Nation*, October 7, 1944, pp. 412–13.

way or another, and it was best all around for this work to be carried out efficiently. Shaw's dictator is simply a business manager, Carlyle's Plugson of St. Dolly Undershot as it were.

Shaw's account in *The Perfect Wagnerite* of the social revolutionary message of the *Ring* evidently came as an unpleasant surprise to some of his readers. Three years later in a second, unrevised edition of the work, Shaw offered a tongue-in-cheek apology to the offended readers, describing them as "people who cannot bear to be told that their hero was associated with a famous Anarchist . . . that he wrote revolutionary pamphlets; and that his picture of Nibelunghome under the reign of Alberic is a poetic vision of unregulated industrial capitalism as it was made known in Germany in the middle of the nineteenth century by Engels's Condition of the Laboring Classes in England."[9] In 1907 Shaw's friend Siegfried Trebitsch translated the second edition into German. Shaw provided the first German edition with a special preface. In addition he inserted a new chapter. An English version of the first German edition appeared in New York in 1909.[10]

A third English edition of *The Perfect Wagnerite* appeared in London and, under the Tauchnitz imprint, Leipzig in 1913. Its preface does not contain Shaw's remarks to the Germans contained in the preface to the first German edition, but it is otherwise unchanged. Passing over the New York version of the first German edition, Shaw states that the new chapter, "Why He Changed His Mind," has hitherto been available only in the German edition. As before, he explains that the new chapter or section has been added in order to show "how the revolutionary history of Western Europe from the Liberal explosion of 1848 to the confused attempt at a popular and *quasi* Socialist military and municipal administration by the Commune of Paris in 1871 . . . had demonstrated practically that the passing away of the present capitalistic order was going to be a much more complicated business than it appeared in Wagner's dramatization." But Shaw's account of things to come was promptly upset by the Great War, a catastrophe he seems not to have anticipated. In consequence, a fourth edition of *The Perfect Wagnerite*

9. Cited from the preface to the second edition contained in George Bernard Shaw, *The Perfect Wagnerite: A Commentary on the Niblung's Ring* (3rd rev. ed.; Leipzig, 1913), 12. This is a copyright edition.

10. George Bernard Shaw, *The Perfect Wagnerite: A Commentary on the Niblung's Ring* (New York, 1909). I have not seen the German edition.

made its appearance in 1923. In a new preface, Shaw says that the message of Wagner's *Ring* remains valid and important, even though the world is now such that "its craziness can be fitted into no allegory." What he does *not* tell the reader is that he has altered the second half of "Why He Changed His Mind" to conceal his disappointed hopes. The fourth edition, which is the only one in print today, contains the four prefaces written for the English editions.[11]

3. SHAW ON THE "RING"

In his remarks on the opening of *The Rhinegold*, Shaw displays some degree of sympathy with the plight of Alberich. Rejected and ridiculed as he was by those slippery females the Rhine maidens, what else could Alberich do, asks Shaw, than curse love and turn to the quest for gold and power? Alberich forswore love "as thousands of us forswear it every day." He is, says Shaw, like some coarse son of the people who has learned the hard lesson that only as a millionaire can he win a beautiful wife and gain access to refined society. Unlike his fellow Nibelungs, Alberich knows that money-power rules the world. He seizes the gold and makes the other Nibelungs his slaves. They are forced to work by the "invisible whip of starvation." Under the *Tarnkappe*, he himself becomes as invisible as the modern shareholder. All this is not a fable, says Shaw. It is "frightfully real, frightfully present, frightfully modern" and, to Wagner, intolerable as well. If we were a race of poets rather than a race of "moral dwarfs," we would make an end to it at once.[12]

Alberich's drive for limitless riches and power would lead to utter death and destruction were it not countered by an opposing force, that of Godhead represented by Wotan. But Godhead itself has been compromised in the struggle for dominance. At Wotan's behest the giants have built the fortress of Valhalla. Freia, the goddess of love and eternal youth, is their promised reward. The giants are unaware that Wotan and Loge have intended from the start to trick them out of their payment. Yet Wotan is the guardian of law, order, and contract. Loge—or Loki, as Shaw calls him—is the god of intellect and illusion. He also

11. Shaw, *The Perfect Wagnerite* (1913), 5–6. George Bernard Shaw, *The Perfect Wagnerite: A Commentary on the Niblung's Ring* (4th rev. ed.; London, 1923). The title of Friedrich Engels' book is given correctly in this edition. The fourth edition was reprinted in 1967 by Dover Publications (New York).

12. Shaw, *The Perfect Wagnerite* (1899), 11.

represents the lie—"a European power, as LaSalle said." The giants represent an aspect of the working classes, their power rather than their misery. After hearing from Loge of Alberich's riches, they agree to accept the gold in place of Freia. In doing so they stoop even lower than Alberich, since he "forswore love only when it was denied to him and made the instrument for cruelly murdering his self-respect."[13]

The guardian of law and order must now descend to the nether world and rob Alberich of his treasure. This world, says Shaw, need not be thought of as a mine; it "might just as well be a match-factory, with yellow phosphorus, phossy jaw, a large dividend, and plenty of clergymen shareholders." And in our day Alberich's *Tarnkappe* takes the form of a tall hat that makes a man "invisible as a shareholder, and changes him into various shapes, such as a pious Christian . . . a model husband and father, a shrewd, practical independent Englishman . . . when he is really a pitiful parasite on the commonwealth, consuming a great deal and producing nothing, feeling nothing, knowing nothing, believing nothing and doing nothing except what all the rest do."[14] The reference to the frightful industrial disease "phossy jaw," a scandal of the 1890s, recalls the defense of Sartorius in *Widowers' Houses*. Alberich is, plainly enough, a more malignant version of Sartorius.

Wotan and Loge descend to the underworld, where they are given a hostile reception by Alberich. Improvising rather freely at this point, Shaw says that Alberich boasts of the power that is his and "paints for them the world as it will be when his dominion over it is complete, when the soft airs and green mosses of its valleys shall be changed into smoke, slag and filth; when slavery, disease and squalor, soothed by drunkenness and mastered by the policeman's baton, shall become the foundation of society."[15] (This ugly picture of industrial England at its worst represents Shaw's transposition of Wagner into the key of John Ruskin, William Morris, William Blake, and Oliver Goldsmith.[16]) Wotan's last scruples vanish. With the aid of Loge, Alberich is tricked, bound, brought to the upper world, and forced to disgorge his riches. The giants are paid off in full once Wotan has been persuaded by Erda

13. *Ibid.*, 12–21.
14. *Ibid.*, 21–22.
15. *Ibid.*, 22–23.
16. See Chap. II, note 60 for Wagner's version of London as *Nibelheim*.

to give up the ring, and the gods make their triumphant entry into Valhalla. Loge foresees the coming downfall of the gods and withdraws.

But, at the height of his triumph, understanding has finally come to Wotan. He now sees that he is everywhere "shackled and bound, dependent on the laws of Fricka and the lies of Loki, forced to traffic with dwarfs for handicraft and with giants for strength, and to pay them both in false coin." Although he longs to break through the tangle of conventions and lies, which bind him as securely as ever he was able to bind Alberich, he cannot; they have become the essence of his power. The runes engraved on Wotan's lance, the symbol of his power, are the runes of established law, order, and convention. The best he can do is breed "a race of heroes to deliver the world and himself from his limited powers and disgraceful bargains." This, says Shaw, is the vision that comes to Wotan as he prepares to cross the rainbow bridge into Valhalla.[17]

Siegfried, the ideal hero of Wagner's younger days, was not a suitable hero for Shaw. His hero was, and remained, a figure of the stamp of Caesar. "If the next generation of Englishmen consisted wholly of Julius Caesars," Shaw wrote in 1898, "all our political, ecclesiastical and moral institutions would vanish." Caesar, as idealized by Shaw, is the prototype of the clear-sighted, practical man of affairs, who sets things right in an unsentimental fashion. He is as merciful as possible but cares rather little for the broken eggs, provided the omelet is well made. Napoleon is another such figure. "It seems hardly possible," says Shaw, "that the British army at the battle of Waterloo did not include at least one Englishman intelligent enough to hope, for the sake of his country and humanity, that Napoleon might defeat the allied sovereigns." That Englishman, as a member of the old order, would nonetheless oppose Napoleon, just as Wotan tried to prevent Siegfried from reaching Brünnhilde. Siegfried is as unconventional as Caesar or Napoleon. He is, in fact, "a totally unmoral person, a born anarchist, the ideal of Bakoonin, an anticipation of the 'overman' of Nietzsche."[18] But he is also, in Shaw's eyes, an ignorant young idealist who, like Harry Trench, does not understand how the world's work is done, and that it *must* be done somehow, better badly than not at all.

17. Shaw, *The Perfect Wagnerite* (1899), 31.
18. *Ibid.*, 38, 57, 71.

After Siegfried has rendered Wotan impotent by shattering his upraised lance with the sword *Nothung*, passed through the magic fire, and consummated his union with Brünnhilde, why are we not ushered forthwith into the brave new world dreamt of by Wagner, Bakunin, Marx, and other social revolutionaries in the early nineteenth century? Because, Shaw answers, Wagner changed his mind. When he began work on the *Ring*, he was a "sanguinary revolutionary Meliorist," putting his trust in Siegfried; when he ended it, he had become a Schopenhauerian pessimist, and the "political philosophy of Siegfried is exactly contrary to the political philosophy of Schopenhauer." Remnants of Wagner's discarded youthful idealism, however, remained behind to clutter up the music and action of the *Ring*.[19]

Idealism in social life is, says Shaw, no better than "panacea quackery." The world's ills cannot be cured by love, anarchism, or any other such quack remedy. Wagner's use of the "love panacea," still persisting in the *Ring* despite his revision of its close, had been anticipated by Percy Bysshe Shelley in 1829. Shelley's Jupiter in *Prometheus Unbound* is the "almighty fiend into whom the Englishman's God had degenerated during two centuries of ignorant Bible worship and shameless commercialism." At the same time he is Alberich, Fafner, Loge, and Wotan rolled into one. Both works "lapse into panacea-mongering didacticism by the holding up of love as the remedy for all evils and the solution of all difficulties." But where Shelley had hurled this Old Testament monster shrieking into the abyss, Wagner had not only pardoned him but made the truth and heroism that overthrew him children of his inmost heart.[20]

Anarchism is just another idealistic panacea. Even the modified form of anarchism on which our present order rests, namely unrestricted business competition, has turned out to be a disastrous failure, and the necessities of the case are forcing us in the direction of socialism. "Society," Shaw tells us here, "cannot effectively organize the production of its food, clothes and housing, nor distribute them fairly and economically on any anarchic plan." Society must be managed with a firm and knowing hand. Siegfrieds cannot save us. Individual Siegfrieds have come forward often enough, only to find themselves confronted by the

19. *Ibid.*, 124–25.
20. *Ibid.*, 83–84, 87–89.

alternatives of government or destruction at the hands of their fellows who are not Siegfrieds:

And this dilemma will persist until Wotan's inspiration comes to our governors, and they see that their business is not the devising of laws and institutions to prop up the weaknesses of mobs and secure the survival of the unfittest, but the breeding of men whose wills and intelligences may be depended on to produce spontaneously the social wellbeing which our laws now aim at and miss. The majority of men at present in Europe have no business to be alive. . . . In short, it is necessary to breed a race of men in whom the life-giving impulses predominate, before the New Protestantism becomes politically practicable.[21]

Here, of course, he overlooks the failure of Wotan's inspiration to have any such result, in the world of the *Ring* at least. But at this point Shaw is more concerned with the elucidation of his own ideas than those of Wagner.

4. SHAW ADDRESSES THE GERMANS

In 1907 in the preface to the German translation of *The Perfect Wag-nerite*, Shaw confesses his artistic and spiritual debt to musical Germany. "Do not suppose," he writes, "that I learnt my art from English men of letters. . . . My masters were the masters of a universal language: they were, to go from summit to summit, Bach, Handel, Haydn, Mozart, Beethoven and Wagner." But, he adds, "had the Germans understood any of these men, they would have hanged them." For their sake alone, he looks on Germany as "the Holy Land of the capitalist age," and his one desire is but "to bring the whole world under this sanctification." As for the average modern German, says Shaw, nobody likes him, not even his own countrymen. The typical modern German's worst fault is that he cannot see that it is possible to have too much of a good thing. His craze for work is worse than his craze for drink. Convinced that "duty, industry, education, loyalty, patriotism and respectability are good things . . . he indulges in them on all occasions shamelessly and excessively. He commits hideous crimes when crime is presented to him as part of his duty." As for the German socialists, they are obsessed by the spirit of orthodoxy. When Shaw, who "knew

21. *Ibid.*, 82, 95–96.

Engels personally and rather liked him as a witty and amiable old 1848 veteran," dares to doubt that Marx was infallible and that Engels was his prophet, he is treated by his socialist colleagues in Germany as if he were guilty of "hideous blasphemies." It is plain, says Shaw, that when a German "throws off all the bonds of convention . . . he promptly uses his freedom to put on a heavier set of chains." And so, Shaw admonishes the Germans in closing his preface, "you who used to fear only God and your own conscience, and now fear nothing at all, here is my book for you; and—in all sincerity—much good may it do you."[22] If nothing else, Shaw's caricature of the typical German reveals how far we have come from Heine's early nineteenth-century perception of the German as dreamer and phantast. Striking also is Shaw's confession of the redeeming power of German music, a confession more Wagnerian than Shavian in spirit.

The new chapter, "Why He Changed His Mind," inserted in the German edition of The Perfect Wagnerite is less what we would expect from its title than an account of how Shaw himself would have concluded the Ring. Shaw says that if the history of Germany from 1849 to 1876 had been the history of Siegfried, Wotan, and Alberich transposed into the key of real life, the catastrophic close of the Ring would not be the "operatic anachronism" that it is. In real life no Götterdämmerung took place. What actually happened was that Siegfried failed, while Bismarck succeeded. Bakunin was exiled from Germany, and the "red spectre" of the International, conjured up by Karl Marx, revealed itself as a "turnip ghost." And in France the suppression of the Paris Commune in 1871 had offered us, Shaw writes, "one of the most tragic examples in history of the pitilessness with which capable practical administrators and soldiers are forced by the pressure of facts to destroy romantic amateurs and theatrical dreamers."[23]

Shaw's scenario is as follows. In terms of the allegory of the Ring, Alberich has regained power but thought better of his old threat to dethrone Wotan and Loge. Instead, he has decided to marry into the best

22. Shaw, The Perfect Wagnerite (1909), vi–xi. Engels appears to have regarded Shaw as a rather favorable member of his class (Fabian Socialists). Shaw is a "paradoxical man of letters . . . very talented and witty as a writer but absolutely useless as an economist and politician, although honest and not a careerist," he wrote to Karl Kautsky in September, 1892. See Karl Marx Friedrich Engels Selected Correspondence (3rd ed.; Moscow, 1975), 422–23.
23. Shaw, The Perfect Wagnerite (1909), 101–102.

Valhalla families and to pay Wotan and Loge for improving living conditions in Nibelheim. Fafner, meanwhile, has turned over his gold to Alberich in return for shares, dividends, and the comfortable life. Alberich's self-respect is restored by his success in large-scale business enterprise and the social esteem it wins for him. His character gradually undergoes a favorable change. As a mere moneygrubber, he could turn tens into hundreds. He now discovers that to turn hundreds into thousands calls for "magnanimity and a will to power rather than to pelf." And to turn thousands into millions, he "must make himself into an earthly providence for masses of workmen: he must create towns and govern markets." The Alberich of 1850 may have been Engels' Manchester factory owner, but the Alberich of 1876 was already half-transformed into a "Krupp of Essen or Carnegie of Homestead." Shaw's list of "monarchs, millionaires, landlords and capitalists" who do the world's work *tant bien que mal* also includes the Romanoffs, Hohenzollerns, Levers, and Pierpont Morgans.[24] These men will save us from the *Götterdämmerung* haunting Europe, Shaw thinks.

5. SARTORIUS RECLOTHED

Once again, as he did with Archer's plot for *Widowers' Houses*, Shaw has fished the tainted treasure out of the Rhine and allowed the show to go on. But before writing the new chapter for *The Perfect Wagnerite*, Shaw had already embodied its message in *Major Barbara*, which was first published in 1905. For Carnegie of Homestead, Lever of Port Sunlight, and Krupp of Essen, we have in *Major Barbara* Undershaft and Lazarus of Perivale St. Andrews. Andrew Undershaft—industrial king, financial giant, and munitions manufacturer—is recognizable as a combination of Wotan and Alberich.[25] He is also Sartorius in the clothing of Carlyle's hero as industrialist. His silent (and invisible) partner Lazarus is the Jew as financial scapegoat. He also recalls Lazarus, the Jew *redivivus* of Chamberlain, and may have originated in Shaw's mind as a conflation of Loki and Lickcheese. Perivale St. Andrews is the improved version of Nibelheim promised us in *The Perfect Wagnerite*. To

24. *Ibid.*, 102–106. In the third edition (1913) of *The Perfect Wagnerite* Shaw added "Cadbury of Bourneville," dropped Pierpont Morgan, and changed "Levers" to "Lever of Port Sunlight." In the fourth edition (1923) none of these names appears.
25. I have been anticipated here in part by J. L. Wisenthal, "The Underside of Undershaft: A Wagnerian Motif in *Major Barbara*," *The Shaw Review*, XV (May, 1972), 56–64. For bringing this paper to my attention I am indebted to Sidney P. Albert.

Barbara Undershaft—who, Brünnhilde-like, had rebelled against her father and joined the Salvation Army, only to wage a futile, idealistic war
against poverty and human degradation—Perivale St. Andrews had
seemed a "sort of pit where lost creatures with blackened faces stirred
up smokey fires and were tormented by my father."[26] She learns, however, that Nibelheim has been transformed into—or, should we say,
disguised by the Shavian *Tarnkappe* as—an earthly paradise inhabited
by happy, hardworking (moral) dwarfs. Unlike Barbara, neither her
mother, the relentlessly conventional Lady Britomart, nor her brother,
the priggish Stephen, had given any more thought to the source of their
dividends than had Harry Trench in *Widowers' Houses*.

The "gospel of St. Andrew Undershaft," as Shaw calls it in the preface to *Major Barbara*, is essentially the same as the implied Wotan-
Alberich gospel in *The Perfect Wagnerite*. It is also a much improved
and updated version of the "Mammon-gospel" of Plugson of St. Dolly
Undershot in Carlyle's *Past and Present*. In *Major Barbara*, we are told
by Lady Britomart that the founder of the Undershaft armaments dynasty was a nameless foundling from the parish of St. Andrew Undershaft in London. Adopted by an armorer, the foundling went on to become a great manufacturer and entrepreneur. The concern was then
passed on through the hands of a succession of foundlings, each one of
whom received the name "Andrew Undershaft." Cusins refers to Undershaft as a "clever devil" and "prince of darkness." Undershaft's name
recalls the rather uncommon German word *Unterschaft*, meaning the
butt of a gun or cannon, or the shaft of a lance—a symbol of Wotan.
Cusins, who is destined to inherit the Undershaft industries and to
marry Barbara-Brünnhilde, is Siegfried. Like Siegfried, he is the product
of an incestuous union—legally at least, since his mother was his father's deceased wife's sister, as he himself points out (in England such a
marriage was illegal). Euphemistically—there is hardly any other justification—he then calls himself a "foundling."[27] This means that he is

26. Shaw, *The Bodley Head Bernard Shaw*, III, 154.
27. *Ibid.*, 154, 164–65. See also Carlyle, *Past and Present*, 217–18. Turco, *Shaw's
Moral Vision*, 250, has pointed out a resemblance between Captain Shotover in Shaw's
Heartbreak House and Wotan in *The Perfect Wagnerite*. To this it may be added that
"Shotover" is a variation on Carlyle's "Undershot." In naming the heroine of *Major
Barbara*, Shaw may have been influenced by the legend of Saint Barbara. The saint was
decapitated by her angry father for refusing to marry the man of his choice and for be-

eligible for adoption by Andrew Undershaft. In marrying Barbara, he will then be marrying the daughter of his adopted father. Siegfried, we recall, united himself with the daughter of his grandfather, Wotan. Shaw has told us in *The Perfect Wagnerite* that Siegfried must learn Alberich's trade and shoulder his burdens; and we have already seen that, for Wagner, Wotan and Alberich are doubles: light-elf (*Lichtalbe*) and dark-elf (*Schwarzalbe*).

But who is the shadowy Lazarus, the secret sharer in *Major Barbara*? We hear Undershaft tell Cusins that Lazarus is a "gentle, romantic Jew," who cares for nothing but music and the theater. He will, however, be blamed for Cusins' "rapacity in money matters," just as he has already been blamed in the past for Undershaft's rapacity. Shaw recognizes that the Jew is no longer the secret ruler of Europe dreamed of by Disraeli and Heine sixty years earlier. Although Undershaft informs his son Stephen—rather in the manner of Sidonia instructing Coningsby, were it not for the "touch of brutality" in the tone of Undershaft's voice— that "*I* am the government of your country: I and Lazarus," there is little other indication that Lazarus plays a leading role in the firm.[28] But the myth of Jewish money power survives, and Lazarus can still play the role of scapegoat in the comedy staged by Undershaft to bemuse the groundlings.

In Shaw's scenario for the film version of *Major Barbara*, first exhibited in the United States in May, 1941, Cusins says that "the scapegoat . . . is the role of the Jew in modern capitalism." To this, Undershaft replies that the role was invented by an Undershaft. By that time the joke had lost whatever savor it may have possessed. In the film itself we hear nothing of Lazarus, although his name still adorns the buildings of the firm. In the film script, Undershaft still informs his son with a "touch of brutality" that he and Lazarus constitute the real government of England. He adds: "You will make war when it suits us, and keep peace when it doesn't. . . . When other people want something to keep my dividends down, you will call out the police and the military." Undershaft refers to his firm on one occasion as a "temple of the Total-

---

coming a Christian convert; the father was promptly consumed by a bolt of fire from above. Barbara is thus the patroness of firearms and may be invoked against lightning.

28. Shaw, *The Bodley Head Bernard Shaw*, III, 151, 167.

itarian State." All this was hardly admissible in the climate of World War II. The climax of Shaw's fantasy is reached when Undershaft plays his "favorite record": Arturo Toscanini conducting Gioacchino Rossini's *Moses in Egypt*, "accompanied by a Wagnerian orchestra."[29]

Another Shavian version of the Jew as scapegoat is worth a brief note at this point. In *Man and Superman* (1903) a London waiter, a Jew by the name of Mendoza (*mendosa* means mendacious; Mendoza, however, is an old and honorable Spanish name), disappointed in love, becomes a brigand in the mountains of Spain. The young woman in question—who had rejected Mendoza's advances and advised him to marry a barmaid named Rebecca Lazarus—is not Jewish. She is, in fact, the sister of the chauffeur of John Tanner, whose party Mendoza has waylaid and is now holding for ransom. Mendoza confesses to Tanner that he had wanted to marry the young woman despite his "pride of race" and his agreement with her objection that "every Jew considers in his heart that English people are dirty in their habits." The attempt at interracial union fails, and Mendoza, brokenhearted, flees to Spain. Mendoza's scapegoat role is evident only in the Don Juan in Hell interlude. There he undergoes a dream-transformation to become a gentle and courteous devil, prince of a "Palace of Lies," lover of music, art, beauty, and sex, and general advocate of the virtues of this-worldly goods against the attack launched by Don Juan Tenorio, alias John Tanner.[30] References to these matters in current productions of *Man and Superman* are apt to be considerably abbreviated.

Shaw had no illusions about nineteenth-century capitalists. Nor did he expect them to undergo a Scrooge-like moral transformation. Like Carlyle, he simply hoped that the capitalists would come to see where their own best interests lay. The Undershafts of the real world, Shaw says in 1906, are "brigands: merciless, unscrupulous, dealing out ruin, death and slavery to their competitors and employees." The villainy of "the English factories, the American trusts, the exploitation of African gold, diamonds, ivory and rubber" make that of the Spanish buccaneers pale by comparison. Shaw agrees with Undershaft that the state is, despite all appearances to the contrary, governed by Mammon.

29. George Bernard Shaw, *Major Barbara: A Screen Version* (New York, 1946), 113, 119–26.
30. Shaw, *The Bodley Head Bernard Shaw*, II, 489–803; see pp. 631–89.

The moral order, represented by the church, has no effective force. Whatever its professed beliefs may be, the church is tolerated only so long as she preaches submission to existing law and order; that is, takes sides with "the police and the military . . . the instruments by which the rich rob and oppress the poor (on legal and moral grounds made for the purpose)."[31] Nevertheless, Shaw had no intention of returning the tainted treasure to the daughters of the Rhine. Even the failure of Cusins and Barbara to meet Shaw's expectations would not have caused him to lose faith in the gospel of St. Andrew Undershaft.[32]

In the light of events since 1905, to read *Major Barbara* today can be a somewhat disconcerting experience. Shaw beats the drums of salvation and looks eagerly into the distance for a glimpse of the paradisiacal land that Undershaft is to reclaim from the watery wastes. Undershaft's methods are at least as suspect as those of the aged, half-blind Faust of Goethe's drama. Shaw is at times prophetic, as in the slogan "Undershaft and Lazarus, Death and Destruction Dealers: address Christendom and Judea."[33] But even the frightfully real death and destruction of the Great War, although profoundly shocking to Shaw, did not cause him to lose faith entirely in Undershaft and Lazarus.

In 1913, we recall, Shaw stated in *The Perfect Wagnerite* that Wagner and Marx had rightly prophesied the end of an epoch but wrongly prophesied a cataclysmic end. Instead (according to Shaw's scenario), Wotan had joined forces with Siegfried and Alberich, "a development of which one gathers no forecast from Wagner or Marx." Despite Shaw's confidence in the future, a *Götterdämmerung* of sorts began one year later. In 1923 in the fourth edition of *The Perfect Wagnerite*, Shaw admitted that "within ten years the centre had fallen out of Europe." The revised version of the chapter, "Why He Went Wrong," states that in 1913 the "epoch seemed so prosperous that the prophecy [of a cataclys-

31. *Ibid.*, III, 45, 50–51. See Winnie Verloc's statement to her weak-minded brother Stevie in *The Secret Agent* that the police are there not to help but "so that them as have nothing shouldn't take anything away from them who have." Joseph Conrad, *The Secret Agent: A Simple Tale* (London, 1907), 246.
32. J. L. Wisenthal suggests in "The Underside of Undershaft" that if Shaw had written a fourth act for *Major Barbara* he would have found "Cusins/Siegfried" and "Barbara/Brunnhilda" not up to their assignment.
33. L. J. Rather, "Some Reflections on the Philemon and Baucis Episode in Goethe's *Faust*," *Diogenes*, XXV (1959), 60–73; Shaw, *The Bodley Head Bernard Shaw*, III, 72.

mic downfall of the present order] seemed ridiculously negligible." We must suppose that the First World War took Shaw, like so many others, by surprise. What went wrong? Alberich, Shaw answers, had prospered so greatly that he began to think himself immortal; further, by marrying into the best families of Valhalla, he had brought his sons and daughters under the influence of "feudal militarist ideals" highly dangerous to commerce. Marching off sword in hand with his feudal sons-in-law, "blasting his way with cyclopean explosives," Alberich had "crashed into the abyss he had not believed in." At this point Shaw concludes his revision of "Why He Changed His Mind," the remainder of the chapter being left in its previous form. In the preface to the fourth edition of *The Perfect Wagnerite* we learn—to borrow from the language of *Major Barbara*—that all is not well in Perivale St. Andrews. "Indeed," says Shaw, "the war was more a great tearing off of masks than a change of face: the main difference is that Alberich is richer, and his slaves hungrier and harder worked when they are so lucky as to have any work to do." But Wagner's allegory had not lost its importance or validity.[34]

In a program note written for a production of *Major Barbara* in March, 1929, Shaw explains where Undershaft and Lazarus have gone wrong. Not only have they disappointed his modestly Utopian hopes, they have proved themselves inefficient as munitions makers and bunglers as financiers. Resurrecting his scapegoat, Shaw claims that the shortfall of munitions in the Great War occurred "because Lazarus had gained too much control." As a result, the government was forced to nationalize the munitions industries. When the war ends, however, Undershaft and Lazarus—their newspapers shouting that they have saved the country—ride back into power. Again they blunder: an orgy of overcapitalization is followed by credit failure, the wholesale repudiation of debts, and general unemployment. Undershaft, says Shaw, manages to survive the wreck: later on in the twenties he "emerged in fiction as Clissold and in fact as John Ford."[35] But once again Shaw was

34. Shaw, *The Perfect Wagnerite* (1913), 186; Shaw, *The Perfect Wagnerite* (1923), xii, 92–93.

35. Shaw, *The Bodley Head Bernard Shaw*, III, 198–200. "Henry" Ford was meant. H. G. Wells rescued Lazarus also from the wreck: Clissold, the industrialist hero, has a Jewish partner, Julian Steinhart. Clissold remarks: "Perhaps Julian and I represent a blend that may become very effective in human affairs" (*The World of William Clissold* [2 vols.; New York, 1926], 432). As Shaw says in the screen version of *Major Bar-*

deceived by Clio. Six months after this reaffirmation of faith in the gospel of St. Andrew Undershaft came the Wall Street stock market crash and on its heels a worldwide collapse of credit that began in the Austrian *Kredit-Anstalt* and quickly extended to undermine the financial structure of all Europe and America. The Great Depression had begun.

It may be that Shaw's relatively optimistic outlook for the future, as expressed in *The Perfect Wagnerite* and *Major Barbara* during the period between 1898 and 1913, owed something to developments that had taken place in Germany after the founding of the Second Reich in 1871. Under Bismarck, the German industrial worker found himself, if not in Perivale St. Andrews, at least the citizen of an embryo welfare state. The benefits were real: steady employment and insurance against accidents, illness, and old age. It seemed that Wotan and Alberich had at last made common cause. Loge, too, was—if we accept Shaw's identification of his better side with intellect—preeminent: German science in the state-supported universities and technical schools ran far ahead of its rivals in other countries. But Bismarck was pushed aside by Wilhelm II in 1890, and under his leadership the Germans outdid even their neighbors in chauvinism and saber rattling. The Second Reich collapsed in 1918, and its would-be Siegfried retreated to the Netherlands. Then, after an interregnum of fourteen years, came the Nazi Third Reich, the thousand-year Reich of Hitler that ran its brief course to a catastrophic end in less than half the time it took Wagner to complete the *Ring*. Shaw lived to see Hiroshima and Nagasaki. One wonders what he would think if he were alive today, now that the Wotan-Alberich-Loge complex has achieved worldwide dominance. As Bill Walker asks in *Major Barbara*: "Wot prawce selvytion nah?"[36]

6. WAGNERISM, WAGNER, AND THE THIRD REICH

In 1952 in a study of Wagner as the culmination of German romantic thought, Paul Arthur Loos remarked that his own manuscript had been

---

bara: "It is part of the tradition that they [the Undershafts] should take a partner with a Jewish name." Wells touched on these themes in an earlier novel. His unheroic, obnoxious entrepreneur Sir Isaac Harmon, described as a "peasant mind allied and blended with a Ghetto mind" and a combination of "Norman peasant" and "Jew pedlar," is prodded by his autonomy-seeking wife into imitating the benevolence of "such firms as Lever and Cadbury and Burroughs & Wellcome" (*The Wife of Sir Isaac Harmon* [London, 1914], 188, 307).
36. Shaw, *The Bodley Head Bernard Shaw*, III, 138.

unpublishable in Germany under the Nazis because it did not follow the party line and unpublishable for some years thereafter because the line had been swallowed by the opponents of Nazism.[37] And even today there are those who believe they oppose Nazism and all its works but continue, in effect, to accept Hitler as their *Opernführer*. For a growing number, in the United States at least, Wagner seems to have become a conveniently available whipping boy for the past sins of the Germans.

Perhaps more widely accepted is the relatively temperate assessment of Wagner and Wagnerism in Nazi Germany to be found in William Shirer's *The Rise and Fall of the Third Reich*. Shirer places Wagner, along with Nietzsche, Treitschke, Hegel, and Fichte, under the rubric *Schwarzalben* (dark-elves)—if we may borrow here from the *Ring*—and Leibniz, Kant, Bach, Beethoven, and Goethe among the *Lichtalben* (light-elves), it is true; yet he admits that Wagner "fervently hoped that the Germans . . . would 'become not rulers, but ennoblers of the world.'" According to Shirer, it was not Wagner's "political writings . . . but his towering operas, recalling so vividly the world of German antiquity with its heroic myths, its fighting pagan gods and heroes, its demons and dragons, its blood feuds and primitive tribal codes, its sense of destiny, of the splendors of love and life and the nobility of death, which inspired the myths of modern Germany and gave it a Germanic *Weltanschauung* which Hitler and the Nazis, with some justification, took over as their own."[38]

No doubt, this somewhat overwrought impression of Wagner's operas and music-dramas is widely shared, but it is nonetheless false. From *Rienzi* to *Parsifal* there are heroes in Wagner aplenty, but their disputes rarely involve "primitive tribal codes." Gods and a dragon occur in the *Ring*, but most of the action is carried out by the human principals. There are no demons in the entire corpus of Wagner's work. Melodrama of the kind met with, often enough, in Gaetano Donizetti, Giuseppe Verdi, and Giacomo Puccini is conspicuously absent. The usual pace of Wagner's music-dramas, for example in *Tristan, Parsifal,*

37. Paul Arthur Loos, *Richard Wagner: Vollendung und Tragik der deutschen Romantik* (Bern, 1952), viii–ix.
38. William Shirer, *The Rise and Fall of the Third Reich* (New York, 1960), 97–101.

and most of the *Ring*, is to the uninitiated often unbearably slow—the stage being occupied by two or three immobile personages who, when they are not exchanging prolonged significant "glances," sing back and forth interminably. A widespread belief has it that the grandiose pageantry of the Nazi party rallies was somehow derived from Wagner's *Ring*. In fact, as Siegfried Kracauer pointed out in 1947, Hitler and Goebbels took some of their cues from Fritz Lang's film *Die Nibelungen*, a work that has nothing to do with Wagner's music-drama. The book for the film was written by Lang's wife, Thea von Harbou; like the medieval *Nibelungenlied*, it has two parts: *Siegfried* and *Kriemhilde's Revenge*.[39]

Shirer's account of the genesis of the pagan German *Weltanschauung* favored by some of the Nazis suffers also from its failure to take into account the revival of interest in Norse mythology and medieval poetry—*The Song of Roland, Morte d'Arthur*, and *The Song of the Nibelungs* included—throughout England and northern Europe in the nineteenth century. The phenomenon was by no means confined to Germany. There is, nevertheless, a grain of truth in his charge. The misuse of Wagner's name by people who, if they had rightly understood his message would have hanged him (as Shaw wrote in 1907), was noted by Theodor Lessing as early as 1906. Lessing's words seem to anticipate the oratorical style of Hitler:

The art-historical and national significance of his [Wagner's] achievements stand today beyond all dispute. But when we speak of them we need not do so with bristling hair, gnashing teeth, foaming mouth and a smiting of the stout-hearted, true manly German breast. This is, indeed, the fashion of so-called -ians or -ites, who strike at random on the skulls of their contemporaries with the dead bones of every man of consequence, misusing great names as battle cries, great work as the triumphal flag of an individual or national drive for power. From the stones that they themselves hurl most vehemently against the man of significance while he is still alive they build, for one who has been historically recognized, funeral monuments and memorials, behind which incompetent infallibility and self-righteous absence of distinction can entrench themselves.

According to Shirer, Hitler used to say that whoever wished to under-

---

39. Siegfried Kracauer, *From Caligari to Hitler: A Psychological Study of the German Film* (Princeton, N.J., 1947), 91–95; Thea von Harbou, *Das Nibelungenbuch* (Munich, 1923).

stand National Socialist Germany must first understand Wagner.[40] Again, there is unwitting truth in the statement. Shaw had already said, in effect, that whoever wished to understand the Western world must first understand Wagner's *Ring*. The German *Götterdämmerung* of 1945 may yet prove to have been only the small-scale rehearsal for a coming world catastrophe.

There is evidence that the Nazi authorities became, somewhat belatedly, aware of the peculiar applicability of Wagner's *Ring of the Nibelung* to their own case. Word went out in Germany in 1942 that complete performances of the *Ring*, even in Bayreuth, were no longer welcome. *Parsifal*, too, fell under this partial ban. Commenting from Tel Aviv in 1977 on the reasons why these two works were singled out by the Nazis, Yehuda Cohen writes: "The Nazis rejected the *Ring* obviously because they saw in it a prophecy of their downfall (*Untergang*), *Parsifal* because it is too Christian." Cohen notes that in Israel the works of Wagner (and those of Richard Strauss as well) are still taboo and that all attempts to reinstate them on the stage or in the concert hall have so far been successfully resisted. The Israeli "heroes" who wage the paper war against Wagner are, according to Cohen, for the most part people "who do not know the difference between a violin and a house key" and who bring to bear every anti-Semitic remark Wagner may have made, whether or not he wanted it to be included in his collected works. Like many Germans, these people mistakenly regard Wagner as the "spiritual father of Nazism" and, Cohen adds: "Against prejudgments and second-hand claims, no arguments are effective."[41]

Shirer also expresses a widely held belief when he writes that Wagner "harbored a fanatical hatred, as Hitler did, for the Jews, who he was convinced were out to dominate the world with their money."[42] The

40. Theodor Lessing, *Schopenhauer, Wagner, Nietzsche: Einführung in moderne deutsche Philosophie* (Munich, 1906), 204–205. See page 197 of the same work for my epigraph on the title page: "All these philosophical stars of the second and third magnitude pale when we name the man who, like a force of nature, a storm-center without compare, is transforming the modern world." Shirer, *Rise and Fall of the Third Reich*, 97.

41. Yehuda Cohen, "Wagner und Strauss im Giftschrank: Warum die Musik der beiden Richards in Israel noch immer tabu ist," *Frankfurter Allgemeine Zeitung*, August 13, 1977. Cohen points out also that Wagner's assimilationist solution to the Jewish question, as it is stated in *On Judaism in Music*, "completely contradicts" Nazi racist doctrine, a fact conveniently overlooked by the Nazis.

42. Shirer, *Rise and Fall of the Third Reich*, 101.

belief is nevertheless mistaken. Wagner's anti-Semitism was not of the same character as Hitler's, nor did Wagner believe (whatever Hitler may have believed) that the Jews, as a people, were out to dominate the world with their money. The reason for the misconception is not far to seek: Nazi anti-Semitism, especially after the full horror of the extermination camps became generally known, caused a revulsion of such strength that all fine distinctions were blurred. Wagner's anti-Semitism could wrongly be seen as no different in principle from that of, say, Julius Streicher. Wagner was, of course, opposed to what he, along with Marx and others, perceived as the dominating Judaistic spirit of the times. Like Marx, again, he believed that the so-called Christian civilization of Europe had become thoroughly Judaized. Judeo-Christianity, not the Jewish people, was out to dominate the world through the power of money and arms.

Wagner's Jewish admirers, collaborators, and associates, together with so-called "anti-Semitic Semites" in Germany and elsewhere, can be, and usually are, written off as sycophants, victims of Jewish self-hatred, or both. The Jewish admirers of his music-dramas were legion, and they may have inadvertently helped set off the sporadic anti-Semitic attacks against Wagner himself that first began in the 1870s. Newman has suggested also that Nietzsche, at the time of his break with Wagner, spread the rumor that Wagner was part Jewish. In 1888 Nietzsche stated in writing that Ludwig Geyer, Wagner's beloved stepfather and a Christian thought to be of Jewish origin, was really his father. It was during this period that Wagner was caricatured in the Viennese press as a large-nosed "Rabbi of Bayreuth." He was also called the "God of the Jews," and it was said that "kosher Valkyries" would soon be brought on the stage in performances of the *Ring*.[43]

We have seen that in 1903 Otto Weininger discerned a certain element of "Jewishness" in Wagner's music. The most perspicacious re-

---

43. Newman, *Life*, II, 609–13. In *Der Fall Wagner*, first published in 1888, Nietzsche asks in a footnote: "Was Wagner a German at all? There are some reasons for asking this. It is difficult to discover any German trait in him. Great learner that he was, he learned to imitate much that is German—that is all. His very nature *contradicts* what has so far been felt as German—not to speak of the German musician! His father was an actor by the name of Geyer. A Geyer is almost an Adler." Friedrich Nietzsche, *Der Fall Wagner*, Part 6, Vol. III of *Werke: Kritische Gesammtausgabe*, ed. Giorgio Colli and Mazzino Montinari (8 parts; Berlin, 1967–77), 35. Eduard Fuchs and Richard Kreowski, *Richard Wagner in der Karikatur* (Berlin, 1907), 55, 95, 138.

marks along this line were made a few years later by Theodor Lessing in his study of Schopenhauer, Wagner, and Nietzsche. After pointing out that every feature of Giacomo Meyerbeer's music execrated by Wagner in *Judaism in Music* can be found in his own music as well, Lessing continues:

The tendency toward exaggeration of accent, the inclination toward expressive pathos embodied in Wagner himself has been blamed on Judaism and Asiaticism. Modern culture, the prototype of which Nietzsche sees in Wagner, is supposed to be the after-effect of the Christian era, which was itself the "triumph of the Jew over Europe." Only one striking truth is lodged in this race-psychological construction. If we analyze those souls who today so readily play off the cultural into the race-biological or national question and embrace the just now prevailing dilettante's sport of fetching from all human greatness an Aryan-German element, we shall find that precisely those traits designated "Jewish" and "anti-German" are present nowhere in more purity than in the types who believe that they are rejecting them. Paul de Lagarde, Heinrich von Treitschke, Eugen Dühring, Adolf Stoecker and Houston Chamberlain are, in the sense of their supposed "race-psychology," the typical Jewish souls of our time.[44]

7. *GÖTTERDÄMMERUNG*

Throughout his life, Wagner continued to express dislike and distrust of power-hungry, spiritually empty warriors, despots, and political adventurers. Responding in 1854 to Röckel's comment that the career of Robespierre had a certain tragic pathos, insofar as he had resorted to evil means only in order to reach a desirable goal, Wagner replied that Robespierre had *no* goal. "At the culmination of his struggle for power," wrote Wagner, "Robespierre stood there without any understanding of what he really ought to do with the power won." And it was "in order to conceal the absence of such a goal and his own emptiness that he resorted to the utterly abominable machinery of the guillotine; for it has been shown that the *terreur* was used . . . on purely political, that is on ambitious and egoistic grounds."[45]

In 1880, three years before his death, Wagner spoke of the still possible "fundamental regeneration" of humanity but warned that the "despotic statesmen and rulers" of the world, whose sphere of action never rose above "violent, but always fruitless effectiveness," are the

44. Lessing, *Schopenhauer, Wagner, Nietzsche*, 243–44.
45. Wagner, *Wagner an Röckel*, 32, 33.

last people to be consulted on the matter. Even the mightiest of these men is dissatisfied as long as more power is to be had: "What such a one may have in mind to do with this power, we search to discover in vain. We see before us, as ever, the likeness of Robespierre, who, after all hindrances to the revelation of his Utopian ideas had been swept a- side by the guillotine, had nothing to offer. . . . It now seems, however, that all statesmen are contending for Robespierre's prize." Absolute but empty power is "Robespierre's prize." The restless strivings of the will, whether expressed in that Leviathan the political-national state or in the individual, are forever insatiable. Not long ago, continues Wagner, the last despot of France had thought it necessary for the security of his dynasty, and in the interest of civilization, to administer a rebuff to Prussia. Since Prussia would not accept it, a war for German unity re- sulted:

In consequence, German unity was fought for, won, and contractually se- cured. But what it was supposed to mean, on the other hand, was hard to say. To be sure, we are offered the prospect of receiving information on the sub- ject just as soon as a great deal more power has been procured: German unity must be able to show its teeth in every quarter, even if it should have nothing left to chew on with them. When we picture the strong man toiling in lonely withdrawal, ceaselessly striving for means to increase his power, we believe we see Robespierre before us, presiding over the Committee of Public Safety.

For Wagner, then, Napoleon III and Bismarck are alike "Robespierres."[46]

Many years earlier, Wagner had described Bismarck to his patron Ludwig II of Bavaria as "an ambitious Junker, deceiving his weak- minded king in the most shameless fashion." At the same time, Wagner informed his royal disciple that the "lust to dominate foreign peoples is un-German." The Prussian military caste, above all, is "un-German . . . imitated as it is from the warrior castes of purely conquering peoples." He warns Ludwig that "the maintenance of huge standing armies . . . will possibly someday lead to the downfall of the monarchies." New- man, who cited these passages in 1941, notes that some of them had been omitted from the 1878 edition of Wagner's journal. He suggests that the victory of 1870 had reconciled Wagner to the Prussianism and Bismarckism that he had once loathed. It is true, as we have seen, that Wagner welcomed the penetration into France of the spirit of German

46. Wagner, *Gesammelte Schriften*, X, 254, 255.

music. But if he did indeed harbor any illusions about Bismarck, they were quickly dispelled. In the essay of 1880 he continues:

What there was to be done, and to be told to the world, with the power already won by that man of power [Bismarck] might, on the other hand, have come to him at the right time if he had been enlightened by the knowledge to which we have reference. We gladly believe the assurances of his love of peace, although it involves the inconvenience of being forced to preserve peace by waging war. We sincerely hope that some day a true peace will be won by peaceful means. It ought to have occurred to the mighty subduer of the last disturber of the peace that a peace other than the treaty of Frankfurt—a peace that leads straight to constantly renewed preparations for war—would have more befitted that frivolously provoked and frightful war.[47]

At Frankfurt the French, theretofore the dominant power in Europe, had been forced to surrender Alsace-Lorraine and pay an enormous cash indemnity, jointly negotiated by the Rothschilds in France and the Bleichröders in Germany. If Bismarck had understood the human situation, continues Wagner:

Recognition of the need and possibility of the real regeneration of humanity caught in the toils of a war civilization could instead have prompted a treaty by means of which the path to world peace might well have been paved: fortresses would have been demolished, not conquered; pledges of peace security, not of war security, would have been taken. But instead historical rights alone were weighed and brutally applied against historical claims; all was based on the right of conquest. It seems that, with the best of intentions, the leaders of nations can see no farther. They all have fantasies of world peace. Napoleon III also had peace in mind—provided that the peace would work to the benefit of his dynasty and France. For these men of power can conceive of peace in no other form than under the widely respected shelter of countless cannons.[48]

During his stay in Paris in 1849, if not before, Wagner had read Pierre-Joseph Proudhon's treatise *What Is Property?*, in which unearned property is equated with theft. In 1881 Wagner had this to say of the place of property in the European world:

In our socio-political conscience, property has acquired almost greater sanctity than religion: there is indulgence for an offense against the one, but no pity for damage to the other. Since property is considered the base of all social stability, so much the more harmful must seem the fact that everyone does

47. Newman, *Life*, III, 76–81; Wagner, *Gesammelte Schriften*, X, 255.
48. Wagner, *Gesammelte Schriften*, X, 255.

not possess property, and that the greater part of society indeed comes into the world disinherited. By its own principle, society is so dangerously disturbed that it must calculate all its laws for an impossible settlement of the difference—and the protection of property, even in the widest international sense, for which the armed forces are primarily maintained, can in truth mean nothing more than the protection of the haves (*Besitzenden*) against the have-nots (*Nichtbesitzenden*). . . . It seems indeed that the state's utilization of the concept of property, in itself apparently so simple, has driven a stake into the body of mankind, on which it can but waste away in painful, agonizing disease.

In times past, continues Wagner, property had been won and secured by pure force of arms and had thus come into the possession of a warrior nobility. But in our own day, the power of money has usurped the place of mere force of individual arms. And this strange new power in Europe is protean in its manifestations:

Though much that is ingenious and admirable has been thought, said and written concerning the invention of *money*, and of its value as an all-powerful cultural force, nevertheless the curse to which it has always been subject in song and story should be weighed against its praises. There *gold* appears as the demonic throttler of mankind's innocence; so, too, our greatest poet has the invention of *paper money* take place as a devil's trick. The chilling picture of the spectral ruler of the world might well be completed by the fateful ring of the Nibelung as stock portfolio.[49]

49. Newman, *Life*, II, 51; Wagner, *Gesammelte Schriften*, X, 267, 268. The poet is, of course, Goethe in *Faust*, 6057 ff.:
> Zu wissen sei es jedem, der's begehrt:
> Der Zettel hier ist tausend Kronen wert.
> Ihm liegt gesichert, als gewisses Pfand,
> Unzahl vergrabnen Guts im Kaiserland.

(Be it known to all concerned: This note is worth one thousand crowns. Secured by the immense mass of treasure buried in the imperial lands.)
Wagner's writings on money and property are worth comparing with those of Jakob Wassermann forty years later:
> Gold is not a possession. Gold is a symbol, a fictitious possession, something invisible, incomprehensible, useless, the un-thing (*Unding*) itself. . . . If it is not changed into things, if it does not surrender its pretended role, if it remains a hateful illusion, a will-'o-the-wisp, a mere notion, a mere phantom of possession, then it is logical and excusable that among those who are excluded from the repugnant and secret magic ring of gold, those who are in need because they cannot master a shadow, a formula, something without essence, there arises irritation, unrest, and a dark animosity, and finally madness, a mass-madness that is the precise portrait of our day. . . . No one who possesses is free of greed and desire; only he who, with full understanding, renounces possession.
The realization of this ideal, says Wassermann, involves "not the modern communistic requirement of expropriation (*Enteignung*) but the mythic Buddhistic requirement of

The spokesmen of our progressive civilization even see this spectral ruler as endowed with spiritual and moral powers, says Wagner; a vanished religious faith has thus been replaced by "credit." (A pun is implied here: in German, *Gläubiger* may mean "believer" or "creditor.") With reference, probably, to the widespread economic disaster following financial mismanagement in Germany immediately after the war with France, Wagner adds:

What comes to pass among us under the blessings of this "credit," we are now experiencing. And we seem not undesirous of attributing the guilt to the Jews alone. They are indeed virtuosos, where we are blunderers. But it was our civilization itself, nonetheless, that invented the art of coining money out of nothing. Or, if the Jews are guilty in the matter, it is because our whole civilization is a mixture of Judaism and barbarism, and in no way a Christian creation. Here we are of the opinion that a little self-knowledge would be advisable also for the spokesmen of the Church, especially when they combat the seed of Abraham, in whose name they nevertheless continue to demand the fulfillment of certain promises of Jehovah.[50]

---

renunciation (*Entäusserung*)." See his essay "Was ist Besitz?" in *Imaginäre Brücken: Studien und Aufsätze* (Munich, 1921), 13, 14, 27. Wagner's remarks on property are remarkably like those of the ethnologist Lewis H. Morgan in the United States. Morgan wrote in 1878 that "it [property] has become . . . an unmanageable power. The human mind stands bewildered in the presence of its own creation. . . . The dissolution of society bids fair to become the termination of a career of which property is the end and aim; because such a career contains the elements of self-destruction." See his *Ancient Society; or, Research in the Lines of Human Progress from Savagery, Through Barbarism to Civilization* (New York, 1878), 552.

50. Wagner, *Gesammelte Schriften*, X, 268. This may be the essay referred to by Wagner in 1881, when repudiating anti-Semitic agitators in Berlin. The circumstances were as follows. While negotiating for the first production of the *Ring* in Berlin, Angelo Neumann was told by Georg Davidsohn, a publicist friendly toward Bayreuth, that the agitators were trying "to proclaim Richard Wagner their chief apostle." Fearing possible adverse consequences, Neumann wrote to Cosima Wagner requesting a "statement on the subject by the Master." Wagner himself replied in a letter dated 23 February 1881: "I am completely unconnected with the present 'anti-Semitic' movement: a forthcoming article of mine in the *Bayreuth Papers* will testify to this in a way that ought to make it quite impossible for *people of intelligence* [emphasis in the original] to connect me with that movement" (*Der gegenwärtigen "antisemitischen" Bewegung stehe ich vollständig fern: ein nächstens in den "Bayreuther Blättern" erscheinender Aufsatz von mir wird dies in einer Weise bekunden, dass Geistvollen es sogar unmöglich werden dürfte, mich mit jener Bewegung in Beziehung zu bringen*). Wagner then told Neumann (who was himself Jewish) to cancel the performance: "To have both court nobility and Jews (*Hofadel und Juden*) on our necks at the same time—and really out of a sheer, absurd misunderstanding—not for this were our Nibelungs intended!" Angelo Neumann, *Erinnerungen an Richard Wagner* (Leipzig, 1907), 138–39. See Chamberlain's remarks, Chap. I, note 47 and text. Also see Cosima Wagner, *Die Tage-*

A passing remark by Wagner in 1880 illuminates a pervasively dominant element in his mythic construct of reality, which is present also, although differently voiced, in the mind of Shaw: "Jew and Junker are now reaching agreement over possession of the world" (*über den Besitz der Welt verständigt sich jetzt der Jude mit dem Junker*). This might seem to anticipate Shaw's myth of the Wotan-Alberich or Undershaft-Lazarus collusion. But Shaw's myth is a fairy story with a happy ending. Wagner—like Undershaft's son Stephen before his conversion—sees the two as "Death and Destruction Dealers: address Christendom and Judea." And according to Wagner, the fatal partnership can be traced back to the union of church and state in the early centuries of Christianity. The partnership, for Wagner, is nothing less than Judeo-Christianity, that is, "judaized" Christianity itself. By means of an alliance with a kingdom of this world based on violence and rapine, the Christian Church has sought to extend her own dominion:

Here, to subject decaying races to herself, she needed the help of terror, and the singular circumstance that Christianity could be looked on as having sprung from Judaism led to the adoption of the seemingly necessary terroristic means. There the tribal god of a small nation had promised his own people eventual rule over the whole world and all that lives and moves therein, provided that they adhered strictly to laws the closest compliance with which would keep them separate from all other peoples of the earth.[51]

The God of the Jews (*Judengott*) thus became the real God of the Christians, despite all lip service given by the church to the teachings of Christ. It is notable that Wagner, like Schopenhauer, sees only one aspect of the God of the Jews—not the mature Jehovah of Amos and Isaiah, and later of Hillel, not the universal God of prophetic and ethical Judaism, but only the primitive, angry, revengeful Jahweh of Joshua, the fierce tribal god of a people fighting to preserve its identity and separate life at all costs:

But it was in this way that the Church won her authorization for might and mastery, as we have already pointed out earlier; for wherever the armies of

---

bücher (2 vols.; Munich/Zurich, 1977), II, 699–700, for a brief note on the incident. Wagner's pun on the replacement of "faith" by "credit" recalls a comment made earlier by Karl Marx: "Public credit becomes the *credo* of capital. . . . Want of faith in the national debt takes the place of the blasphemy against the Holy Ghost." See his *Capital* (New York, 1967), I, 754.

51. Wagner, *Gesammelte Schriften*, X, 230, 234.

Christendom, even under the sign of the Cross, were seen to set forth in pursuit of robbery and bloodshed, it was not the name of the All-Sufferer that was invoked; instead Moses, Joshua, Gideon, and whatever else Jehovah's champions of the Israelite nation might be called were the names necessarily invoked to fire up the mood for slaughter. The history of England at the time of the Puritan wars furnishes an instructive example of both this and the whole Old Testament development of the English Church. Without drawing on the spirit of ancient Judaism and giving it equal rank with the purely Christian message, would it otherwise be possible for the Christian Church, even down to the present day, to assert ecclesiastical authority over a "civilized world" whose peoples, armed to the teeth for mutual destruction, squander the fruits of peace to fall upon and tear each other apart at the first sign from their warlords?[52]

In times of peace, or when left fully to themselves, the arts and sciences flourish in their undistorted form. But today the all-encompassing pressure of the warfare state—the incarnation, on an immense scale, of the unregenerate will—has reduced the intellect to near-complete servitude. Speaking for his own time, Wagner continues:

The brute force of the conqueror now steps up to these sciences and arts of peace, saying to them: "What of you is serviceable for war may prosper, what does not may perish." Thus we see that the law of Mohammed has become the fundamental law of all our civilizations, and we have but to look at our sciences and arts to see how they flourish under it. Let a man of intelligence who at the same time is well-meaning at heart rise up anywhere: the sciences and arts of civilization know how to send him about his business soon enough.

52. *Ibid.*, 232–33. Similarly adverse evaluations of Old Testament morality are frequently expressed also by so-called "anti-Semitic Semites": Marcel Proust (see Chap. I, note 51), Karl Kraus (Chap. II, note 71), Simone Weil (who wrote that the Old Testament always "yielded an appropriate quotation every time anybody had a crime he wanted to justify": Simone Weil, "The Iliad, or the Poem of Force," trans. Mary McCarthy, *Politics*, November, 1945, p. 330), and Otto Rank (who wrote in the late 1930s that "in our day it is the Germans, who, to every seeing eye, propound the ideology of the chosen people": Otto Rank, *Beyond Psychology* [New York, 1958], 281). Opposition to the morality of the God of the Old Testament goes back to early Christian times. The case of the Manichaean Christians against the Old Testament God is fully stated by Augustine in his "Reply to Faustus the Manichaean," in Philip Schaff, ed., *A Select Library of the Nicene and Post-Nicene Fathers of the Christian Church*, 1st series (14 vols.; Grand Rapids, Mich., 1956), IV, 155–345.
   Wagner's indictment of European "Judeo-Christianity" (the negation of both Christianity and Judaism in the good sense) was matched in kind and intensity by Karl Kraus forty years later. Germany and Austria were fighting for "the idea of Judeo-Christian world destruction" during the Great War, says *der Nörgler* (Kraus); German militarism and the newspaper press alike were in servitude to "the idea of Judeo-capitalistic world destruction." Kraus, *Die letzten Tage der Menschheit*, 194, 197.

Here it is asked: "Are you of use or not to a heartless and base civilization?" The military authorities have been made aware that through the so-called natural sciences, physics and chemistry in particular, many more destructive forces and substances are yet to be discovered. . . . These sciences are especially favored.[53]

Wagner indeed warns that humanity, under the doubtful guidance of Wotan and Alberich, is marching blindly toward an abyss, to use Shaw's words. Wagner notes also that the substitution, by the so-called civilized countries, of the "abstract" force of gunpowder and cannon for the "concrete" wounding force of swords and spears has allowed cowardice (moral as well as physical) to come to terms with brutality. Humanity can no longer face the bloodbath of the slaughterhouse, but the purchase and consumption of hardly recognizable fragments of animal flesh remains possible. The machinery of death and destruction must perforce become more and more impersonal, more abstract and removed in its workings. Others might view the state as "a kind of mill in which the human grain, after it has been threshed on the field of war, must be ground so as to become edible." But he himself favors a "path from which all violence (*Gewalt*) is completely excluded," a path that requires nothing more than "the invigoration of those seeds of peace that, even though they are as yet scanty and feeble, have taken root everywhere among us."[54]

But matters could well turn out otherwise. Frederick the Great, so it was said, on hearing a princely guest praise the matchless discipline of the Prussian soldiers, told him that the real wonder was "that the fellows don't shoot us dead." It is more than unlikely, says Wagner, that "the war machine was about to use itself up from within and collapse," leaving a Frederick the Great with nothing more to marvel at. And the essay of 1880 closes with these words:

Nevertheless it must arouse our misgivings that the advancing art of war continues to turn away from the mainsprings of moral forces toward the development of mechanical force. Here the rawest forces of the underlying powers of nature are brought into artificial play, into which, despite all mathematics and arithmetic, the blind will, breaking loose after its fashion with elemental power, could someday mix itself. The armored Monitors, against which the

---

53. Wagner, *Gesammelte Schriften*, X, 234–35.
54. *Ibid.*, 233, 251–52.

proud and stately sailing ship can no longer hold its own, already offer us a spectral, gruesome sight. Silent obedient men, who no longer resemble human beings, serve these monsters; no longer will they desert, not even from the frightful stokehole. Just as every natural thing has its destroying enemy, so also art has fashioned torpedoes in the sea, and everywhere else dynamite cartridges and the like. One is forced to believe that all this, together with art, science, bravery and point of honor, life and goods, could one day fly into the air due to some incalculable oversight. After the fruits of peace were thus blown away, to such events in the grand style there would be needed only the outbreak of general famine that is slowly but with blind infallibility being readied. Then we would perhaps stand again where our historical development began, and it could really seem "as if God created the world so that the Devil might take it"—which our great philosopher found stated in Judeo-Christian dogma.[55]

The destruction of the self and its world, in this crudest of senses, will then have been translated from dream into suicidal reality.

55. *Ibid.*, 252–53.

Epilogue
WAKING FROM
THE NIGHTMARE

The Ring of the Nibelung, so Wagner wrote to Liszt in 1853, encompassed the beginning and the end of the world.[1] We have seen that Wagner derived the essential substructure of the *Ring* from Sophocles' Oedipus trilogy. Borrowing Wagner's assessment of the Oedipus myth itself, we may say that the *Ring,* if rightly understood, presents the "entire history of humanity, from the beginning of society to the necessary downfall (*Untergang*) of the state."[2] Wagner's *Ring* is at the same time the supreme artistic expression of a nightmare that began increasingly to haunt the conscience of Europe early in the nineteenth century—the dream of a day of judgment lying in wait for a race that had lost touch with the source of truly human life in its frenzied quest for gold and power without end, a quest for a false Grail in which the ruthless, self-seeking male principle had been given free rein and the communal, nourishing, female principle, although becoming increasingly restive, sharply held in check and confined to the home. Only a handful of visionaries sensed the approaching *Götterdämmerung* at first. Then the motif of the coming downfall, a ground bass growing ever louder, began to sound through European art, literature, and philosophy. The male-dominated upper world of finance, industry, and politics, increasingly disturbed by rumblings in the depths of the European heartland, took defensive, ameliorative, and repressive measures.[3] The Great War of 1914–1918 suddenly and unexpectedly reasserted the male principle in its most brutal form. The apocalypse seemed to have arrived. War, pestilence, famine, and death rode abroad. When the war ended, a brief critical period of convalescence was followed by an apparent recovery, but one of short duration. A few years later a severe worldwide depression, following in the wake of another credit

1. See Chap. II, note 27.
2. See Chap. II, note 15.
3. Arthur Drews, *Der Ideengehalt von Richard Wagners "Ring des Nibelungen,"* 121: "The voices of those who believe they hear in the distance the tread of the workers' legions grow louder every day. . . . In the depths Nibelheim forges its weapons against Valhalla."

failure, crippled Western industry and soon brought it to a near halt. And now, sounding from the world beyond the confines of the still-dominant West, the motif of the Nibelung's hate became audible to the seer: "Wherever there is coal, oil and water power, new weapons can be forged against the heart of Faustian culture; now begins the plundered world's revenge on its masters," wrote Spengler in 1930.[4]

Until the onset of World War II, Western industry continued to function sluggishly. It then quickly recovered. War, it seemed, was not only the health of the state but the health of industry as well. Before the conflict ended, Loge had conferred almost limitless destructive power on the war machine. Afterward, convinced again of their invulnerability and immortality, Wotan and Alberich marched on as before. Again they blundered into the abyss. And so it is today—in a time of expanding armaments, decreasing natural resources, sporadic and unending wars, terrorism, separatism, racial unrest, collapsing credit, and a justified but crippling loss of faith in governmental authority—that in the dreamworlds of cinema, television, and the novel our thoughts walk abroad, caressing images of ruin and destruction. Kali is in the house of the ascendant.

In reality, neither Wagner nor his mentor Schopenhauer ever succumbed to self-indulgent pessimism. Schopenhauer, who is the philosopher as educator par excellence, teaches us how we may face the world at its worst and yet triumph over it in spirit. He is a wise elder brother, perhaps a guru, rather than an academic philosopher. "Today," said Max Horkheimer in 1960, on the occasion of the hundredth anniversary of Schopenhauer's death, "there is no thought more needed than his, with all its hopelessness, and, because it expresses the hopelessness, none that knows more of hope."[5] And Wagner's final utterance in The Ring of the Nibelung knows nothing of despair. Instead we hear in its closing bars a harmonious blending of motifs associated with Brünnhilde and Siegfried, with the feminine and masculine principles, a triumphant synthesis of opposites, the promised union of *prakriti* and *purusha*.

4. Oswald Spengler, *Der Mensch und die Technik: Beitrag zu einer Philosophie des Lebens* (Munich, 1930), 86–87.

5. Max Horkheimer, "Die Aktualität Schopenhauers," in Max Horkheimer and Theodor Adorno, *Sociologica II: Reden und Vorträge* (Frankfurt, 1962), 141.

GERMAN-ENGLISH CONCORDANCE OF CITED WORKS BY WAGNER AND SCHOPENHAUER

Unless otherwise shown, the German titles refer to Wagner's *Gesammelte Schriften*, 2nd ed. (Leipzig, 1877–78) and to Schopenhauer's *Sämtliche Werke*, ed. W. von Löhneysen (Stuttgart, 1960–65). The English titles refer to *Richard Wagner's Prose Works*, trans. W. A. Ellis (2nd ed.; London, 1895–99) and E. F. J. Payne's translations of Schopenhauer, as listed in the bibliography.

WAGNER

Aufklärungen über das Judenthum in der Musik (*Gesammelte Schriften*, ed. Julius Kapp, XIII, 29–51): Some Explanations Concerning "Judaism in Music" (III, 75–78, 101–22).

Ausführungen zu Religion und Kunst: 1. "Erkenne dich selbst" (X, 263–74): Continuations of "Religion and Art": 1. "Know Thyself" (VI, 264–74).

Autobiographische Skizze (I, 4–19): Autobiographic Sketch (I, 1–19).

Beethoven (IX, 61–126): Beethoven (V, 57–126).

Einleitung zum dritten und vierten Bande (III, 1–17): Introduction to Art and Revolution (I, 23–29).

Jesus von Nazareth: Ein dichterischer Entwurf (*Gesammelte Schriften*, ed. Julius Kapp, VI, 194–247): Jesus of Nazareth (VIII, 283–340).

Das Judenthum in der Musik (3rd ed.; V, 66–85): Judaism in Music (III, 79–100).

Die Kunst und die Revolution (III, 8–41): Art and Revolution (I, 30–65).

Das Kunstwerk der Zukunft (III, 42–177): The Art-Work of the Future (I, 67–213).

Eine Mittheilung an meine Freunde (IV, 230–344): A Communication to My Friends (I, 267–392).

Der Nibelungen-Mythus als Entwurf zu einem Drama (II, 156–66): The Nibelungen-Myth As Sketch for a Drama (VII, 299–311).

Offenes Schreiben an Herrn Ernst von Weber, Verfasser der Schrift, "Die Fol-

terkammern der Wissenschaft" (X, 194–210): Against Vivisection (VI, 193–210).

Oper und Drama; Erster Theil: Die Oper und das Wesen der Musik (III, 222–320): Opera and Drama; First Part: Opera and the Nature of Music (II, 1–115).

Oper und Drama; Zweiter Theil: Das Schauspiel und das Wesen der dramatischen Dichtkunst (IV, 1–103): Opera and Drama; Second Part: The Play and the Nature of Dramatic Poetry (II, 117–236).

Oper und Drama; Dritter Theil: Dichtkunst und Tonkunst im Drama der Zukunft (IV, 103–229): Opera and Drama; Third Part: The Arts of Poetry and Tone in the Drama of the Future (II, 237–376).

Religion und Kunst (X, 211–53): Religion and Art (VI, 211–52).

Die Sarazenin (*Gesammelte Schriften*, ed. Julius Kapp, VI, 68–93): "The Saracen Woman" (VIII, 249–76).

"Was nützt diese Erkenntnis?" Ein Nachtrag zu: Religion und Kunst (X, 253–63): "What Boots This Knowledge?" A Supplement to "Religion and Art" (VI, 253–63).

Die Wibelungen: Weltgeschichte aus der Sage (II, 115–55): The Wibelungen: World-History As Told in Saga (VII, 257–98).

Wollen wir hoffen? (X, 118–136): Shall We Hope? (VI, 111–130).

Wagner's correspondence with Franz Liszt, Angelo Neumann, and Mathilde Wesendonck is currently in print in English translation. The letters to August Röckel are available in English (see annotated bibliographic supplement), but long since out of print.

SCHOPENHAUER

Die beiden Grundprobleme der Ethik (III, 481–815): On the Basis of Morality.

Transzendente Spekulation über die anscheinende Absichtlichkeit im Schicksale des Einzelnen (IV, 243–72): Transcendent Speculation on the Apparent Deliberateness in the Fate of the Individual (*Parerga and Paralipomena*, I, 199–223).

Über den Willen in der Natur (III, 299–471): On the Fourfold Root of the Principle of Sufficient Reason and On the Will in Nature. (Trans. Mme. Karl Hildebrand; London: George Bell & Sons, 1881.) *De la volonté dans la nature* (See bibliography under Schopenhauer.)

Über die vierfache Wurzel des Satzes vom zureichenden Grunde (III, 7–189): On the Fourfold Root of the Principle of Sufficient Reason.

Versuch über das Geistersehn und was damit zusammenhängt (IV, 273–372): Essay on Spirit Seeing and Everything Connected Therewith (*Parerga and Paralipomena*, I, 225–309).

Die Welt als Wille und Vorstellung (I, II): The World as Will and Representation.

BIBLIOGRAPHY

Adorno, Theodor W. *Philosophie der neuen Musik.* Tübingen: J. C. B. Mohr, 1949.
———. *Versuch über Wagner.* Berlin: Suhrkamp Verlag, 1952.
Anscombe, G. E. M. *An Introduction to Wittgenstein's "Tractatus."* London: Hutchinson University Library, 1959.
Archer, William. *About the Theater: Essays and Studies.* London: T. F. Unwin, 1886.
———. "Widowers' Houses." *World,* December 14, 1892, pp. 14–15.
Arendt, Hannah. Introduction to *Illuminations,* by Walter Benjamin. Translated by Harry Zohn. New York: Harcourt, Brace & World, 1968.
———. *The Origins of Totalitarianism.* 2nd ed. Cleveland & New York: World Publishing Co., 1958.
Arnim, Sophie Gräfin von. *Carl Gustav Carus: Sein Leben und Wirken.* Dresden: Zahn und Jaensch Nachf. Verlag, n.d.
Asher, David. *Arthur Schopenhauer als Interpret des Goethe'schen Faust.* Leipzig: Arnold'sche Buchhandlung, 1859.
Augier, Émile. *Théâtre Complet.* 6 vols. Paris: Calman-Lévy, 1885–86.
Bachofen, Johann Jacob. *Das Mutterrecht: Eine Untersuchung über die Gynaikokratie der alten Welt nach ihrer religiösen und rechtlichen Natur.* 2nd ed. Basel: Benno Schwabe, 1897.
Bardas, Willy. "Zur Problematic der Musik." *Imago,* V (1917), 364–71.
Bauer, Bruno. *Disraelis romantischer und Bismarcks sozialistischer Imperialismus.* 1882; reprinted, Darmstadt: Scientia Verlag Aalen, 1969.
Becker, Werner. "'Demokratie des socialen Rechts': Die politische Haltung der Frankfurter Zeitung, der Vossischen Zeitung und des Berliner Tageblattes." Doctoral dissertation, Munich, Ludwig Maximilian University, 1965.
Béguin, Albert. *L'Âme romantique et le rêve: essai sur le romantisme allemand et la poésie française.* Paris: Librairie Jose Corti, 1946.

Bekker, Paul. *The Story of the Orchestra*. New York: W. W. Norton, 1936.

Brain, W. Russell. *Mind, Perception and Science*. Oxford: Blackwell's, 1951.

Brophy, Brigid. *A Black Ship to Hell*. New York: Harcourt, Brace & World, 1962.

Brown, Norman O. *Life Against Death: The Psychoanalytic Meaning of History*. Middleton, Conn.: Wesleyan University Press, 1959.

Carlyle, Thomas. Review of Karl Simrock's translation of "Das Nibelungenlied" (1827). *Westminster Review*, July, 1831, pp. 1–45.

———. *Past and Present*. Introduction and Notes by Edwin Mims. New York: C. Scribner's Sons, 1918.

———. *Thomas Carlyle on Heroes, Hero-Worship, and the Heroic in History*. Edited by H. D. Gray. New York: Longmans, Green, 1906.

Carpenter, William B. *Principles of Human Physiology*. Philadelphia: Lea & Blanchard, 1853.

———. *Principles of Mental Physiology*. New York: Appleton, 1875.

Carus, Carl Gustav. *Gedanken über grosse Kunst*. Leipzig: Insel Verlag, 1944.

———. *Lebenserinnerungen und Denkwürdigkeiten*. 4 vols. in 2. Leipzig: F. A. Brockhaus, 1865–66.

———. *Psyche*. Edited by Ludwig Klages from the 2nd ed. (1860). Jena: Eugen Diderichs, 1926.

———. *Vorlesungen über Psychologie gehalten im Winter 1829/30 zu Dresden*. Special ed. of the 1931 centennial reprint; edited by Edgar Michaelis. Darmstadt: Hermann Gentner Verlag, 1958.

Chamberlain, Houston Stewart. *The Foundations of the Nineteenth Century*. Translated by John Lees; introduction by Lord Redesdale. 2 vols. London: John Lane, 1911.

———. *Die Grundlagen des neunzehnten Jahrhunderts*. 2 vols. Munich: F. Bruckmann Verlag, 1899.

Cohen, Yehuda. "Wagner und Strauss im Giftschrank: Warum die Musik der beiden Richards in Israel noch immer tabu ist." *Frankfurter Allgemeine Zeitung*, August 13, 1977.

Collected Papers on Eugenic Sterilization in California: A Critical Study of the Results in 6000 Cases. Introduction by E. S. Gosney. Pasadena, Calif.: Human Betterment Foundation, 1930.

Conrad, Joseph. *The Secret Agent: A Simple Tale*. London: J. C. Methuen, 1907.

Cottle, Amos Simon, trans. *Icelandic Poetry; or, The Edda of Saemund*. Bristol: Printed by N. Briggs for Joseph Cottle, 1797.

Disraeli, Benjamin. *Coningsby; or, The New Generation*. Introduction by Philip Guedalla. London: P. Davies, 1927.

———. *Tancred; or, The New Crusade*. Introduction by Philip Guedalla. London: P. Davies, 1927.

Dostoevsky, Fedor M. *The Diary of a Writer*. Translated and annotated by

B. Brasol. New York: G. Braziller, 1954.

Drews, Arthur. *Der Ideengehalt von Richard Wagners "Ring des Nibelungen" in seiner Beziehung zur modernen Philosophie.* Leipzig: H. Haacke, 1898.

Dumas, Alexandre, *père.* "Les merveilleuses aventures du comte Lyderic." *Musée des familles,* September, 1841, pp. 373–77; October, 1841, pp. 1–14; November, 1841, pp. 33–44.

Eckermann, Johann Peter. *Conversations of Goethe with Eckermann.* Translated by John Oxenford. London: Everyman's Library, 1930.

Eichler, Max. "Jewish Eugenics." A paper read before the New York Board of Jewish Ministers. New York, 1916.

Eisler, Robert. *Man into Wolf.* London: Spring Books, n.d.

Eliot, George [Marian Evans]. *Daniel Deronda.* 2 vols. New York: Harper & Brothers, 1876.

Encyclopaedia Judaica. 16 vols. Jerusalem: Keter Publishing Co., 1971–72.

Engels, Friedrich. *The Origin of the Family, Private Property and the State, in the Light of the Researches of Lewis H. Morgan.* London: Lawrence & Wishart, 1940.

Eshleman, Lloyd Wendell. *A Victorian Rebel: The Life of William Morris.* New York: C. Scribner's Sons, 1940.

Ettmüller, Ludwig. *Die Lieder der Edda von den Nibelungen.* Zurich: Orell, Füssli, 1837.

Feuerbach, Ludwig. *Sämtliche Werke.* Edited by Wilhelm Bolin and Friedrich Jodl. 13 vols. in 12. Stuttgart: Fromman Verlag, 1959–64.

Fletcher, Harris F. *Milton's Rabbinical Readings.* Urbana: University of Illinois Press, 1930.

Frauenstädt, Julius. *Briefe über die Schopenhauer'sche Philosophie.* Leipzig: F. A. Brockhaus Verlag, 1854.

———. *Schopenhauer-Lexikon.* 2 vols. in 1. Leipzig: F. A. Brockhaus, 1871.

Freud, Sigmund. *Collected Papers.* Authorized translation under the supervision of Joan Riviere. 5 vols. New York: Basic Books, 1959.

———. *Gesammelte Werke.* 17 vols. London: Imago Publishing Co., 1941–49.

———. *New Introductory Lectures on Psycho-Analysis.* New York: W. W. Norton, 1933.

———. *Sigmund Freud: The Origins of Psychoanalysis: Letters to Wilhelm Fliess, Drafts and Notes, 1887–1902.* Translated by Eric Mosbacher and James Strachey. New York: Basic Books, 1954.

———. *Standard Edition of the Complete Psychological Works.* Translated under the editorship of James Strachey. 23 vols. London: Hogarth Press, 1953–74.

Friedell, Egon. *Kulturgeschichte der Neuzeit.* 3 vols. Munich: C. H. Beck Verlag, 1927–32.

Fromm, Erich. *The Anatomy of Human Destructiveness.* New York: Holt, Rinehart & Winston, 1973.

Fuchs, Eduard, and Richard Kreowski. *Richard Wagner in der Karikatur.* Berlin: B. Behr's Verlag, 1907.

Gardiner, Patrick. *Schopenhauer.* London: Penguin Books, 1967.

Garland, Henry, and Mary Garland. *The Oxford Companion to German Literature.* Oxford: Clarendon Press, 1976.

Ginzburg, Christian D. *The Kabbalah.* 1863; reprinted, London: Routledge & Kegan Paul, 1970.

Glasenapp, Carl. *Das Leben Richard Wagners.* 6 vols. Leipzig: Breitkopf & Härtel, 1904–12.

Glover, Edward. *War, Sadism and Pacifism: Further Essays on Group Psychology and War.* London: G. Allen & Unwin, 1946.

Gobineau, Arthur de. *The Inequality of the Human Races.* Translated by Adrian Collins; introduction by Dr. Oscar Levy. New York: G. P. Putnam's Sons, 1915.

Goethe, Johann Wolfgang. *Faust.* Edited by Erich Trunz. Hamburg: Christian Wegner Verlag, 1949.

———. *Goethes Gespräche.* Edited by Wolfgang Herwig. 4 vols. Zurich: Artemis Verlag, 1965–.

Goetschius, Percy. *The Material Used in Musical Composition.* New York: G. Schirmer, 1913.

Grant, Madison. *The Passing of the Great Race; or, The Racial Basis of European History.* Prefaces by Henry Fairfield Osborn. 4th ed. New York: Charles Scribner's Sons, 1922.

Groddeck, Georg. *Das Buch vom Es.* 2nd ed. Leipzig: Insel Verlag, 1926.

Grundmann, Herbert. *Studien über Joachim von Floris.* Leipzig: B. G. Teubner, 1927.

Gwinner, Wilhelm von. *Schopenhauers Leben.* Leipzig: F. A. Brockhaus, 1910.

Hamilton, William. *Lectures on Metaphysics.* 2 vols. Boston: Gould & Lincoln, 1859–64.

Harbou, Thea von. *Das Nibelungenbuch.* Munich: Drei Masken Verlag, 1923.

Hartmann, Eduard von. *Philosophy of the Unconscious.* Authorized translation by William C. Coupland. 3 vols. in 1. London: Routledge & Kegan Paul, 1931.

Heidegger, Martin. *Sein und Zeit.* Tübingen: Max Niemeyer Verlag, 1953.

Heine, Heinrich. "De l'Allemagne depuis Luther." *Revue des deux mondes,* 1. *trimestre* (1834), 473–505; 4. *trimestre* (1834), 373–408, 633–78.

———. *Werke.* Edited by Hermann Friedemann, Helene Herrmann, Erwin Kalischer, Raimund Pissin, and Veit Valentin. 15 vols. in 5. Berlin: Bong, 1927.

Hoffmann, E. T. A. "Der Sandmann." In *Fantasie- und Nachtstücke.* Munich: Winkler Verlag, n.d.

Hoffmann, Géza von. *Die Rassenhygiene in den Vereinigten Staaten von Nordamerika*. Munich: J. F. Lehmann, 1913.

Hook, Sidney. Review of Eric R. Bentley's *A Century of Hero-Worship*. *Nation*, October 7, 1944, pp. 412–13.

Horkheimer, Max. "Die Aktualität Schopenhauers." In Max Horkheimer and Theodor Adorno, *Sociologica II: Reden und Vorträge*. Frankfurt: Europäische Verlagsanstalt, 1962.

James, William. *The Varieties of Religious Experience*. New York: New American Library, 1958.

Kaiser, Georg. *Gas. Drei Akte*. Potsdam: G. Kiepenhauer, 1925.

Kant, Immanuel. *Werke*. 6 vols. Frankfurt: Insel, 1956–64.

Knust, Herbert. *Wagner, the King and "The Waste Land."* University Park: Pennsylvania State University Press, 1967.

Koch, Ernst. *Richard Wagners Bühnenfestspiel Der Ring des Nibelungen in seinem Verhältnis zur alten Sage wie zur modernen Nibelungendichtungen betrachtet*. Leipzig: C. F. Kahnt, 1875.

Kracauer, Siegfried. *From Caligari to Hitler: A Psychological Study of the German Film*. Princeton, N.J.: Princeton University Press, 1947.

Kraus, Karl. *Die letzten Tage der Menschheit*. Vol. IV of *Werke*. Edited by H. Fischer. 14 vols. Munich: Kosel Verlag, 1952–67.

Leon, Abram. *The Jewish Question: A Marxist Interpretation*. 1950; reprinted, New York: Pathfinder Press, 1970.

Lessing, Theodor. *Schopenhauer, Wagner, Nietzsche: Einführung in moderne deutsche Philosophie*. Munich: C. H. Beck, 1906.

Levy, Oscar. Introduction to *The Inequality of the Human Races*, by Arthur de Gobineau. Translated by Adrian Collins. New York: G. P. Putnam's Sons, 1915.

Loos, Paul Arthur. *Richard Wagner: Vollendung und Tragik der deutschen Romantik*. Bern: Francke, 1952.

Lowry, Malcolm. *Under the Volcano*. New York: Reynal & Hitchcock, 1947.

Lucka, Emil. *Otto Weininger: sein Werk und seine Persönlichkeit*. Vienna & Leipzig: Wilhelm Braumüller Verlag, 1905.

Ludmerer, Kenneth. *Genetics and American Society: A Historical Appraisal*. Baltimore: Johns Hopkins University Press, 1972.

Lück, Rudolf. *Richard Wagner und Ludwig Feuerbach: eine Ergänzung der bisherigen Darstellungen der inneren Entwicklung Richard Wagners*. Breslau: H. Fleischmann Verlag, 1905.

Magnússon, Eiríkr, and William Morris. *The Volsunga Saga*. Translated from the Icelandic . . . with introduction by H. Halliday Sparling, supplemented with Legends of the Wagner Trilogy by Jessie L. Weston, and old Norse sagas kindred to the Volsung and Niblung tale. London and New York: Norroena Society, 1906.

Magnússon, Finnur. *Den aeldre Edda: En samling af de nordiske folks aeldste sagn og sange, ved Saemund Sigfüsson kaldet hin Frode.* 4 vols. Copenhagen: n.p. 1821–23.

Mallarmé, Stéphane. "Hommage (à Richard Wagner)." In *Oeuvres Complètes.* Edited and annotated by Henri Mondor and G. Jean-Aubry. Paris: Gallimard, 1945.

Mallet, Paul Henri. *L'Introduction à l'histoire de Dannemarc, où l'on traite de la religion, des lois, des moeurs et des usages des anciens Danois.* 2 vols. Copenhagen: Berlin, 1755–56.

Mann, Thomas. *Doktor Faustus.* Stockholm: S. Fischer Verlag, 1951.

———. *Freud, Goethe, Wagner.* I, "Freud and the future"; II, "Goethe's career as a man of letters"; III, "The sufferings and greatness of Richard Wagner." New York: Alfred A. Knopf, 1937.

———. "Schopenhauer." In *Adel des Geistes.* Stockholm: Bermann-Fischer Verlag, 1948.

———. "Wälsungenblut." In *Erzählungen.* Stockholm: S. Fischer Verlag, 1960.

Marx, Karl. *Capital.* 3 vols. New York: International Publishers, 1967.

———. *Writings of the Young Marx on Philosophy and Society.* Translated and edited by L. D. Easton and K. H. Guddat. Garden City, N.Y.: Doubleday, 1967.

Marx, Karl, and Friedrich Engels. *Karl Marx Friedrich Engels Collected Works.* 10 vols. Moscow: Progress Publishers, 1975–.

———. *Karl Marx Friedrich Engels Selected Correspondence.* 3rd ed. Moscow: Progress Publishers, 1975.

———. *Karl Marx Friedrich Engels über Kunst und Literatur; eine Sammlung aus ihren Schriften.* Edited by Michail Lifschitz. Berlin: Henschel & Son, 1948. Most of the excerpts in this book are to be found, in abridged form, in Karl Marx and Friedrich Engels. *Marx Engels on Literature and Art.* Moscow: Progress Publishers, 1976.

Massow, Wilhelm von, ed. *Fürst Bülows Reden.* 5 vols. Leipzig: P. Reclam, Jr., 1910–15.

Maudsley, Henry. *The Physiology and Pathology of Mind.* New York: Appleton, 1897.

Merleau-Ponty, Maurice. *Phenomenology of Perception.* Translated by Colin Smith. London: Routledge & Kegan Paul, 1962.

Micheletti, Mario. *Lo Schopenhauerismo di Wittgenstein.* Bologna: Zanchielli, 1967.

Mill, John Stuart. *An Examination of Sir William Hamilton's Philosophy.* London: Longmans, Green, Reader & Dyer, 1867.

Mitford, Algernon Bertram, Lord Redesdale. Introduction to *The Foundations of the Nineteenth Century,* by Houston Stewart Chamberlain and translated by John Lees. 2 vols. London: John Lane, 1911.

Mochulsky, Konstantin. *Dostoevsky: His Life and Work.* Translated by Michael A. Minihan. Princeton, N.J.: Princeton University Press, 1967.

Morgan, Lewis H. *Ancient Society; or, Research in the Lines of Human Progress from Savagery, Through Barbarism to Civilization.* New York: Henry Holt, 1878.

Morris, William. *The Collected Works of William Morris.* Introduction by his daughter, May Morris. 24 vols. London: Longmans, Green, 1910–15.

Neumann, Angelo. *Erinnerungen an Richard Wagner.* Leipzig: L. Staackmann, 1907. Translated by Edith Livermore as *Personal Recollections of Wagner by Angelo Neumann.* New York: Henry Holt, 1908.

Newman, Ernest. *The Life of Richard Wagner.* 4 vols. New York: Alfred A. Knopf, 1933–47.

Nietzsche, Friedrich. *Der Fall Wagner.* Part 6, Vol. III of *Werke: Kritische Gesamtausgabe.* Edited by Giorgio Colli and Mazzino Montinari. 8 parts. Berlin: Walter de Gruyter, 1967–77.

Oxenford, John. "Iconoclasm in German Philosophy." *Westminster Review,* April, 1853, pp. 388–407.

Paul, Jean [Johann Paul Richter]. *Werke.* 7 vols. Munich: Hanser Verlag, 1960–.

Percy, Thomas, trans. *Northern antiquities: or, A description of the manners, customs, religion and laws of the ancient Danes, and other northern nations; including those of our own Saxon ancestors.* Translated from Mons. Mallet's *l'Introduction à l'histoire de Dannemarc;* with additional notes by the English translator and Goranson's Latin version of the Edda. 2 vols. London: T. Carnan, 1770.

Proust, Marcel. *À la recherche du temps perdu.* 3 vols. Paris: Gallimard, 1968.

Rank, Otto. *Beyond Psychology.* Published privately by friends and students of the author. Camden, N.J.: Haddon Craftsmen, 1941; reprint ed., New York: Dover Publications, 1958.

———. *Das Inzest-Motiv in Dichtung und Sage: Grundzüge einer Psychologie des dichterischen Schaffens.* 2nd ed. Leipzig: Franz Deuticke, 1926.

———. "Schopenhauer über den Wahnsinn." *Zentralblatt für Psychoanalyse,* I (1910), 69–71.

Rather, L. J. "Alchemistry, the Kabbala, the Analogy of the 'Creative Word', and the Origins of Molecular Biology," *Episteme,* VI (1972), 83–103.

———. "Some Reflections on the Philemon and Baucis Episode in Goethe's *Faust,*" *Diogenes,* XXV (1959), 60–73.

Roazen, Paul. *Freud and His Followers.* New York: New American Library, 1971.

Rosenberg, Alfred. *Houston Stewart Chamberlain als Verkünder und Begründer einer deutschen Zukunft.* Munich: H. Bruckmann, 1927.

Rühl, Hans. *Disraelis Imperialismus und die Kolonialpolitik seiner Zeit.* Leipzig: Meyer & Müller, 1935.

Sans, Edouard. *Richard Wagner et la pensée Schopenhauerienne.* Paris: Éditions Klincksieck, 1969.

Schaff, Philip, ed. *A Select Library of the Nicene and Post-Nicene Fathers of*

the Christian Church. 1st series. 14 vols. Grand Rapids, Mich.: W. B. Eerd-
mans, 1956.
Schelling, Friedrich. *Sämmtliche Werke.* 14 vols. Stuttgart: J. B. Cotta Verlag,
1856–61.
Scholem, Gershom. *Sabbatai Ṣevi, the Mystical Messiah.* Princeton, N.J.:
Princeton University Press, 1973.
————. *Ursprung und Anfänge der Kabbala.* Berlin: Walter de Gruyter, 1962.
Schopenhauer, Arthur. *De la volonté dans la nature.* Translated, with intro-
duction and notes, by Edouard Sans. Paris: Presses universitaires de France,
1969.
————. *On the Basis of Morality.* Translated by E. F. J. Payne. Indianapolis,
Ind.: Bobbs-Merrill, 1965.
————. *On the Fourfold Root of the Principle of Sufficient Reason.* Translated
by E. F. J. Payne; introduction by Richard Taylor. La Salle, Illinois: Open
Court Publishing Co., 1974.
————. *Parerga and Paralipomena: Short Philosophical Essays.* Translated by
E. F. J. Payne. 2 vols. London: Oxford University Press, 1974.
————. *Sämtliche Werke.* Edited by Wolfgang Freiherr von Löhneysen. 5 vols.
Stuttgart: Insel Verlag, 1960–65.
————. *The World as Will and Representation.* Translated by E. F. J. Payne. 2
vols. Indian Hills, Colorado: The Falcon's Wing Press, 1958; republished,
with minor corrections, New York: Dover Publications, 1969.
Shaw, George Bernard. *The Bodley Head Bernard Shaw: Collected Plays and
Prefaces.* Edited by Dan H. Laurence. 7 vols. London: The Bodley Head,
1970–74.
————. *The Complete Prefaces of Bernard Shaw.* London: Hamlyn, 1965.
————. "A Degenerate's View of Nordau." *Liberty,* July 27, 1895, pp. 2–10.
————. *Major Barbara: A Screen Version.* New York: Penguin Books, 1946.
————. *Major Critical Essays: The Quintessence of Ibsenism; The Perfect
Wagnerite; The Sanity of Art.* London: Constable, 1948.
————. *The Perfect Wagnerite: A Commentary on "The Ring of the Nib-
lungs."* London: Grant Richards, 1898; Chicago & New York: Herbert S.
Stone, 1899.
————. *The Perfect Wagnerite: A Commentary on the Niblung's Ring.* New
York: Brentano's, 1909.
————. *The Perfect Wagnerite: A Commentary on the Niblung's Ring.* 3rd
rev. ed. Leipzig: Bernard Tauchnitz, 1913.
————. *The Perfect Wagnerite: A Commentary on the Niblung's Ring.* 4th
rev. ed. London: Constable, 1923.
————. *The Sanity of Art: An Exposure of the Current Nonsense About Art-
ists Being Degenerates.* London: New Age Press, 1908.
Shirer, William. *The Rise and Fall of the Third Reich.* New York: Simon &
Schuster, 1960.

Simrock, Karl, trans. *Das Nibelungenlied.* 54th ed. Stuttgart: J. B. Cotta Verlag, 1898.

Sparling, H. Halliday. Introduction to *The Volsunga Saga.* Translated by Eiríkr Magnússon and William Morris. London and New York: Norroena Society, 1906.

Spengler, Oswald. *Der Mensch und die Technik: Beitrag zu einer Philosophie des Lebens.* Munich: C. H. Beck'scher Verlag, 1930.

————. *Der Untergang des Abendlandes.* 2 vols. Munich: C. H. Beck'scher Verlag, 1920.

Spielrein, Sabina. "Die Destruktion als Ursache des Werdens." *Jahrbuch für psychoanalytische und psychopathologische Forschungen,* IV (1912), 464–503. (See the annotation in the bibliographic supplement.)

Spinoza, Baruch. *Benedicti de Spinoza opera quotquot reperta sunt.* Edited by J. van Vloten and J. P. N. Land. 4 vols. in 2. The Hague: Martin Nijhoff, 1914.

Stark, W. *The Sociology of Knowledge.* London: Routledge & Kegan Paul, 1958.

Stein, Leon. *The Racial Thinking of Richard Wagner.* New York: Philosophical Library, 1950.

Teller, Frieda. "Musikgenuss und Phantasie." *Imago,* V (1917), 8–15.

Turco, Alfred. *Shaw's Moral Vision: The Self and Salvation.* Ithaca, New York: Cornell University Press, 1976.

Virchow, Rudolf. "Anthropology in the Last Twenty Years." *Smithsonian Report,* 1889, pp. 555–70.

————. "The Founding of the Berlin University and the Transition from the Philosophic to the Scientific Age." *Smithsonian Report,* 1894, pp. 681–85.

Wagner, Cosima. *Die Tagebücher.* Edited and annotated by Martin Gregor-Dellin and Dietrich Mack. 2 vols. Munich & Zurich: R. Piper, 1977.

Wagner, Gustav Friedrich. *Schopenhauer-Register.* Edited by Arthur Hübscher. Stuttgart: Fromman Verlag, 1962.

Wagner, Richard. *Beethoven; With a Supplement From the Philosophical Works of Arthur Schopenhauer.* Translated by Edward Dannreuther. London: Reeves, 1880.

————. *Gesammelte Schriften und Dichtungen.* 3rd ed. 10 vols. Leipzig: E. W. Fritzsch Verlag, 1898. (2nd ed.; 10 vol.; 1877–78.)

————. *Mein Leben.* 2 vols. Munich: List Verlag, 1969.

————. *My Life.* 2 vols. New York: List & Dodd Mead, 1911.

————. *Richard Wagner an August Röckel.* Edited by La Mara [Ida Maria Lipsius]. Leipzig: Breitkopf & Härtel Verlag, 1903.

————. *Richard Wagners Briefe.* Edited by Erich Kloss. 17 vols. in 9. Leipzig: Breitkopf & Härtel Verlag, 1910–13.

————. *Richard Wagners Gesammelte Schriften.* Edited by Julius Kapp. 14

vols. in 5. Leipzig: Hesse & Becker Verlag, 1914.

———. *Richard Wagner's Prose Works*. Translated by William Ashton Ellis. 8 vols. London: Kegan Paul, Trench, Trübner, 1895–99.

———. *Wagner an Mathilde Wesendonck*. Berlin: A. Duncker Verlag, 1906.

———. *Wagner-Encyclopädie: Haupterscheinungen der Kunst- und Kulturgeschichte im Lichte der Anschauung Richard Wagners*. Edited by Carl Fr. Glasenapp. Leipzig: E. W. Fritzsch, 1891.

———. *Wagner-Lexikon: Hauptbegriffe der Kunst- und Weltanschauung Richard Wagners*. Compiled by Carl Fr. Glasenapp and Heinrich von Stein. Stuttgart: Cotta, 1883.

———. "The Work and Mission of My Life." *North American Review*, August, 1879, pp. 107–24; September, 1879, pp. 238–58.

Warren, Robert Penn. *Homage to Theodore Dreiser*. New York: Random House, 1971.

Wassermann, Jakob. *Imaginäre Brücken: Studien und Aufsätze*. Munich: Kurt Wolff Verlag, 1921.

———. *Rede an die Jugend über das Leben im Geiste*. Berlin: S. Fischer Verlag, 1932.

Weil, Simone. "The Iliad, or the Poem of Force," translated by Mary McCarthy. *Politics*, November, 1945, pp. 321–31.

Weininger, Otto. *Dr. Otto Weininger über die letzten Dinge*. Biographical preface by Moriz Rappaport. 6th ed. Vienna & Leipzig: Wilhelm Braumüller Verlag, 1920.

———. *Geschlecht und Charakter*. 21st ed. Vienna: W. Braumüller, 1926.

———. *Sex and Character*. Authorized translation from the 6th German ed. London: W. Heinemann, 1906. (Incomplete and not always accurately translated.)

Wells, H. G. *The Wife of Sir Isaac Harmon*. London: Macmillan, 1914.

———. *The World of William Clissold*. 2 vols. New York: George H. Doran, 1926.

Westernhagen, Curt von. *The Forging of the "Ring": Richard Wagner's Composition Sketches for "Der Ring des Nibelungen."* Translated by Arnold and Mary Whittall from *Die Entstehung des "Ring"* (Zurich: Atlantis Musikbuch-Verlag, 1973). Cambridge: Cambridge University Press, 1976.

———. *Richard Wagners Dresdener Bibliothek 1842–1849*. Wiesbaden: F. A. Brockhaus, 1966.

———. *Wagner: A Biography*. Translated by Mary Whittall. Cambridge: Cambridge University Press, 1978.

Weston, Jessie Laidlay. *From Ritual to Romance*. Cambridge: Cambridge University Press, 1920.

———. *The Legends of the Wagner Drama: Studies in Mythology and Romance*. 1903; reprint ed., Boston: Longwood Press, 1977.

———. "Legends of the Wagner Trilogy and old Norse Sagas kindred to the

Volsung and Niblung Tale." In *The Volsunga Saga*, translated by Eiríkr Magnússon and William Morris. London & New York: Norroena Society, 1906.

White, Victor. *God and the Unconscious*. London: Harvill Press, 1952.

Whitehead, Alfred North. *Modes of Thought*. Cambridge: Cambridge University Press, 1938.

Wilson, Pearl Cleveland. *Wagner's Dramas and Greek Tragedy*. New York: Columbia University Press, 1919.

Wisenthal, J. L. "The Underside of Undershaft: A Wagnerian Motif in *Major Barbara*." *Shaw Review*, XV (May, 1972), 56–64.

THEMATIC
BIBLIOGRAPHY

Andreevsky, Alexander. *Der Weg zum Gral: Richard Wagners Kämpferleben* [The Way to the Grail: Richard Wagner's Embattled Life]. Berlin: Verlagshaus Bong, 1941. A rather pedestrian novel based on Wagner's career from 1823 to 1883. Far less emphasis on Wagner's anti-Semitism than might have been expected, given the time. Giacomo Meyerbeer appears as a scheming intrigant, but Carl Tausig (the Jewish musician and piano virtuoso who worked with Wagner at Bayreuth) is presented with respect and sympathy. Angelo Neumann, Hermann Levi, and Joseph Rubinstein, however, are not in evidence. Begins with Richard at home "in the Voigt's house on Jews-Court in Dresden," where, according to Mrs. Burrell (Newman, *Life*, I, 44), the family never lived.

Arendt, Hannah. Introduction to *Illuminations*, by Walter Benjamin and translated by Harry Zohn. New York: Harcourt, Brace & World, 1968. "The main work consisted in tearing fragments out of their context and arranging them afresh in such a way that they illustrated one another. . . . Benjamin's ideal of producing a work consisting entirely of quotations, one that was mounted so masterfully that it could dispense with any accompanying text, may strike one as whimsical in the extreme and self-destructive to boot" (47).

Benjamin, Walter. *Schriften*. 2 vols. Frankfurt a.M.: Suhrkamp Verlag, 1955. The epigraph on the title page of the present book is taken from Vol. I, p. 571: "Citations in my work are like robbers on the highway who rush out armed and deprive the leisurely traveler of conviction."

Bergonzi, Bernard. *The Early H. G. Wells*. Manchester: Manchester University Press, 1961. The young Wells exhibited as a *fin de siècle* if not *"fin du globe"* writer. The "fin du globe myth" is the "fearsome" myth of the *Götterdämmerung* presented in the English translation (1895) of Max Nordau's *Degeneration*.

Bernfeld, Siegfried. "Freud's Earliest Theories and the School of Helmholtz."

Psychoanalytic Quarterly, XIII (1944), 341–62. A study of the influence on Freud of his feared and admired teacher Ernst Brücke, who, with Emil du Bois-Reymond and Hermann Helmholtz, studied under Johannes Müller in Berlin.

Clemens, Samuel L. [Mark Twain]. *King Leopold's Soliloquy: A Defense of His Congo Rule.* Boston: P. R. Warren, 1905. Conrad's Heart of Darkness: the Belgian Congo (now Zaïre), scene of one of the world's great genocides at the end of the nineteenth century. Mark Twain cites from the debate in the Belgian Parliament, July, 1903: "This work of 'civilization' is an enormous and continual butchery. . . . All the facts we brought forward in this chamber were denied at first most energetically; but later, little by little, they were proved by documents and official texts." Leopold's reputation for posterity is not endangered, says Twain; the human race will soon forget that "this ghastliest episode in all human history is the work of *one man alone*" (41–44).

Cohn, Robert Greer. *Toward the Poems of Mallarmé.* Berkeley & Los Angeles: University of California Press, 1965. An interpretation of Stéphane Mallarmé's poem of homage to Richard Wagner, cited in part on the title page of the present book, appears on pp. 177–85. Cohn's translation: "Trumpets aloud of gold fainted on the vellums, / The god Richard Wagner radiating a sacrament / Ill hushed by ink itself in sybilline sobs."

Conrad, Joseph. *Geography and Some Explorers.* New York: Doubleday Page, 1926. Conrad on the Congo affair and the European exploitation of the Americas four centuries earlier.

——. *Two Tales of the Congo: An Outpost of Progress; Heart of Darkness.* London: Folio Society, 1952. A transposition into politico-economic reality, and back again into metaphor, of Immanuel Kant's region "on the great map of the heart" where "only a few places are lit up" and Jean Paul's "huge realm of the unconscious, that real inner Africa."

Donington, Robert. *Wagner's "Ring" and Its Symbols: The Music and the Myth.* London: Faber & Faber, 1963. An interesting and valuable interpretation along Jungian lines of both the musical themes and the story of the *Ring.*

Drews, Arthur. *Der Ideengehalt von Richard Wagners dramatischen Dichtungen im Zusammenhange mit seinem Leben und seiner Weltanschauung, nebst einem Anhang: Nietzsche und Wagner* [The Thought Content of Richard Wagner's Dramatic Poems in Relation to His Life and World Outlook, with an Appendix: Nietzsche and Wagner]. Leipzig: E. Pfeiffer, 1931. An extended, updated version of his earlier book on Wagner (see bibliography), but quite without its characteristic élan.

Faure, Gabriel. "La mort de Wagner à Venise." In *Les rendez-vous italiens.* Paris: Bibliothèque-Charpentier Fasquelle Éditeurs, n.d. Wagner's death in Venice, remembered by Faure on the occasion of a visit to the city in 1932.

Franklin, H. Bruce. "Chic Bleak in Fantasy Fiction." *Saturday Review*, July 5, 1972, pp. 42–45. Marxist-oriented correlation of "doomsday-literature" with critical periods in economic history, when an old form of production is shattered by a new. The doomsday-writer is a Chicken Little who mistakes "an act of creation (the fall of an acorn) for cosmic destruction (the fall of the sky)." Franklin's own title was "The Sky Is Falling" (personal communication, H. B. F.).

Fussell, Paul. *The Great War and Modern Memory*. New York and London: Oxford University Press, 1975. Myths, rituals, and remembrances of the *Götterdämmerung*, 1914–1918.

Gérard, René. *L'Orient et la pensée romantique allemand*. Paris: Marcel Didier, 1963. Influence of Eastern thought (chiefly Buddhistic and Brahmanic) on Johann Herder, the Schlegels, Wilhelm von Humboldt, Karl Ritter, Arthur Schopenhauer, and others. The revolt against "Jewish" or "Judeo"-Christianity in favor of "Aryan" or "Eastern" Christianity extends from Herder to the Romantic school. The sui generis character of Schopenhauer's thought, and its lack of accordance with Buddhism or Brahmanism, is pointed out.

Gissing, George. *The Nether World*. 3 vols. London: Smith, Elder, 1889. Gissing's frightful vision of London as Nibelheim is Dantesque in spirit, but his redemptive measures are Wagnerian: "For, work as you will, there is no chance of a new and better world until the old be utterly destroyed. Destroy, sweep away, prepare the ground; then shall music the holy, music the civiliser, breathe over the renewed earth" (I, 264–65).

Gross, Otto. "Über Destruktionssymbolik" [On Symbols of Destruction]. *Zentralblatt für Psychoanalyse*, IV (1914), 525–34. Another psychoanalytic interpretation of Sabina Spielrein's question: Why are symbols of rape and destruction associated with ideas of sex and motherhood in the unconscious? Gross finds that the social and sexual domination of women by men is the root cause of the present sufferings of humanity. A "basic ethical instinct" is also a driving force in the unconscious. Overcompensation and distortion of conflicting drives take place in such a way that "the play of forces between the self-preserving drive 'not wanting to be raped' (*Nichtvergewaltigtwerdenwollen*) and the ethical drive 'not wanting to rape' (*Nichtvergewaltigenwollen*) expresses itself in modified form . . . as an inner conflict between the 'will to power' (*Wille zur Macht*) and the 'will to self-abolition' (*Wille zur Selbstaufhebung*)." (Neither a victim nor an executioner, as Albert Camus will say.)

Grove's Dictionary of Music and Musicians. Edward Dannreuther's article on Wagner in the first edition (1904) of this reference work contrasts interestingly with Percy M. Young's in the fifth edition (1954). Young finds it appropriate to cite William Shirer on Wagner in relation to Hitler and Nazi Germany.

Janik, Allen, and Stephen Toulmin. *Wittgenstein's Vienna*. New York: Simon & Schuster, 1973. Vienna (Karl Kraus's "proving ground for world-destruction") and Ludwig Wittgenstein. "An account of the life, the times and the culture of Habsburg Vienna before World War One—the Vienna of Sigmund Freud, Arnold Schönberg, Adolph Loos, Oskar Kokoschka, 'modernism,' Mayerling, and Ludwig Wittgenstein, the great philosopher whose epochal work was formed in the decline and fall of the Austro-Hungarian Empire."

Jullian, Philippe. *Esthètes et magiciens: l'art fin de siècle*. Paris: Librairie académique Perrin, 1969. This study of *fin de siècle* art is illustrative throughout of what Wagnerism meant in late nineteenth-century France. Jullian himself finds that "Wagner, qui n'avait pas trouvé de peintre digne de lui, trouvait en Fritz Lang le metteur en scène des Niebelungen" (272).

Larisch, Marie (Countess). *My Past*. London: Eveleigh Nash, 1913. Daughter of Duke Ludwig of Bavaria, niece and confidante of Elisabeth empress of Austria. Marie's role in T. S. Eliot's *The Waste Land* was pointed out by George L. K. Morris in "Marie, Marie, Hold on Tight," *Partisan Review*, March–April, 1954, pp. 231–33. See her account of Elisabeth's prophetic dream of the drowned king, Ludwig II, and of her own and her sister's death. Wagner, then near the height of his fame, makes a brief, good-humored appearance.

Lévi-Strauss, Claude. *The Raw and the Cooked*. Translated from *Le Cru et le cuit* (1964) by John and Doreen Weightman. New York: Harper & Row, 1975. Lévi-Strauss expresses his "reverence, from childhood on, for 'that God, Richard Wagner,'" whom he regards as the "undeniable originator of the structural analysis of myths . . . *in music*."

Lorenz, Alfred. *Das Geheimnis der Form bei Richard Wagner* [The Secret of Form in Richard Wagner]. 4 vols. Leipzig: M. Hesse, 1924–33; reprint ed., Tutzing: H. Schneider, 1966. An elaborate and demanding study of the architectonics of Wagner's orchestral and vocal music.

Lowry, Malcolm. *Under the Volcano*. London: Jonathan Cape, 1947. The self-destructive drive now overmastering the Western world luridly depicted in this carefully planned parable, the story of the downfall and death (with a hint of salvation at the end) of a drunkenly lucid British "Consul" in Mexico, near the close of the Civil War in Spain. The patently Wagnerian elements in the structure of the novel have been generally overlooked. Echoes of Kant, Jean Paul, and Joseph Conrad are heard also; for example, when the "Consul" likens himself to a "great explorer who has discovered some extraordinary land from which he can never return to give his knowledge to the world: but the name of this land is hell . . . not Mexico of course but in the heart."

Mann, Klaus. *Mephisto*. Translated by Robin Smyth. New York: Random House, 1977. A *roman à clef* by the oldest son of Thomas Mann, who committed suicide in 1949. A bitter indictment (written in the 1930s) of

Germany and the Germans during Hitler's rise to power, when Nazi "philosophers . . . considered 'Race' to be the only objective truth." "Hendrik Höfgen" (the actor Gustav Gründgens, whose most successful role was that of Mephistopheles in Goethe's *Faust*) is the prototypical trimmer throughout. His estranged wife, "Barbara Bruckner" (Erika Mann), daughter of the "invulnerable . . . Privy Councillor," hears the approaching catastrophe as "the underworld crying out for power." Another master trimmer, the poet "Benjamin Pelz," calls Hitler "the god of the Underworld." The "Privy Councillor" is conflated from Thomas Mann's father-in-law, *Geheimrat Professor Doktor* Alfred Pringsheim, mathematician, Wagner enthusiast, and son of a rich Jewish railroad magnate, and Thomas Mann himself. The attraction of the god Hermes for the "Privy Councillor" seems to foreshadow Thomas Mann's confession of his own kinship with the underworld, in the novel *Felix Krull* (1954) and the essay *Brother Hitler* (1938).

Mann, Thomas. *Der Erwählte*. Stockholm: S. Fischer Verlag, 1951. Based on the medieval French *Vie du pape Grégoire*, the life of a fictitious Pope Gregory. In this retelling Mann comes to cheerful terms with one of his lifelong preoccupations, the theme of incest. Gregory is the product of a brother-sister union, brought up in ignorance of his parentage, who rescues and marries a woman who turns out to be his mother. After prolonged penance, Gregory is crowned pope. The Oedipus legend given a happy ending.

Müller, Johannes. *Über die phantastischen Gesichtserscheinungen: eine physiologische Untersuchung mit einer physiologischen Urkunde des Aristoteles über den Traum, den Philosophen und Aerzten gewidmet* [On Subjective Visual Phenomena: A Physiological Study with a Physiological Document by Aristotle on Dreams, Dedicated to Philosophers and Physicians.]. Coblenz: Jacob Hölscher, 1826. A rationalization of the irrational by the most famous biologist of his time (1801–1858). Teacher of the Vienna physiologist Ernst Brücke, whom Freud called "the greatest authority who ever impressed himself on my mind."

Northcote-Bade, James. *Die Wagner-Mythen im Frühwerk Thomas Manns*. Bonn: Bouvier Verlag, 1975. A careful examination of the Wagnerian myths in Mann's writings up to the time of his "Wagner-crisis" in 1909–1911. Especially illuminating is the detailed analysis of the novella *Wälsungenblut*, including its suppressed ending. *Wälsungenblut*, a parody of Wagner's *Die Walküre* in which an incestuous relationship between twins of Jewish "blood" is substituted for the similar relationship between Siegmund and Sieglinde, first appeared in 1906, but was not included in the collected works until after Mann's death in 1955.

Polanyi, Karl. *The Great Transformation*. New York: Farrar & Rinehart, 1944.

Although all societies are limited by economic factors, according to Polanyi: "Nineteenth-century civilization alone was economic in a different and distinctive sense, for it chose to base itself on a motive only rarely acknowledged as valid in the history of human societies, and certainly never before raised to the level of a justification of action in everyday life, namely gain."

Pynchon, Thomas. *Gravity's Rainbow.* New York: Viking Press, 1973. Myths, rituals, and remembrances of the *Götterdämmerung,* 1939–1945.

Raff, Joachim. *Die Wagner Frage: Kritisch beleuchtet; Erster Theil, Wagner's letzte künstlerische Kundgebung im "Lohengrin"* [The Wagner Question: A Critical Study; Part 1, Wagner's Latest Artistic Pronouncement in *Lohengrin*]. Braunschweig: Friedrich Vieweg und Sohn, 1854. Raff, a prolific but now forgotten composer, was at various times associated with Felix Mendelssohn, Franz Liszt, and Hans von Bülow. His book, in the form of thirty-five letters to a friend who has asked for light on the "Wagner question," is probably the first of its kind. *Lohengrin* was initially produced in 1850 in Weimar. When Lohengrin is faced with the choice of "becoming a whole human being" (*ganz Mensch zu werden*) by devoting himself to Elsa, "his egoism conquers" (*siegt sein Egoismus*); and he chooses to withdraw to Monsalvat, says Raff (243). Raff does not refer at this point to Wagner's reevaluation of *Lohengrin* in his *Mittheilung an meine Freunde* (1851).

Rank, Otto. *Die Lohengrinsage: Ein Beitrag zu ihrer Motivgestaltung und Deutung* [The Lohengrin Saga: A Contribution to Its Motivational Structure and Interpretation]. 1911; reprint ed., Nendeln/Liechtenstein: Kraus, 1970. A survey of the literary background of the saga and a fascinating, if orthodox, psychoanalytic study of Wagner's treatment of the saga in *Lohengrin,* and of Wagner himself. Rank points to hidden Oedipal elements in the saga, accentuated and altered by Wagner in *Lohengrin,* and to strong Oedipal elements in Wagner's psyche.

Roussel, Royal. *The Metaphysics of Darkness.* Baltimore: Johns Hopkins University Press, 1971. Conrad's victory, after a lifetime struggle with the "darkness," came at last in *Under Western Eyes* when he recognized and accepted "the fact that the darkness is, finally, the source of life, and if he [the human being] wishes ever to transcend the ephemerality and abstractness of his initial, orphaned state, then he can do so only by returning to this source. . . . It is only by such a voyage that man can make the necessary and saving contact with the reality which has brought him into existence" (182).

Sans, Edouard. *Richard Wagner et la pensée Schopenhauerienne* [Richard Wagner and the Thought of Schopenhauer]. Paris: Éditions Klincksieck, 1969. A superb full-scale study (478 pages) of Wagner's thought and Schopenhauer's philosophy, with special emphasis on the *Ring.* Seven chapters on the central ethical importance of "compassion" (*Mitleid, universelle pitié*) in the writings of Schopenhauer and Wagner.

Spielrein, Sabina. "Die Destruktion als Ursache des Werdens" [Destruction As the Basis of Becoming]. *Jahrbuch für psychoanalytische und psychopathologische Forschungen*, IV (1912), 464–503. "Why this mightiest of all drives, the reproductive drive, harbors within itself negative feelings, such as anxiety and disgust, as well as the a priori to-be-expected positive feelings." She finds two antagonistic components in the self-reproductive drive: a life-oriented (*Werdetrieb*) and a death-oriented destructive drive (*Zerstörungstrieb*), the latter anticipating Sigmund Freud's "death instinct" (see *Beyond the Pleasure Principle* in Freud, *Standard Edition*). Spielrein draws heavily on Richard Wagner's music-dramas in illustrating her views. The typical Wagnerian heroes and heroines are self-sacrificing savior types: "The similarity between the Nordic Siegfried and the Oriental Christ is striking," she writes.

Stern, Fritz. *Gold and Iron: Bismarck, Bleichroeder and the Building of the German Empire*. New York: A. A. Knopf, 1977. The prototype of Wagner's "Jew and Junker" combine.

Stevenson, Robert Louis. *The Strange Case of Dr. Jekyll and Mr. Hyde, With other Fables*. London: Longmans, 1896. Mr. Hyde, like Wells's invisible man, is the invisible id made visible by the power of science. Stevenson's Hyde, a cross between a Morlock and a Nibelung, is "troglodytic" and "pale and dwarfish," inspires "loathing," and inhabits a part of Soho seeming to Mr. Utterson like "a district of some city in a nightmare."

Teller, Charlotte. *The Cage*. New York: D. Appleton, 1907; reprint ed., New York: AMS Press, 1977. From the heights of an aristocratic but mysteriously veiled background, Lohengrin-von Harden arrives in Chicago to become involved in a bitter dispute between capital and labor, culminating in the Haymarket Square bomb explosion of May 4, 1886. Frederica-Elsa asks the "forbidden question." But when the offended Lohengrin seeks to withdraw, Frederica confronts him with his theatrical self-conceit and at the same time attains full, independent womanhood. Containing overt references to *Lohengrin*, Teller's story is in harmony with Wagner's (and Raff's) reevaluation of the Lohengrin-Elsa relationship that led to the figure of Brünnhilde.

Wagner, Gottlob Heinrich Adolf. "Übersicht des mythischen Systems" [Survey of Mythical System]. In Johann Arnold Kanne, *System der indischen Mythe*. Leipzig: Weyand, 1813. Adolf Wagner, Richard's uncle, was a private scholar interested in, among other things, myths. Richard, who admired his uncle greatly, spent some time with him in Leipzig in 1822 (Newman, *Life*, I, 43, 59).

Wagner, Richard. *Richard Wagner's Letters to August Roeckel*. Translated by Eleanor C. Sellars; introductory essay by Houston Stewart Chamberlain.

.:....

Bristol: J. W. Arrowsmith, 1897. The forty-page introductory essay is enlightening. Chamberlain writes that the words and action in Wagner's music-dramas furnish only an "allegory" of the real action, expressed by the music, in the "depths" and that a corrupt art, to Wagner's way of thinking, is the logical outcome of a corrupt society. In this sense "Wagner may be said to have been a revolutionist ever since 1840, and his very latest writings leave no doubt that he continued to be a revolutionist to the day of his death." Points out Wagner's opposition to Bismarck.

Wassermann, Jakob. *Christian Wahnschaffe* [Christian Madshape, or Christian Create Illusion!]. 2 vols. S. Fischer Verlag, 1919. The Morocco crisis in Germany and the Potemkin mutiny in Russia date the action, but the novel is in fact a powerful evocation of the apocalyptic *Götterdämmerung* spirit abroad in Europe at the time of the Great War. Christian's first lodestar is Eva, a self-willed, non-Jewish *première danseuse* who meets her death in Russia at the hands of the revolutionary sailors; then Ruth, a self-abnegating Jewess who meets her death in Berlin at the hands of a rapist-murderer. Christian vanishes into legend in the end, but not before telling his multimillionaire-industrialist father, whose name is (almost predictably) Albrecht: "You cannot see me; the father does not see the son. The world of sons must rise up against the world of fathers; in no other way can things change" (II, 439). Translated into English as *The World's Illusion*.

Wells, H. G. "A Dream of Armageddon." In *Twelve Stories and a Dream*. London: Macmillan, 1903. A dream of *Götterdämmerung* as an air war in the future: "A darkness, a flood of darkness that opened and spread and blotted out all things. . . . 'Nightmares,' he cried; 'nightmares indeed!'"

———. *The Invisible Man: A Grotesque Romance*. London: C. A. Pearson, 1897. Griffin (beast-guardian of the Scythian treasure), the invisible man, reveals what lies within: his headlong course of rapine, murder, and destruction is the id made visible (by science) in action. Whereas Schopenhauer asserts (*Sämtliche Werke*, II, 167) that the body is simply the "will" become visible, Wells in effect makes the counterassertion: the "will" is the body become invisible.

———. *The Island of Dr. Moreau*. London: W. Heinemann, 1896. Man as the creator's failure: the beast hidden within makes its way out.

———. *Mind at the End of Its Tether; and The Happy Turning, A Dream of Life*. New York: Didier, 1946. A "menace of darkness," an "unknown implacable," an "Antagonist," has turned its face against life and reason in our time.

———. *The Time Machine: An Invention*. London: W. Heinemann, 1895. The "revenge of the Nibelungs" theme transposed from London's nineteenth-century Nibelheim to a distant future. The cannibal-technician Morlocks prey at night on the surface-dwelling Eloi, who attempt in daytime to repress all knowledge of these suppressed men, now become underground monsters. The Morlocks, described by Wells as "small . . . stooping white creatures [with] the half-bleached colour of worms," recall the Nibelungs of Wagner's *Sketch* of 1848: "Ceaselessly active, they churn through the bowels of the earth, like worms in a dead body" (*Gesammelte Schriften*, 2nd ed., II, 156; Ellis, VII, 301).

The Morlocks, Stevenson's Mr. Hyde, and Wagner's Nibelungs somewhat resemble the *homo terribilis* or *homo troglodytes* of Linnaeus, described in the 1771 *Encyclopaedia Britannica* (II, 789) as "white . . . about one half human size . . . lives about 25 years . . . conceals himself in caves during the day, and searches for his prey at night." Early in the nineteenth century it was recognized that this supposed species of primitive man was represented in fact only by the immature orangutan, *pongo pygmaeus*. That Wagner was familiar with the story is evident from a letter to Theodor Uhlig written in September, 1852. The letter begins with the salutation, "O Thou Human Being! *Homo terribilis* (Lin. II, 53)." Wagner had been upset by the mistreatment of animals that he had witnessed while on his way to Spezia, and he confided to Uhlig his doubts as to the future of the human race. He was, he said, "constrained to believe that this species must perish utterly" (*Richard Wagners Briefe*, IV, 203–206).

Werfel, Franz. *Barbara, oder die Frömmigkeit* [Barbara, or Piety]. Berlin, Vienna, Leipzig: Paul Szolnay Verlag, 1929. (Translated by Geoffrey Dunlop as *The Pure in Heart*. New York: Book League of America, 1931.) The ship's physician Ferdinand R., who as an Austrian officer on the East Front during the Great War defied authority by refusing to carry out a military execution, consigns to the ocean depths the gold accumulated for him by his childhood guardian angel, the maid Barbara, since he desires to "withdraw . . . it from the profanement of circulation" (808)."Gebhart" (Otto Gross), the "man of destruction," plays an important part in the novel, especially in the chapter entitled "Babylonisches Zwischenspiel," as spokesman for the needed "sexual revolution," revolt against the father, and restoral of "mother-right."

―――. *Verdi: Roman der Oper*, [Verdi: A Novel of the Opera]. Berlin, Vienna, Leipzig: Paul Szolnay Verlag, 1926. (Translated by Helen Jessiman as *Verdi*. London: Jarrolds, 1926.) A story of Verdi's desperate struggle with the spirit of Wagner. The two men never meet. The story takes place in 1882–1883, culminating in Verdi's release following Wagner's death in Venice.

INDEX

Adorno, Theodor, 102n, 147n
Alberich: the *Ring*, xvii, 60, 62, 67, 103,
179, 182; Norse mythology, 1, 11, 12;
Ring outline, 44–47, 100, 101; Shaw,
155–67 *passim*, 177
Andreevsky, Alexander, 197
Animal rights, 96–97, 205
Annihilation, 70, 73, 78, 88–89, 105,
106, 109, 116, 128, 130–31, 140, 141.
See also Death; Destruction; Self-
abolition; Self-destruction
Anscombe, G. E. M., 75, 84
Antigone: Oedipus myth, 51–55 *passim*,
107, 144; as savior, 56, 59, 61, 63–64,
104, 110
Antigone (Sophocles), 48
Anti-Semitism: and Chamberlain, 28,
32–34, 95; as trend, 34–35; German,
35n–36n, 97–98; and Schopenhauer,
90–91, 96, 97–98; and Marx, 91; and
Weininger, 92–95, 97; Jewish, 95; and
Wagner, 89–91, 94, 96, 97, 98n, 102n,
170–71, 176n. *See also* Jews; Nazism
Archer, William, 149–51
Arendt, Hannah, 15, 197
Aristotle, 77, 128, 133
Art, xviii, 10, 48–49, 50, 55–56, 103–
105, 108, 113–14, 131, 143–44, 147–
48
Artemidorus, 123
The Art-Work of the Future, 66, 142–44
Asher, David, 90–91
Augier, Emile, 150–51

Bach, Johann Sebastian, 139, 159, 168
Bachofen, Johann, 110–11

Bähr, Karl, 90
Bakunin, Michael, 20, 142, 158, 160
Baudelaire, Charles, 119
Bauer, Bruno, 17
Beethoven: Schopenhauer on, 139; Wag-
ner on, 139–48; C-sharp Minor String
Quartet, 140–41; Ninth Symphony,
141–45; Feuerbachian interpretation,
142–44; Schopenhauerian interpreta-
tion, 144–45, 147; mentioned, 41, 136,
159, 168
Benjamin, Walter, xx, 197
Bergonzi, Bernard, 197
Berkeley, George, 75
Berlioz, Hector, 142
Bernfeld, Siegfried, 197
Beyond the Pleasure Principle (Freud),
203
Bismarck, 15–16, 32, 85, 97, 108, 160,
173–74, 203, 204
Blake, William, 156
Bleichröder, Gerson, 15–16, 174, 203
Bois-Reymond, Emil du, 198
Börne, Ludwig, 101
Brahmanism, 89, 96, 109, 130, 199
Brahms, Johannes, 115
Brain, W. Russell, 76
Breuer, Josef, 94
Brophy, Brigid, xix
Brother Hitler (Mann), 201
Brown, Norman O., xix
Brücke, Ernst, 198, 201
Brünnhilde: the *Ring*, xvii, 103, 106, 107,
151, 182, 203; Norse myths, 1–2; *Ring*
outline, 45–47, 100; as savior, 46, 47,
67, 108; perfected human, 59, 60, 61;
Shaw, 157, 162

Buber, Martin, 66
Buddhism, 89, 96, 100–101, 109, 130, 175, 199
Bülow, Hans von, 202

The Cage (Teller), 203
Calderón, Pedro, 120
Camus, Albert, 199
Capitalism, 8, 10, 11, 59, 91, 103, 154, 160–61, 164–65
Carlyle, Thomas: on Norse mythology, 4–8; anti-Semitism, 90; industrialist-hero, 93, 154, 161, 162; mentioned, 9, 17, 23, 164
Carus, Carl Gustav, 114–15
Ceinture Dorée (Augier), 150–51
Chamberlain, Houston Stewart: on Judaism, 20, 33–34, 98; and Gobineau, 24, 28, 30, 31; Oscar Levy on, 27, 28; on race, 28–39; and Disraeli, 28, 29, 31, 33; on Germans, 30–31; called anti-Semite, 32, 33–34, 95; and Marx, 34; mentioned, xviii, 18, 97, 161, 172, 203–204
Christ, 38, 59, 94, 203
Christian God, 37–38. *See also* God
Christianity: destruction of, 12–15; and Judaism, 16–17, 21, 23–24, 27, 34, 91, 171, 177–78, 199; and Norse myths, 42–43; mentioned, 49, 50, 89, 96, 130, 147, 176
Church. *See* Religion; names of religions
Civilization: development, 25–27, 37–39; destruction, *see* Destruction
Civilization and Its Discontents (Freud), xix
Clemens, Samuel L., 198
Cohen, Yehuda, 170
Cohn, Robert, 199
A Communication to My Friends, 58, 63
Compassion, 96–97, 104, 144, 203. *See also* Love
Coningsby (Disraeli), 18–21, 22, 29, 33
Conrad, Joseph, 165, 198, 200, 202
Consciousness. *See* Unconscious
Cottle, Amos, 3
Creativity, 48–49, 74, 113–14, 148
Credit, 176, 177n
Creon, 51–54, 64, 144
Critique of Pure Reason (Kant), 13

Daniel Deronda (Eliot), 33
Dannreuther, Edward, 199

Darwin, Charles, 99
Davidsohn, Georg, 176n
Death: instinct, xix, 203; of God, 12–15, 17, 80; of civilization, 26–27; mentioned, xvii, 65, 68, 127–28. *See also* Annihilation; Destruction; Self-abolition; Self-destruction
Decline of the West (Spengler), 29
"The Defence of Guenevere" (Morris), 9
"A Degenerate's View of Nordau" (Shaw), 152
Degeneration (Nordau), 197
Descartes, René, 75, 77–78, 79, 81
Destruction: in the *Ring*, xvii, 43, 60, 102–103, 107; of civilization, xx, 7, 8, 26–28, 39, 116, 197, 199, 204; in Norse myths, 2, 4–5; of capitalism, 10, 11, 154; of Christianity, 12–15; Wagner on, 48, 145, 179–80; of state, 49–56 *passim*, 60–62, 181; Juggernaut, 146; today, 181–82; and sex, 199, 203. *See also* Annihilation; Death; Self-abolition; Self-destruction
The Diary of a Writer (Dostoevsky), 93
Dickens, Charles, 10
Disraeli: on race, 18–24, 90, 98; and Wagner, 22–24; and Marx, 24; on Jews, 28–29; and Chamberlain, 28, 29, 31, 33; mentioned, xviii, 16, 27, 163
Doktor Faustus (Mann), xx, 147n
Donington, Robert, 198
Donizetti, Gaetano, 168
Dorn, Heinrich, 41
Dostoevsky, Fedor, 92
Dreams, xviii, 79–80, 113–14, 119–24, 136–37, 201
Dreiser, Theodore, 64n
Drews, Arthur, 62–63, 198
Dühring, Eugen, 172
Dumas, Alexandre *père*, 41–42

Eddas, xviii, 2, 3, 6, 43, 56
Eddington, Arthur, 76
Egoism. *See* Male egoism
Eichler, Max, 98–99
Eliot, George, 33
Eliot, T. S., 86n
Engels, Friedrich, 8n, 24n, 159–61
"Essay on the Spirit Seeing" (Schopenhauer), 122–23
The Essence of Christianity (Feuerbach), 64
Ettmüller, Ludwig, 3

Europe, destruction of. *See* Destruction

Fafner, 11, 12, 60, 158
Faure, Gabriel, 198
Faust (Goethe), 65, 69, 91, 137, 143, 165, 175n, 201
Felix Krull (Mann), 201
Female-male elements. *See* Male-female elements
Female-male savior. *See* Savior
Female-male union. *See* Male-female union; Perfected human
Feuerbach, Ludwig, xviii, 17, 63, 64–70, 86, 142–44
Fichte, J. G., 14–15, 17, 71, 77, 97, 111, 168
Fliess, Wilhelm, 116
The Flying Dutchman, 58, 102, 105
The Foundations of the Nineteenth Century (Chamberlain), 28–39
Franklin, H. Bruce, 199
Frauenstädt, Julius, 72, 85, 90, 97
Freia, 62, 155–56
Freud, Sigmund, xviii, xix, 51, 64, 94, 110, 116–18, 153n, 198, 200, 201, 203
Fricka, 45, 61, 62, 63n, 67, 157
Friedell, Egon, 118
Fromm, Eric, xix
Fundamentals of the Philosophy of the Future (Feuerbach), 66–67
Fussell, Paul, 199

Galton, Sir Francis, 99
George, Stefan, 38
Germany: racial pride, 3–6, 17, 30–31; nature of, 12–15, 30–31, 108, 159–60, 200–201; philosophers, 13–15, 71–72; racism, 35n–36n, 97–98; musicians, 159, 160
Geyer, Ludwig, 40, 171
Gissing, George, 199
Gobineau, Arthur de, xviii, 18, 24–28, 30, 31
God: death of, 12–15, 17, 80; in Norse myth, 13, 15; of the Jews, 23, 36–37, 93, 130, 177–78; of Christians, 37–38; mentioned, 121, 155, 158, 177
Goethe, 32, 50, 69, 71, 72, 90, 91, 97, 98, 143, 165, 168, 175n, 201
Gold. *See* Money
Goldsmith, Oliver, 156
Görres, Joseph, 14
Gravity's Rainbow (Pynchon), 202

Groddeck, Georg, 118
Gross, Otto, 199
Guedalla, Philip, 21, 22, 23
Gunther, 1–2, 6, 45–46

Hagen, 1–2, 6, 45, 47, 100, 101
Hall, Marshall, 124
Hamilton, Sir William, 112–13
Hamlet (Shakespeare), 116
Handel, George Frederick, 159
Harbou, Thea von, 169
Hartmann, Eduard von, 38–39, 110–18 *passim*
Haydn, Franz Joseph, 139, 140, 159
Heart of Darkness (Conrad), 198
Hegel, Georg Friedrich, 14, 17, 37, 71–72, 97, 168. *See also* Young Hegelians
Heidegger, Martin, 84
Heine, Heinrich, 12–17, 23, 57, 71, 80, 90, 91, 101, 119, 160, 163
Helmholtz, Hermann, 198
Herder, Johann, 32, 199
Heroes: Carlyle, 6, 8, 93, 154; male-female, 42, 46, 47, 67; Brünnhilde, 42, 46, 47, 67, 203; Siegfried, 42, 55, 56, 67; Antigone, 52–56 *passim*, 61, 63–64, 104, 203; Elsa, 58–59; Shaw, 153–54, 157, 166–67
Herwegh, Arthur, 85
History and myth, 49, 50, 55, 56
Hitler, Adolf, 3, 97, 102, 153, 167–70, 171, 200
Hobbes, Thomas, 78
Hoffmann, E. T. A., 41, 119
Homer, 37
Hook, Sidney, 153
Horkheimer, Max, 182
Hugo, Victor, 119
Humans, perfected. *See* Perfected humans
Humboldt, Wilhelm von, 25, 119
Hume, David, 71, 72, 78

Ibsen, Henrik, 152
Id, 118
Incest motif: Otto Rank, xix, 117n; the *Ring*, 23, 43, 47, 53, 55; Oedipus legend, 53, 55, 56, 61–62; Siegfried legend, 56, 61–63; Shaw, 162–63; mentioned, 48, 57, 63n, 201
Invisible Man (Wells), 203, 204
Islam, 89, 130
The Island of Dr. Moreau (Wells), 204

James, William, 74, 82–83
Janet, Pierre, 116
Janik, Allen, 199
Jean Paul, 112, 114, 119, 198, 200
Jesus. *See* Christ
Jesus of Nazareth, 59
Jewish-Aryan union, 20, 21, 28–29, 31–34, 36–37
Jewish characteristics of Wagner, 94–95, 171–72
Jewish God, 23, 36–37, 93, 130, 177–78. *See also* God
Jews: racial purity, xviii, 17–33 passim, 36n, 98–99, 164; money-power, 15–17, 19–20, 23–24, 29, 31, 36–37, 89–91, 163, 176, 203; and Christianity, 16–17, 21, 23–24, 27, 34, 91, 171, 177, 199; Sephardic, 18, 29, 33; and Disraeli, 20, 21, 28–29; and Marx, 23–24, 91, 102, 171; self-destruction, 24, 24n, 94, 101–102; and Gobineau, 27, 28; and Chamberlain, 28–37 passim, 95; Ashkenazim, 29, 33; embodiment of will, 36–37, 89, 130–31; and materialism, 89–91, 93; and Wagner, 89–102 passim, 170–71, 176n; and Schopenhauer, 90–91, 96–98, 130–31; and Weininger, 92–95, 97, 102; self-hatred, 95; and Shaw, 161–66 passim, 177; as scapegoat, 161, 166; mentioned, 35, 36, 96, 166n–167n. *See also* Anti-Semitism
Joachim of Floris, 38
Jocasta, 51, 53, 55
Judaism in Music, 24, 101, 102, 172
Juggernaut, 146
Jullian, Philippe, 199
Jung, Carl, 57, 198

Kabbala, 126, 128–31
Kant, Immanuel, 12–14, 17, 71, 75, 77, 78, 80, 86, 111, 118, 120, 125, 126, 139, 168, 198, 200
King Leopold's Soliloquy (Twain), 198
Kleist, Heinrich von, 119
Kokoschka, Oskar, 200
Kracauer, Siegfried, 169
Kraus, Karl, xx, 95, 200

Lagarde, Paul de, 172
Laius, 51, 52–53, 61–62
Lang, Fritz, 169
Language and music, 55, 56, 143–45

Language as world, 87, 131
Larisch, Marie, 200
Lectures on Psychology (Carus), 114
Legend. *See* Eddas; Myth; Norse mythology; Oedipus legend; Siegfried legend; *The Song of the Nibelungs*
Leibniz, Gottfried von, 78, 111–13, 131–32, 168
Lessing, Theodor, 95, 97, 169, 170n, 172
Levi, Hermann, 91, 95, 197
Lévi-Strauss, Claude, 200
Levy, Oscar, 27–28, 34
Lindner, Ernst, 85, 90
Liszt, Franz, 60, 61, 103, 135, 181, 202
Locke, John, 75
Loge, 11, 155–58, 167, 182
Lohengrin, 58–59, 94, 105, 202, 203
London as Nibelheim, 86, 154, 199
Loos, Adolph, 200
Loos, Paul Arthur, 167–68
Lorenz, Alfred, 200
Love: and death, xix; selfless, 54, 63–64, 110; sexual, 64–67, 104, 106, 111, 126–28; Wagner on, 65–66, 103–104; Feuerbach on, 66–67; compassion, 96–97, 104, 144, 203; Schopenhauer on, 104, 126–29; types of, 106, 129; Kant on, 126; Shaw on, 158. *See also* Male-female union; Perfected human; Self-destruction
Lowry, Malcolm, 200
Lucka, Emil, 95
Luther, Martin, 130, 146

Magnússon, Eiríkr, 9, 35
Magnússon, Finnur, 3, 35
Major Barbara (Shaw), 161–67
Male egoism, 58–59, 61, 65–66, 71, 107, 110, 181
Male-female elements, 37–38, 55, 92, 181
Male-female savior. *See* Savior
Male-female union, 15, 21, 26, 104, 109, 182. *See also* Love; Perfected human; Savior
Mallarmé, Stéphane, 119, 198
Mallet, Paul Henri, 3
Man and Superman (Shaw), xix, 164
Mann, Erika, 201
Mann, Klaus, 200–201
Mann, Thomas, xx, 63n, 118, 147n, 200–201

Marx, Karl: on money, 7, 177n; on Jews, 23–24, 24n, 34, 90, 91, 94, 102, 171; on incest, 63n; on the *Ring*, 63n; on proletariat, 94; Shaw on, 149, 159–60; Marxist writings on destruction, 199; mentioned, 10, 17, 92, 158, 160, 165
Masculine. *See* headings beginning with Male
Mathematics and music, 131–33
Maudsley, Henry, 113–14
Men. *See* headings beginning with Male
Mencken, H. L., 64n
Mendelssohn, Felix, 41, 202
Merleau-Ponty, Maurice, 83–84
Meyerbeer, Giacomo, 172, 197
Micheletti, Mario, 84
Militarism, 59, 71, 93, 98, 146, 171–74. *See also* War
Mill, John Stuart, 113, 113n
Money-power, xviii, 7, 8, 10, 11, 15–17, 19–20, 23–24, 29, 31, 36–37, 68, 89–91, 151, 163, 171, 175–76, 181, 202, 203
Morality, 52–55
Morgan, Lewis H., 176n
Mosley, Oswald, 28
Morris, William, 6, 8–12, 17, 23, 35, 152, 156
Mozart, Wolfgang, 139, 140, 151, 159
Müller, Johannes, 198, 201
Music: united with word, xviii, 55, 56, 57, 131, 143–45; Wagner on, xviii, 136–39, 147–48, 159, 160; Jewish, 20; and mathematics, 131–33; as voice of will, 132, 133, 137–38, 145; Schopenhauer on, 132–33, 136, 139; as salvation, 147–48, 199; German, 159, 160. *See also* names of musicians
Music-drama, xviii, 57, 109, 151, 204
Myth, 49, 50, 55–57, 119. *See also* Eddas; Norse mythology; Oedipus legend; Siegfried legend; *The Song of the Nibelungs*

Napoleon I, 50, 71, 98, 157
Napoleon III, 173–74
Nature-philosophers, 14–15, 17, 34–35, 72, 111, 119
Nazism: and Wagner, 168–72, 199; mentioned, 3, 4, 85, 90, 92, 95, 98, 99, 167, 200
Nerval, Gerard de, 119

Netherlands, 1, 167
The Nether World (Gissing), 199
Neumann, Angelo, 176n, 197
Newman, Ernest, 47, 62, 68, 102, 114, 142, 171, 173
Nibelungenlied. See The Song of the Nibelungs
Nibelung legend. *See The Ring of the Nibelung;* Siegfried legend; *The Song of the Nibelungs*
Nietzsche, Friedrich, 64, 64n, 71, 117, 118, 157, 168, 171, 172
Nordau, Max, 152, 197
Norse mythology: revival of interest, xviii, 1–6, 169; translations of, 1, 3, 4, 9; and race, 3–4, 17; used by Morris, 8–12; used by Wagner, 9, 50, 56–57; and Christianity, 13, 15, 42–43, 49; incest motif, 62–63. *See also* Eddas; Siegfried legend; *The Song of the Nibelungs*; names of characters
Northcote-Bade, James, 201
Northern Antiquities (Percy), 3
Novalis, 119
Numbers, significance of, 37–39

Occult, 119, 124–26
"Ode to Joy," (Schiller), 142–44
Oedipus, 51, 53, 55, 61–62
Oedipus legend: Wagner's analysis, xviii, 48, 52–55, 59, 117, 117n; summary, 51–52; and Siegfried legend, 61–62; and Freud, 116–17; mentioned, 56, 104, 110–11, 140, 181, 201, 202
On the Fourfold Root of the Principle of Sufficient Reason (Schopenhauer), 71, 73, 75, 77–79
On the Will in Nature (Schopenhauer), 81
Ontologia (Wolff), 77
Opera and Drama, 48–51, 55–56, 63
Oresteia (Aeschylus), 62n
Osborn, Henry Fairfield, 100
Our Mutual Friend (Dickens), 10
Oxenford, John, 72–73, 85

Palestrina, Giovanni, 139
Paralipomena (Schopenhauer), 72
Parerga (Schopenhauer), 72
Paris commune, 160
Parsifal, 94, 168, 170
Past and Present (Carlyle), 7, 8n, 162

Percy, Thomas, 3
Perfected human, xviii, 50–61 *passim*, 65–67, 73, 94, 108, 110, 142–44. *See also* Love; Savior
The Perfect Wagnerite (Shaw), 152–67 *passim*
Phenomenology, 83–84. *See also* World-as-representation
Philosophy, German, 13–15, 71–72. *See also* Nature-philosophers; names of philosophers
Philosophy of the Unconscious (Hartmann), 115
Plato, 77, 133
Plotinus, 119
Polanyi, Karl, 201–202
Politics, 6, 50–51, 172–74
Polynices, 51, 53, 54
Proletariat, 24n, 94
Prometheus Unbound (Shelley), 158
Property, 174–75, 175n, 176n
Proudhon, Pierre-Joseph, 174
Proust, Marcel, 36n, 109, 119
Psyche (Carus), 114
Psychoanalysis, xix, 116–17, 202
Puccini, Giacomo, 168
The Pure in Heart (Werfel), 205
Pynchon, Thomas, 202

Race: supremacy, xviii, 3–4, 24–25, 31, 50; pride, 3–4, 17; Disraeli on, 18–24, 98; as "truth," 21, 33, 201; Gobineau on, 24–28; intermixture, 27, 29–31, 98; Chamberlain on, 28–35, 98; purity, 30, 99–100. *See also* Anti-Semitism; Jews; headings beginning with Jewish
Racism, 4, 35n–36n, 97–98
Raff, Joachim, 202, 203
Rank, Otto, xix, 117, 117n, 202, 205
Rape, 199
Rathenau, Walther, 16
Reality, nature of. *See* World-as-will; World-as-representation
Redesdale, Lord, 28–29, 33
Religion, 12–17, 38, 49–50. *See also* Christianity; God; and names of other religions
Remembrance of Things Past (Proust), 109
Revolution. *See* Annihilation; Destruction; Self-abolition; Self-destruction
Rienzi, 40, 168

Rimbaud, Arthur, 119
The Ring of the Nibelung: sources, xvii–xviii; 62–63; themes, xvii–xx, 105–106, 281–82; Schopenhauerian influence, xviii, 89, 104–109, 158; similar works, 11, 41, 62n, 161–67; Feuerbachian influence, 39, 67–70, 103; closing, 43, 47, 70, 89, 100–109; 1848 outline, 43–47, 62; as music-drama, 56; Wagner's comments, 59–60; parody, 63n, 201; opening, 86, 135–36; interpreted by Shaw, 155–59, 160–61; criticism, 198, 202–203. *See also* names of characters
The Rise and Fall of the Third Reich (Shirer), 168
Ritter, Karl, 199
Robespierre, 172, 173
Röckel, August, 20, 60, 62, 64–65, 67–70, 86, 89, 102, 104–106, 172, 203–204
Rosenberg, Alfred, 32
Rossini, Gioacchino, 139, 151
Rothschilds, 15–16, 91, 174
Roussel, Royal, 202
Rubinstein, Joseph, 91, 95, 197
Ruskin, John, 156
Russell, Bertrand, 76

Salvation: by art, 10, 108, 109; of Jews, 24, 24n, 94, 101–102; through sympathy, 88–89; in music, 147–48, 199. *See also* Savior; Self-abolition; Self-destruction
Sans, Edouard, 202–203
The Saracen Woman, 22–23
Savior: as industrialist, 8, 161, 162, 166–67; Christ, 38, 94, 203; male-female, 42, 46, 47, 67; Siegfried, 42, 55, 56, 67, 203; Brünnhilde, 46, 47, 67, 203; Antigone, 52–56 *passim*, 61, 63–64, 104; Elsa, 58–59
Schelling, Friedrich, 111–12, 126
Schiller, Friedrich, 97, 142–45
Schlegels, 199
Schönberg, Arnold, 200
Schopenhauer, Arnold: and Wagner, xviii, 39, 48, 63–64, 64n, 70–89, 135; influenced the *Ring*, xviii, 104–109, 158; misunderstood, xx, 70–71; influenced Hartmann, 38, 39; and other philosophers, 71–72; reviewed by Oxenford, 72–73; philosophy of, 73–82;

on dreams, 79–80, 119–24, 136; Wagner's explanation of, 86–89; anti-Semitism, 90–91, 96–98; animal rights, 96–97; on love, 96, 97, 104, 126–28; on the occult, 124–26; on death, 127–28; use of Kabbala, 128–31; on music, 132–33, 136, 139, 141; influenced Wagner's interpretation of Beethoven, 144–45, 147; mentioned, 71, 84, 90, 94, 109, 117, 134–35, 138–39, 172, 177, 182, 199, 202–203. *See also* Will; World-as-representation; World-as-will
Schroeder-Devrient, Wilhelmine, 22, 115
Schumann, Robert, 115
Science, xix, 178–79
Scotus Erigena, 121
The Secret Agent (Conrad), 165n
Self-abolition: of proletariat, 24n; of Jews, 24n, 94; of women, 24n, 94. *See also* Self-destruction
Self-destruction: in the *Ring*, xviii, 59, 103, 107, 108, 179–80; Jews, 24, 24n, 94, 101–102; in Oedipus legend, 52, 54, 63–64, 104, 110; through sympathy, 54, 63–64, 88, 89, 104, 110; of male egoism, 58–59, 61, 63, 67, 70, 107, 110; versus suicide, 59, 73, 128; mentioned, xix, xx, 52, 102, 107, 110, 116, 127, 176n, 200. *See also* Annihilation; Death; Destruction; Self-abolition; Will
Sex, 64–67, 104, 106, 111, 126–28, 199. *See also* Love
Sex and Character (Weininger), 92
Sexes, differences between. *See* Male-female elements
Sexes, union of. *See* Male-female union; Perfected human
Shakespeare, William, 50, 116, 120, 141
Shaw, George Bernard: Wagnerian themes, 149–52, 161–67; as interpreter of Wagner, 152–54; heroes, 153–54, 157; interprets the *Ring*, 155–59, 160–61; on Germans, 159–60; on Marx and Engels, 159–61; on Jews, 177; mentioned, xix, 179
Shelley, Percy Bysshe, 158
Shirer, William, 168, 169, 170, 199
Siegfried: the *Ring*, xvii, 55, 144, 182; Norse myths, 1–2, 6, 42–43, 47, 62–63; as savior, 42, 55, 56, 59, 67, 70, 203; *Ring* outline, 43, 45–47, 100, 101; as

perfected human, 59, 60, 61; Shaw, 157–59, 160, 162, 165, 167
Siegfried, 42, 59
Siegfried legend, 41–43, 47, 56–57, 61–63
Siegfried's Death, 47, 100, 101, 102
Sieglinde, 1, 43, 45, 47, 53, 55, 61, 62–63, 201
Siegmund, 1, 43, 45, 47, 53, 55, 61, 62–63, 201
Sigurd the Volsung (Morris), 9, 11–12
Simrock, Karl, 1, 4
The Song of the Nibelungs, xviii, 1–2, 4–7, 9, 17, 41, 42, 47, 49, 56, 62, 103, 169
Sophocles, xviii, 48, 56, 110, 116–17, 181
Sparling, H. Halliday, 9
Spengler, Oswald, 24, 28, 29, 182
Spezia, Italy, 134–35
Spielrein, Sabina, 199, 203
Spinoza, Baruch, 78, 96
State, destruction of. *See* Destruction
State versus individual, 38, 50–55
State versus church, 49–50
Stein, Leon, 96, 97–98
Sterilization, 99
Stern, Fritz, 203
Stevenson, Robert Louis, 203, 205
Stoecker, Adolf, 172
The Strange Case of Dr. Jekyll and Mr. Hyde (Stevenson), 203, 205
Strauss, Richard, 170
Suicide, 59, 73, 128
Sympathy and self-destruction. *See* Self-destruction

Tancred, 18, 19, 21–23, 33
Tannhaüser, 105
Tausig, Carl, 91, 197
Teller, Charlotte, 203
The Tempest (Shakespeare), 141
Thoughts on Death and Immortality (Feuerbach), 64
Three, significance of number, 37–39
Tichatschek, Joseph, 115
The Time Machine (Wells), 204–205
Tolstoy, Leo, 94, 152
Toulmin, Stephen, 199
Toynbee, Arnold, 24
Tractatus (Wittgenstein), 75, 84
"Transcendent Speculation on the Apparent Deliberateness in the Fate of the Individual"(Schopenhauer), 119–21

Trebitsch, Siegfried, 154
Treitschke, Heinrich von, 168, 172
Trinities, examples, 37–38
Tristan and Isolde, 134, 137, 149, 168
Turco, Alfred, 153
Twain, Mark, 198

Uhlig, Theodor, 205
Ullstein, Leopold, 85
Unconscious: raise to consciousness, 54, 66, 82, 106, 110, 115–16, 143; versus consciousness, 57; and self-destruction, 59, 110, 116; and creativity, 74; development of the concept, 111–18; in dreams and waking life, 120–21, 122–24; and the occult, 125
Under the Volcano (Lowry), 200
Under Western Eyes (Conrad), 202
United States, 4, 7, 10, 17, 99–100

Valéry, Paul, 84
The Varieties of Religious Experience (James), 82–83
Verdi (Werfel), 205
Verdi, Giuseppe, 168, 205
Virchow, Rudolf, 34–35, 85
Vischer, Friedrich, 41
The Volsunga Saga (Morris), 9n
Voltaire, 71

Wagner, Cosima, 85, 176
Wagner, Eva, 28
Wagner, Gottlob Heinrich Adolf, 203
Wagner, Minna, 85
Wagner, Richard: psychoanalytic interpretation, xix, 202; use of myth, 9, 41–42, 48, 56–57, 203; Levy on, 27, 28; early life, 40–41; as revolutionist, 41, 47–48, 107–108, 204; as artist, 55–56, 104–105, 109; comments on the Ring, 59–60; parody, 63n, 151, 201; introduced to Schopenhauer, 84–86, 135; explanation of Schopenhauer, 86–89; and anti-Semitism, 89–91, 97, 98n, 101n, 102n, 170–71, 176n; Jewish friends, 90–91, 95, 102n, 171; admirers, 94, 198, 200; "Jewish" characteristics, 94–95, 171–72; and Nazism, 96, 168–72, 199; on Germany, 108; Carus on, 115; on Beethoven, 139–48; themes in Shaw, 149–52, 161–67; Archer on, 151n; Max Nordau attack,

152; defended by Shaw, 152–53; Shirer on, 168; Hitler on, 169–70; works banned, 170; break with Nietzsche, 171; critical studies on, 172, 198, 199, 200, 202–203; and Bismarck, 173–74, 204; appearances in novels, 197, 200, 205; death, 198; themes in Gissing, 199; themes in Lowry, 200; themes in Thomas Mann, 201; themes in Spielrein, 203; themes in Wells, 204–205. See also Feuerbach; Schopenhauer; The Ring of the Nibelung
War, xix, 173–75, 204. See also Militarism; World War I; World War II
Warfare state, 178–80, 182
Wassermann, Jakob, 35n–36n, 175n, 204
Wealth. See Money
Weber, Ernst von, 96–97
Weininger, Otto, 92–96, 97, 102, 171
Wells, H. G., 166n–167n, 197, 203, 204–205
Werfel, Franz, 205
Wesendonck, Mathilde, 71, 85
What Is Property? (Proudhon), 174
Whitehead, Alfred North, 76, 84
Die Wibelungen, 42
Widowers' Houses (Shaw), 149–52, 156, 161, 162
Wieck, Clara, 115
The Wife of Sir Isaac Harmon (Wells), 167n
Will: versus intellect, 36–37; will to power, 36–37, 70, 71; Jews embody, 36–37, 89, 130–31; Schopenhauer's concept, 70, 71, 74, 79, 81, 84, 87–88, 118, 134, 204; denial of, 70, 73, 78, 88–89, 105, 106, 109, 116, 128, 130–31, 140, 141; transcendence, 73, 78; in nature, 81; in dreams and waking life, 120–21, 122–24, 136–37; and sex, 127; and self-destruction tendency, 127; and suicide, 128; expressed in music, 132, 133, 137–38, 145; in warfare state, 178–80. See also World-as-will
Wille, Eliza, 85
Wilson, Pearl, 62
Wisenthal, J. L., 161n
Wittgenstein, Caroline von, 103
Wittgenstein, Ludwig, 75, 84, 87, 131, 199–200
Wolff, Christian, 77, 78

Women. *See* Perfected human; Self-abolition; headings beginning with Male-female
World as art, 148
World as language, 87, 131
World-as-representation, 74–80, 84, 86–87, 125–26, 132–34, 139
World-as-will, 74, 77–82, 86–87, 125–26, 131–34. *See also* Will
The World as Will and Representation (Schopenhauer), 71–73, 79, 82, 83, 85, 100, 108–109, 117, 123, 139
World destruction. *See* Destruction
The World of William Clissold (Wells), 166n
The World's Illusion (Wassermann), 204
World War I, xx, 166–67, 181, 199, 204, 205
World War II, xx, 182, 202
Wotan: *Ring* outline, 44, 45, 100, 101; the *Ring*, 47, 59–63 *passim*, 63n, 67, 68, 70, 144, 179, 182; Shaw, 155–67 *passim*

Young, Percy M., 199
Young Hegelians, 17, 38. *See also* Hegel

Zuyder Zee, 118, 143